ENCYCLOPEDIA

OF

Technology and Applied Sciences

7

Military vehicles – Plant hormone

Marshall Cavendish
New York • London • Toronto • Sydney

England
Research
Fellow, Department of Materials Science and Metallurgy, University of
Cambridge, Cambridge, England

Martin Campbell-Kelly, Department of Computer Science, University of
Warwick, Coventry, England

Mark S. Coyne, Associate Professor, Department of Agronomy,
University of Kentucky, Lexington, Kentucky

R. Cengiz Ertekin, Professor, Department of Ocean Engineering,
University of Hawaii at Manoa, Honolulu, Hawaii

Donald R. Franceschetti, Ph.D., Distinguished Service Professor,
Departments of Physics and Chemistry, The University of Memphis,
Memphis, Tennessee

Colin Harding, Curator of Photographic Technology, National Museum of
Photography, Film, and Television, Bradford, England

Lee E. Harris, Ph.D., P.E., Associate Professor, Division of Marine and
Environmental Systems, Florida Institute of Technology,
Melbourne, Florida

Deborah Korenstein, Instructor in Medicine, Mount Sinai School of
Medicine, New York, New York

John Liffen, Associate Curator, The Science Museum, London, England

Robert C. Mebane, Ph.D., Professor, Department of Chemistry
University of Tennessee at Chattanooga, Chattanooga, Tennessee

Peter R. Morris, Visiting Fellow, Bath University, Bath, England

Christopher M. Pastore, Director of Research, Philadelphia College of
Textiles and Science, Philadelphia, Pennsylvania

Sunday Popo-Ola, Ph.D., Department of Civil Engineering, Imperial
College, London, England

Marc D. Rayman, Ph.D., Principal Engineer, National Aeronautics and
Space Administration (NASA) Jet Propulsion Laboratory at the
California Institute of Technology, Pasadena, California

John M. Ritz, Ph.D., Professor, Department of Occupational and
Technical Studies, Old Dominion University, Norfolk, Virginia

John Robinson, Former Curator, The Science Museum, London, England

Thomas R. Rybolt, Professor, Department of Chemistry, University
of Tennessee at Chattanooga, Chattanooga, Tennessee

Mark E. Sanders, Associate Professor, Department of Technology
Education, College of Human Resources and Education, Virginia Tech,
Blacksburg, Virginia

Anthony E. Schwaller, Ph.D., Professor, Department of Environmental
and Technological Studies, College of Science and Engineering,
St. Cloud State University, St. Cloud, Minnesota

J. Derek Smith, Ph.D., Department of Engineering, University of
Cambridge, Cambridge, England

Colin Uttley, Programmes Manager, The Science Museum, London,
England

Phil Whitfield, Professor, School of Life, Basic Medical, and Health
Sciences, King's College London, London, England

Cover illustration: illustration of a communications satellite
Title page illustration: huge drilling rigs are used to extract and
distribute Earth's reserves of oil and natural gas. Kevin R. Morris/Corbis

Marshall Cavendish Corporation
99 White Plains Road
Tarrytown, New York 10591-9001

© 2000 Marshall Cavendish Corporation

Created by **Brown Partworks Ltd.**

Library of Congress Cataloging-in-Publication Data

Encyclopedia of technology and applied sciences.
    p.   cm.
    Includes bibliographical references.
    Contents: 1. Abacus–Beverages—2. Bicycle–Codes and ciphers—3. Color–Engine—4. Engineering–Gyroscope—5. Hand tools–Leather—6. Light and optics–Military communications and control—7. Military vehicles–Plant hormone—8. Plastics–Sailing—9. Satellite–Tank—10. Technology in ancient civilizations–Wood and woodworking—11. Indexes.
      ISBN 0-7614-7116-2 (set)
    1. Technology Encyclopedias, Juvenile. [1. Technology Encyclopedias.]
T48.E52   2000
603—dc21

                        99-14520
                        CIP

      ISBN 0-7614-7116-2 (set)
      ISBN 0-7614-7123-5 (vol. 7)
Printed in Malaysia
Bound in U.S.A.
    06 05 04 03 02 01 00 54321

CONTENTS

USEFUL INFORMATION

Use this table to convert the English system (or the imperial system), the system of units common in the United States (e.g., inches, miles, quarts), to the metric system (e.g., meters, kilometers, liters) or to convert the metric system to the English system. You can convert one measurement into another by multiplying. For example, to convert centimeters into inches, multiply the number of centimeters by 0.3937. To convert inches into centimeters, multiply the number of inches by 2.54.

To convert	into	multiply by
Acres	Square feet	43,560
	Square yards	4840
	Square miles	0.00156
	Square meters	4046.856
	Hectares	0.40468
Celsius	Fahrenheit	First multiply by 1.8 then add 32
Centimeters	Inches	0.3937
	Feet	0.0328
Cubic cm	Cubic inches	0.06102
Cubic feet	Cubic inches	1728
	Cubic yards	0.037037
	Gallons	7.48
	Cubic meters	0.028317
	Liters	28.32
Cubic inches	Fluid ounces	0.554113
	Cups	0.069264
	Quarts	0.017316
	Gallons	0.004329
	Liters	0.016387
	Milliliters	16.387064
Cubic meters	Cubic feet	35.3145
	Cubic yards	1.30795
Cubic yards	Cubic feet	27
	Cubic meters	0.76456
Cups, fluid	Quarts	0.25
	Pints	0.5
	Ounces	8
	Milliliters	237
	Tablespoons	16
	Teaspoons	48
Fahrenheit	Celsius	First subtract 32 then divide by 1.8
Feet	Centimeters	30.48
	Meters	0.3048
	Kilometers	0.0003
	Inches	12
	Yards	0.3333
	Miles	0.00019
Gallons	Quarts	4
	Pints	8
	Cups	16
	Ounces	128
	Liters	3.785
	Milliliters	3785
	Cubic inches	231
	Cubic feet	0.1337
	Cubic yards	0.00495
	Cubic meters	0.00379
	British gallons	0.8327
Grams	Ounces	0.03527
	Pounds	0.0022
Hectares	Square meters	10,000
	Acres	2.471
Horsepower	Foot-pounds per minute	33,000
	British thermal units (Btu) per minute	42.42
	British thermal units (Btu) per hour	2546
	Kilowatts	0.7457
	Metric horsepower	1.014
Inches	Feet	0.08333
Inches (continued)	Yards	0.02778
	Centimeters	2.54
	Meters	0.0254
Kilograms	Grams	1000
	Ounces	35.274
	Pounds	2.2046
	Short tons	0.0011
	Long tons	0.00098
	Metric tons (tonnes)	0.001
Kilometers	Meters	1000
	Miles	0.62137
	Yards	1093.6
	Feet	3280.8
Kilowatts	British thermal units (Btu) per minute	56.9
	Horsepower	1.341
	Metric horsepower	1.397
Kilowatt-hours	British thermal units (Btu)	3413
Knots	Statute miles per hour	1.1508
Leagues	Miles	3
Liters	Milliliters	1000
	Fluid ounces	33.814
	Quarts	1.05669
	British gallons	0.21998
	Cubic inches	61.02374
	Cubic feet	0.13531
Meters	Inches	39.37
	Feet	3.28083
	Yards	1.09361
	Miles	0.000621
	Kilometers	0.001
	Centimeters	100
	Millimeters	1000
Miles	Inches	63,360
	Feet	5280
	Yards	1760
	Meters	1609.34
	Kilometers	1.60934
	Nautical miles	0.8684
Miles nautical, U.S. and International	Statute miles	1.1508
	Feet	6076.115
	Meters	1852
Miles per minute	Feet per second	88
	Knots	52.104
Milliliters	Fluid ounces	0.0338
	Cubic inches	0.061
	Liters	0.001
Millimeters	Centimeters	0.1
	Meters	0.001
	Inches	0.03937
Ounces, avoirdupois	Pounds	0.0625
	Grams	28.34952
	Kilograms	0.0283495
Ounces, fluid	Pints	0.0625
	Quarts	0.03125
	Cubic inches	1.80469
	Cubic feet	0.00104
	Milliliters	29.57353
	Liters	0.02957
Pints, fluid	Ounces, fluid	16
	Quarts, fluid	0.5
Pints, fluid (continued)	Cubic inches	28.8745
	Cubic feet	0.01671
	Milliliters	473.17647
	Liters	0.473176
Pounds	Ounces	16
	Grams	453.59237
	Kilograms	0.45359
	Tons	0.0005
	Tons, long	0.000446
	Metric tons (tonnes)	0.0004536
Quarts, fluid	Ounces, fluid	32
	Pints, fluid	2
	Gallons	0.25
	Cubic inches	57.749
	Cubic feet	0.033421
	Liters	0.946358
	Milliliters	946.358
Square centimeters	Square inches	0.155
Square feet	Square inches	144
	Square meters	0.093
	Square yards	0.111
Square inches	Square centimeters	6.452
	Square feet	0.0069
Square kilometers	Hectares	100
	Square meters	1,000,000
	Square miles	0.3861
Square meters	Square feet	10.758
	Square yards	1.196
Square miles	Acres	640
	Square kilometers	2.59
Square yards	Square feet	9
	Square inches	1296
	Square meters	0.836
Tablespoons	Ounces, fluid	0.5
	Teaspoons	3
	Milliliters	14.7868
Teaspoons	Ounces, fluid	0.16667
	Tablespoons	0.3333
	Milliliters	4.9289
Tons, Long	Pounds	2240
	Kilograms	1016.047
	Short tons	1.12
	Metric tons (tonnes)	1.016
Tons, short	Pounds	2000
	Kilograms	907.185
	Long tons	0.89286
	Metric tonnes	0.907
Tons, Metric (tonnes)	Pounds	2204.62
	Kilograms	1000
	Long tons	0.984206
	Short tons	1.10231
Watts	British thermal units (Btu) per hour	3.415
	Horsepower	0.00134
Yards	Inches	36
	Feet	3
	Miles	0.0005681
	Centimeters	91.44
	Meters	0.9144

MILITARY VEHICLES

Military vehicles used in combat are highly specialized, while noncombat vehicles resemble civil vehicles

The German Marder was one of the first infantry fighting vehicles (IFVs). Developed in the 1970s for the West German Panzer Grenadiers, it was adapted from an armored personnel carrier (APC) by mounting an automatic cannon, with a 2-cm (¾-in) caliber, on its turret. Weighing 29.2 tons (26.5 tonnes), it carried up to nine men in its interior.

Until the latter part of the 19th century, the method of moving military equipment was exactly the same as moving civil equipment—on horse-drawn wagons. Until the 18th century, it was common to hire, or impress, civilian wagons—complete with horses and drivers—to carry army supplies when a campaign was under way. The drawback was that civilian drivers felt that they were under no obligation to get shot, and they tended to flee when they were needed most.

The development of a military vehicle that could be used in combat came even later. Until the 20th century, there were only a few historical examples of attempts to produce a type of war cart (a wagon in which soldiers could ride into the thick of battle and, with some degree of protection, add their weight to the combat), and few of these lasted beyond their first use. All of them were horse-drawn, and horses were highly vulnerable to arrows or firearms. Mechanical propulsion was necessary before the military fighting vehicle could become sufficiently effective (see HORSE-DRAWN TRANSPORT).

CORE FACTS

- Prior to the 20th century, military and civil vehicles were exactly the same—horses and wagons.
- The ability to carry heavy loads across rough country is the prime military requirement.
- Concealment of military vehicles in the face of modern electronic surveillance technology, such as high-frequency microwave radar, is almost impossible.

THE RAILROAD

The development of railways made rapid mass transportation of troops possible. In 1846, the Prussian Sixth Corps (12,000 men with their guns, wagons, and horses) were moved from Berlin to Poznań by rail, and in 1851 an Austrian division (14,500 men, 2000 horses, 48 guns, and 464 wagons) went from Kraków to the Hungarian border in two days—a journey that would have taken 15 days to march.

Yet railroad transportation had its drawbacks. After arriving at the railroad's end, a further method of transportation had to be found, or there might not be any railroad lines running where the army needed to go. Also, in wartime, armies might find the lines so damaged as to be unusable. Therefore, armies developed their own railroad equipment and staffs.

Military railroads

Military railroads came in two kinds: full-sized, which could be used to put a damaged railroad system back into operation, and narrow-gauge or trench railways, which could be laid in the combat zone to move ammunition and other supplies quickly. Military lines were also laid to extend commercial tracks to move railroad artillery into place. These exceptionally heavy guns—far too big to be moved by motor vehicles—were mounted on railroad trucks designed to move easily over hurriedly laid tracks. In World War I (1914–1918), railroad lines were laid out behind the Allied trenches and used for gas attacks. By parking freight cars filled with gas cylinders, an immense cloud of gas could be launched downwind and into enemy lines.

CONNECTIONS

- **AUTOMOBILE** innovations in **STEERING SYSTEMS, SUSPENSION SYSTEMS** and **TIRES** were used in military vehicles.

- **ARTILLERY** was moved by **HORSE-DRAWN TRANSPORT** in **LAND WARFARE** up until the 1940s.

TANK CONCEALMENT

A U.S. Army M2 IFV with camouflage was designed to blend in with its background.

Concealment of military vehicles has become an increasing problem because of advances in detection technology. The necessity for concealment arose when aerial reconnaissance became standard practice. The first attempt to solve the problem was sought in camouflage—painting the vehicle a color or a disruptive pattern that would blend with its background, and providing each vehicle with a camouflage net (a large openwork net threaded with brown and green strips of sack cloth). To the aerial observer, however, it is not its color that gives the vehicle away, but its angular shape and the shadows it casts. The camouflage net could help to conceal these, but soldiers were rarely given sufficient instruction. They tended to regard the net as a cloak of invisibility that would conceal anything simply by throwing it over an object, without considering whether the net actually blended into the surroundings.

Training and experience eventually improved this situation, but aerial photography made great strides during and after World War II. It introduced such things as color film and infrared film, which could distinguish between natural and manufactured objects with great clarity. The recent arrival of thermal imaging made the slightest change of temperature between a vehicle and its background visible through camouflage nets and trees. Even a vehicle parked inside a barn could be detected by aerial photography. Special paints and net garnish that absorb infrared—thus defeating the thermal-imaging camera—have been developed, but in the 1990s the use of extremely high-frequency radars (millimetric-wave radar) was proposed as another method of defeating camouflage. Only time will tell whether this system will pose a new threat, but one thing is certain: disruptive camouflage painting is now of no use.

A CLOSER LOOK

Military railroads are used less today due to improvements in automobiles and the development of short-distance air transport capable of lifting most heavy military equipment.

NONCOMBAT VEHICLES

Mechanical transport was first used in 1854 during the Crimean War. The British sent a steam road vehicle to Crimea to haul wagon supply trains. It had special wheels for operating in mud, but the wagons it needed to pull didn't, so they sank, defeating the engine's power. Steam engines were used again in the South African War (1899–1902), but the smoke and engine noise produced when towing artillery up to the front drew artillery and long-range rifle fire, so the steam engine was abandoned (see STEAM-POWERED ROAD VEHICLES).

Early motor vehicles

The motor vehicle appeared—both as a passenger conveyance and as a method of hauling freight—in the early 20th century. A 1913 census of motor vehicles in Germany counted 7700 heavy trucks and 50,000 cars and light trucks, and the German army had sufficient vehicles to provide a transport column of 50 trucks for each of their 25 Army Corps. Most armies had subsidy plans by which a civil firm could receive money toward the purchase of a truck plus an annual retainer fee for five years, during which period the truck could be taken by the army should mobilization take place. All these plans were called into action in August 1914, and a large proportion of commercial vehicles were impressed into service all over Europe.

World War I demonstrated that the commercial truck or car was satisfactory for military use only outside the combat zone. Within the combat zone, it was necessary for vehicles to be designed for their task. Commercial vehicles were designed to run on roads, whereas military vehicles had to be capable of going anywhere an army might find itself, negotiating mud, snow, farmland, moorland, sand, and swamps. They also had to withstand much harder usage and minimum attention and maintenance, and they had to be simple to repair in the field without highly specialized equipment and tools.

Military vehicle innovations

Between the world wars, there was no financial incentive for automobile manufacturers to develop military vehicles. It was therefore up to military establishments to experiment as cheaply as possible with such things as cross-country suspension, half-tracked vehicles, and all-wheel drive. By the time World War II broke out in 1939, they were able to provide manufacturers with designs for gun-towing tractors, cross-country trucks, amphibious vehicles, and other similar machines. These experiments formed the basis for converting commercial vehicles into specialized military vehicles.

All-wheel drive. All-wheel drive allowed military vehicles to go anywhere, on or off roads. It had been achieved in several commercial vehicles before 1914, but building an all-wheel-drive vehicle that could stand up to the stress of cross-country work and incorporate steering joints took several years (see STEERING SYSTEMS). Because the vehicle needed to have ample ground clearance, improved suspension and robust tires were also developed.

Low-pressure wide-tread tires. Mud—sometimes deep enough to swallow horses and men, as in France during World War I—was a major obstacle to cross-country vehicle operation. Postwar research led to the adoption of low-pressure wide-tread tires, which spread the weight of a vehicle over a larger area, and were therefore less liable than conventional tires to sink into mud and soft ground (see TIRE).

Half-track. The half-track vehicle also avoided sinking into mud by spreading the vehicle's weight over a greater area. It had front wheels for steering, but a tracked assembly at the rear for driving and distributing the weight. Pioneered around 1912 by a Russian engineer using the French Charron armored car as his test bed, it was developed further in the 1920s by the French Citroen company, who successfully sent a convoy of half-tracks across the Sahara (see TRACKED VEHICLE).

Cargo vehicles

About this time, a range of cross-country cargo vehicles, graduated in a series based upon the weight they could carry, were developed. Beginning with a light truck of about one-ton (0.9-tonne) capacity, it ran through 3, 5, 7, 10, 12 and 15 tons (2.7, 4.5, 6.3, 9.1, 10.9 and 13.6 tonnes). The 3- and 5-ton (2.7- and 4.5-tonne) groups were used for general work, while the heavier vehicles were used to tow heavy artillery or trailers or to carry bridging components.

Motorcycles and horses

Individuals who needed to be mobile—couriers, guides, and liaison personnel—generally used motorcycles. Officers still used horses well into World War II, but in the combat zone, horses were too vulnerable and motorcycles were deemed inappropriate for senior officers.

Jeeps

Demand for a light car with cross-country capabilities resulted in the U.S. Army jeep—a rugged go-anywhere four-seater that rapidly became indispensable. The German army, which had originally adopted a very luxurious and complicated car, rapidly abandoned it for a cross-country version of their Volkswagen, and similar vehicles have since been developed in most countries.

Bridging and amphibious vehicles

One of the oldest military formations is the bridging train. Water has always posed obstructions to army movement. From the earliest times, wagons carrying boats accompanied any military operation, since existing bridges could be easily defended or destroyed. Despite boats' becoming lighter and wagons' becoming trucks, little changed until World War II, when modular bridges appeared. Built with good load-bearing capacity in prefabricated sections, they could be bolted together to provide a bridge of any length. Yet, they needed specialized vehicles to carry them and launch them across the obstacle.

The next step—the development of specialized bridge or ferry vehicles—generally came about in the 1960s. Resembling flatbed cargo trucks, but with a deep buoyant body, they carried two buoyancy chambers on a hinged bed that folded out and down to lie alongside the body. Unfolded and driven into

water, they could be used as a ferry—the flat bed being able to float and take the weight of cargo or vehicles. If a number were launched, they could be hooked up, side by side, to form a continuous bridge across a river or to form a pier for landing equipment on a beach.

Another World War II innovation was the amphibious truck, notably the American DUKW or "Duck"—a floating version of the standard 2½-ton (2.3-tonne) truck (see the photograph on page 872). Used to ferry loads on rivers or to move troops in flooded areas, it was also a vital link on beaches for moving cargo from deep-draft vessels to the shore.

Another notable U.S. development during World War II was a series of amphibious assault vehicles. Lightly armored and tracked, they were capable of being launched from a ship offshore, swimming ashore, and clambering across beaches and rough country to deliver troops or supplies where needed. As with bridging equipment, these were improved upon in postwar years and now equip many armies.

COMBAT VEHICLES

The 20th century brought about the invention of the combat vehicle—a vehicle that, when driven into battle, stood a chance of surviving enemy fire.

Armored cars

Armored cars were the earliest combat vehicles. In 1901, the French army bought a number of automobiles for staff officers. The Charron, Girardot and Voigt company, which made several of these vehicles, produced an armored combat car by placing a machine gun in an armored shield in the rear seat area of an ordinary open touring car. The French army bought the car and shipped it to Algeria, where it was all but forgotten. However, the Russian army heard about it, examined the drawings, and then issued the Charron company with their own

A motorcycle and sidecar with a fitted cannon are on patrol as part of a German reconnaissance unit prior to World War II. Military motorcycles could be very flexible vehicles. Used on their own, they were quick and easy to maneuver, making them ideal for reconnaissance and messenger work. Yet they could also be fitted with sidecars to carry extra persons and guns for defense, as shown above.

During a World War II Allied invasion that took place on August 18, 1944, DUKW amphibious trucks were unloaded from military transport vessels to "swim" across the water, propelled by their tracks, and land on the beach in southern France.

specification, ordering 36 cars. The result was a boxy, steel-bodied car weighing just over 3 tons (2.7 tonnes), with a revolving turret on the roof, mounting a Maxim machine gun. The first one was delivered to Russia in 1904 and was immediately used to disperse rioters in St. Petersburg. Yet, for some unknown reason, Russia then canceled the contract. Charron built only one more car, which was sold to the French army. Yet the idea had taken hold: the Austro-Daimler company produced a design in 1904, as did several other European firms, and most armies acquired one or two.

In the opening phase of World War I, troops moved swiftly in battle, while armored cars acted as cavalry in a scouting and reconnaissance role. The British, French, and Belgian armies acquired vehicles and armored them with steel plates. When the war became mired in trench fighting, there was no longer any scope for these vehicles and they were generally forgotten, particularly after the tank appeared.

In the postwar years, however, armored cars were widely used by the British forces in the Middle East and India for patrolling dissident areas. When armored forces began to be established in armies, the scouting cavalry role was recalled and armored cars were recommissioned; they have retained their military role ever since. Cheaper to build and easier to maintain than tanks, these multiwheeled armored cars are capable of negotiating difficult terrain as easily as tracked vehicles.

Armament on armored cars has also improved. The first cars carried machine guns and, by the start of World War II, were mounting light cannon of 0.8-in (2-cm) caliber. By the end of the war, however, this had improved to 3-in (7.6-cm) guns. Today, some large 8- and 10-wheeled armored cars mount 4.7-in (12-cm) guns of the type used in tanks. Indeed, it is frequently difficult to see much difference between the bodies of some tanks and some armored cars, the principal difference being that armored cars run on wheels while tanks run on tracks (see TANK; TRACKED VEHICLE).

Artillery tractors

The greatest restriction on artillery weapon designers was the limited pulling power of a controllable horse team. Field artillery was therefore restricted to 3-in- (7.6-cm-) caliber guns weighing about 3000 lbs (1360 kg), pulled by six horses. Bigger guns had to be split into their components and assembled at the firing position. Thus, mechanical traction was developed for artillery.

German and Austria began using Benz and Austro-Daimler tractors just before 1914. It was these that took the famous Big Bertha 16½-in (42-cm) howitzers to batter the Belgian fortress of Liège into submission in 1914. The "caterpillar" tractor (invented by Benjamin Holt, owner of the U.S. heavy-equipment Holt Manufacturing Company, later the Caterpillar Tractor Company) ran on metal-belted tracks instead of wheels and was adopted by the Allies to tow heavy guns. It inspired the designers of tanks, but most field artillery was still horse-drawn and remained so until the 1940s.

Britain led the field in tracked artillery vehicles with its effective, yet expensive and complicated, Dragons (from "drag guns"). When a private contractor produced a powerful four-wheel-drive tractor—the "Quad"—with room for six gunners and ammunition, it became the standard towing vehicle in the late 1930s for the 25-lb (11.3-kg) field gun. It remained virtually the world's only specialized artillery tractor. Soon after, heavy trucks appeared, with most other nations finding that a six-wheel truck of about 3 tons' (2.7 tonnes') cargo capacity made an excellent gun tractor and could carry everything the gun needed. The only major army to deviate from this was the German army, which developed a useful range of half-track trucks of various sizes to draw heavier guns. Field guns were still horse-drawn.

APC to IFV tanks

The tank was originally designed to assist the infantry in their assault. As firepower increased, it became obvious that there was little point in having the tank crew safely encased in armor while the infantry walked alongside, exposed to all kinds of enemy fire. When the German panzer divisions invaded Poland and France in 1939 and 1940, the marching infantry were in relatively little danger, but when the war spread to the Russian front, things changed. The Germans designed half-track armored vehicles in which the motorized infantry could ride into battle. They could fire their weapons through ports in the side, and the vehicle had extra machine guns; but it was not, of itself, a fighting vehicle. Its job was simply to take the soldiers in relative safety to their required location, whereupon they got out of the vehicle and operated as normal foot infantry. These were the first armored personnel carriers (APCs).

In postwar years, the APC became popular in all armies. The American M113 was the standard model—a simple, boxy vehicle on tracks with aluminum armor, giving lightweight but adequate protection against small-arms fire and shell splinters. Some nations preferred their own designs. Yet it was eventually realized that if APCs had better armament, they could attack enemy APCs and relieve the heavy tanks from a job. Turrets with heavier weapons were developed. The German Marder, for example, had strong armor and a turret mounting a ¾-in (2-cm) automatic cannon.

These new vehicles took various names, but eventually the standard term for them became the infantry fighting vehicle (IFV). Among today's best examples are the American M2 Bradley and the British Warrior, both of which have powerful automatic cannon and heavy machine guns in their turrets and sufficient space inside for up to six fully equipped soldiers, an antitank missile, an air-defense missile, mines, and other equipment. The infantry could now fight their way to their objective, dismount for an assault on foot, and have their IFV acting as their personal tank, keeping up with them and giving them covering fire and protection.

Tank transport vehicles

The tank's greatest weakness is its track. Designed to provide grip on soft ground, it wears rapidly when running on paved roads. Once this defect was discovered in the 1930s—when tanks had become reliable enough to drive long distances without breakdowns—it became common practice to carry the tank as far as possible by loading it onto a truck. At first, any heavy commercial truck could do this job, but once tanks increased in weight and size, specialist vehicles had to be developed. Commercial trucks capable of carrying the weight were far too slow and ponderous for military use.

Two approaches to the problem were used. The first, adopted by most armies, was a heavy truck that pulled a strengthened trailer. The trailer had ramps so that the tank could be driven on and off, and the truck—usually weighing 10 to 15 tons (9.1 to 13.6 tonnes)—was ballasted at the rear to keep the wheels on the ground and ensure maximum pulling ability. A typical example was the U.S. M19 trailer, towed by a 12-ton (10.9-tonne) truck—a combination that could carry any tank weighing up to 45 tons (40.8-tonnes), but only on fairly hard surfaces.

The second type of tank transporter was the semitrailer. It is a wheeled trailer unit attached to the rear of a powerful tractor, which forms a very flexible combination. The Tractor Truck M26 was armored, with two front and eight rear wheels, and the semitrailer M15, also with eight rear wheels, was attached to it. It, too, could carry up to 45 tons (40.8 tonnes), but it had the added ability to carry the tank across rough country. Similar vehicles of both types, but capable of carrying even heavier loads, have since been developed.

I. HOGG

See also: LAND WARFARE; OFF-ROAD AND AMPHIBIOUS VEHICLES; RAILROAD CONSTRUCTION AND TRACK; RAILROADS, HISTORY OF; TRACTOR; TRUCK.

SELF-PROPELLED ARTILLERY

The U.S. M7, used in World War II, was the first successful self-propelled artillery.

Self-propelled (SP) artillery is a conventional artillery gun mounted on a motorized chassis, which may be wheeled or tracked to give it mobility. Used in the same way as towed artillery, only quicker to maneuver, it gave fast-moving armored divisions artillery that could move just as fast. SP guns were tried out by the French army in World War I and by the U.S. and British armies in the 1920s. However, at the outbreak of war in 1939, the only such guns in use were a small number of German assault guns—5.7-in (15-cm) howitzers mounted on tank chassis to accompany infantry and deliver direct fire against obstacles.

Several attempts were made to produce an SP field artillery weapon. The first successful design was the American M7—a modified M3 medium tank chassis with an open-topped body carrying a standard 4-in (10-cm) field howitzer (see the photograph above). First used by the British at the Battle of El Alamein in October 1942, it proved an immediate success. It was closely followed by the British Sexton, which mounted a 25-lb (11.3-kg) field gun on a similar open-topped body, built on the chassis of the Canadian Ram tank—a slightly modified version of the U.S. M3 medium tank. The German Hummel 5.7-in (15-cm) howitzer was a similar weapon, but Germany and the Soviet Union were more inclined to build assault guns and tank destroyers than pure SP guns.

In postwar years, SP guns became widely used because they claimed to be able to protect crews from radioactive fallout resulting from the possible future use of battlefield nuclear weapons. In the 1960s stripped-down versions emerged that could be air-lifted. In turn, this gave way to something between the two—not excessively armored but not lightweight either. The objective was to allow the gun to displace and move very rapidly after firing in order to avoid return fires that, due to electronic methods of detection, could pinpoint an artillery piece after a few shots from the same place. Moreover, with improved communication and navigation equipment, SP guns can be dispersed over a wide area and yet still be able to concentrate their fire on a single target when necessary.

A CLOSER LOOK

Further reading:
Citino, R. M. *Armored Forces: History and Sourcebook.* Westport, Connecticut: Greenwood Press, 1994.
Horb, I. V. *The American Arsenal.* Mechanicsburg, Pennsylvania: Greenhill Books, 1996.
Polk, A. *Technology Transfer from Military Applications to Intelligent Vehicle Highway Systems.* Washington, D.C.: IVHS America, 1993.

MINING AND QUARRYING

Mining and quarrying are processes used to extract rocks and minerals from under the ground

A vast bucket-wheel excavator works a surface coal mine in Kazakhstan.

Mines and quarries have evolved from the simple, scratched-out holes of prehistoric times to complex surface and underground designs requiring enough electric power to supply a small town and teams of highly skilled engineers and laborers. Mining exists because of humans' continuous demand for raw materials from rocks and minerals. The gold on computer contacts, the copper or aluminum in electric wires, the coal used to generate power, and the cement in sidewalks and buildings all come from mines or quarries.

What is mining?

Mining operations are usually designated by the methods used to extract the target minerals or rocks. The most simple division is between surface mining and underground mining. These two possibilities are easily imagined and classified.

Surface mining requires that a large excavation or pit be dug to obtain the minerals. Since the sides of the pit often cannot stand vertically, the pit becomes a large bowl. Some large pits are a mile or two in diameter and thousands of feet deep. They are mined in a steplike progress. The steps are called benches and are connected by ramp roads.

Surface mines are economic because very large drilling, loading, and hauling equipment can be used. A single truck may transport 300 tons (270 tonnes) or more on roads that are 200 ft (60 m) wide. The disadvantage of surface mines is the unfortunate fact that tons of barren waste rock must be removed to expose the mineral-bearing veins of ore or coal.

Deep mineral deposits cannot be mined by surface methods because there is simply too much waste rock overlying the deposit.

Underground mines are developed by vertical shafts from the surface or through steep inclines connecting to horizontal tunnels. These tunnels are called drifts in metal mines or entries in coal mines. Usually these openings are limited to 20 ft (6 m) in width because unmined rock or coal is left as support pillars to carry the load of the rock above the mine. Even then, the roof, known as the back by miners, must be supported by wooden or steel posts and cross beams called sets. Modern operations use rock bolts or hollow friction tubes called split sets to hold the roof material in a solid mass. Since underground openings are limited in size, smaller equipment must be used; this increases the cost of operating the mine, since smaller amounts can be extracted at a time.

Other cost-increase factors include having smaller drill holes for explosive charges—therefore more charges are required than in surface mines.

CONNECTIONS

● Mining is the first part of **ORE EXTRACTION AND PROCESSING**, since minerals must be removed from the ground before being turned into **METALS**.

● Many **CANALS AND INLAND WATERWAYS** were built to carry coal and ore away from mines to factories and refineries.

CORE FACTS

■ Mining provides metals, energy, and construction materials for human use.
■ Minerals and rocks are extracted either from surface mines or underground mines.
■ Mining methods optimize material handling.
■ Mines require sophisticated planning for stability, power, and ventilation.

In addition, more explosives are needed for blasting underground seams since there is only one free surface to break into. Underground, this surface is the end of the drift in the direction that the miner is going, and it is called the face. Surface mines can have three free faces on a bench—one on the top of the bench, one on the side, and one at the end—each of which can be blasted with explosives. Underground mines have an important advantage in cost, however, because little or no waste rock is mined. An underground coal mine in a flat-lying coal seam has all of its workings in the coal seam.

Types of mines

Most mines are either classified as hard rock or coal. *Hard rock* refers to metal mining where the veins exist in many orientations, from vertical to horizontal, and can be relatively thin or very wide. Coal mines normally have seams or beds that lie close to the horizontal and are more easily mined in grid patterns like the streets, alleys, and roads that make up a modern planned city or town. Other flat-lying, sedimentary deposits, such as gypsum, rock salt, and potash (potassium carbonate), are included in the coal-mining classification. Hard rock and coal mines use surface or underground methods.

The historical development of metal mines and coal mines has created differing sets of names for similar areas in the mine. Each type has a face, but coal mines have a roof overhead and ribs for sidewalls and a floor. Metal mines have the same physical appearance, but the coal mine floor is a metal mine sill, like in a windowsill in a house. The roof and rib of a coal mine are described as a single unit, known as the back, in a hard rock metal mine.

Quarries are sites from which materials such as aggregates, limestone, sandstone, or building stones such as granite or marble are extracted. Quarries have benches similar to other surface mines, but they are not as deep and the sides stand vertically. They have little or no waste rock and perhaps only a little soil cover. Most quarries are on the surface, but a few quarries are vast underground openings.

Valuable minerals such as gold, platinum, tin, and even diamonds may be mined from erosional deposits found in the gravel along rivers and streams.

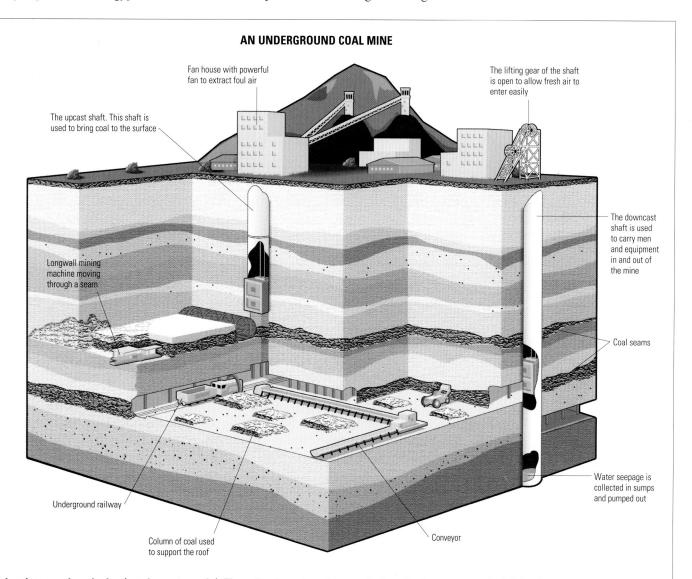

AN UNDERGROUND COAL MINE

Fan house with powerful fan to extract foul air

The lifting gear of the shaft is open to allow fresh air to enter easily

The upcast shaft. This shaft is used to bring coal to the surface

The downcast shaft is used to carry men and equipment in and out of the mine

Longwall mining machine moving through a seam

Coal seams

Underground railway

Column of coal used to support the roof

Conveyor

Water seepage is collected in sumps and pumped out

A typical underground coal mine (not drawn to scale). The soft nature of coal means that much of a seam must be left in place to support underground drifts. However, longwall mining removes the whole seam and lets the roof fall into the space where the coal used to be.

GEORGIUS AGRICOLA

A windlass hoisting system as illustrated in Agricola's historic book.

Georgius Agricola wrote the first printed book on mining, which was published posthumously in 1556. Born in 1494, two years after Columbus sailed to the New World, Agricola lived in what is now Germany. He was a scholar and a scientific observer of life. His fascination with the mining activities that were commonplace in the area of Saxony, the province in which he lived, caused him to author many scientific texts. His most famous, *De re metallica* (literally, *Of metals*) explained mining and metallurgy practice from the earliest time to his day. *De re metallica* is remarkable for its content and detailed illustrations.

PEOPLE

This activity is known as placer (pronounced *plasser*) mining and was the main form of mineral excavation until the advent of large-scale mechanized mines. Many of the first mines and those that began the great gold rushes to California, Australia, and the Yukon were placer mines.

Since metals or gems are heavy compared to other rocks in gravel, they accumulate or concentrate in layers at the bottom of flowing water. As the streams meander back and forth, these layers become crossed and stacked. In the days of the gold rushes, the gravel banks were washed down (sluiced) by jets of water from a nozzle mounted on a swivel called a monitor. This hydraulic mining method recovered millions of dollars of gold.

As the gravel overlying the mineral becomes harder or deeper, or if not enough water is available to sluice the gravel, floating dredges with buckets connected by chain links are used to dig the gravel and bring the mineral to the surface. As the dredge

works upstream, it digs its own small lake and fills behind itself with the new gravel. Dredges are still being used in Alaska and in South America, where vast gravel and gold deposits exist.

Mining through the ages

Mining began when humans needed specific mineral commodities. Early efforts at digging a specific rock called chert to make tools began when simple collection from an exposed bed could no longer satisfy demand. The first miners were part-timers who began to dig down to meet their mineral needs. Throughout the Bronze Age and then into the Iron Age, mining became a full-time occupation. Trade and commerce around these commodities became one of the first global businesses.

The Greeks, Romans, and Persians were the first civilizations to mine on a significant scale. Although arming and armoring a Roman army cohort of 300 soldiers required about 3 tons (2.7 tonnes) of iron, this is little more than required by a single automobile. Demands for metals for domestic use also lead to the creation of mines. On Cyprus, in Spain, and in Cornwall, England, miners followed surface exposures (called leads or outcrops) underground. Ancient underground mines lacked forethought and sophistication. The miners followed the veins, and the mine openings took the path of the extracted ore. Little surface mining was done in those days because too much waste rock was in the way and was as hard to break with primitive picks and shovels as was the ore. The broken ore was hauled up ladders to the surface in bags and baskets.

The importance of mining in the Middle Ages is demonstrated by *De re metallica*, published in 1556. This illustrated tome shows the principles of mining and was originally published only forty years after the first printed books.

With the rise of the industry from 1800 on, the demand for metals derived from mineral ores rose dramatically. Simultaneously, energy to smelt and work metals was found in another minable source, coal. Although the miners still depended on hand tools and baskets, they had acquired black-powder explosives similar to gunpowder to break the rock. This in turn required miners to use a rock drill and drilling hammer to create a hole for the powder.

A bit of sophisticated planning kept the mine from wandering along the vein. The mineral deposit was reached with vertical openings called shafts or horizontal tunnels called adits. Shaft buckets to lift the ore required hoisting towers and demanded more power than horses could provide. Coal-burning steam engines were used. Adits, or drifts as they are called underground, were driven straight to the ore veins. They were made large enough for carts and horses; rails were laid to keep the wagons out of the mud. With increased mining depth, more planning and power were needed to pump water out and clean air into the mines. The need for pumps for water removal inspired the development of efficient steam engines (see STEAM ENGINE).

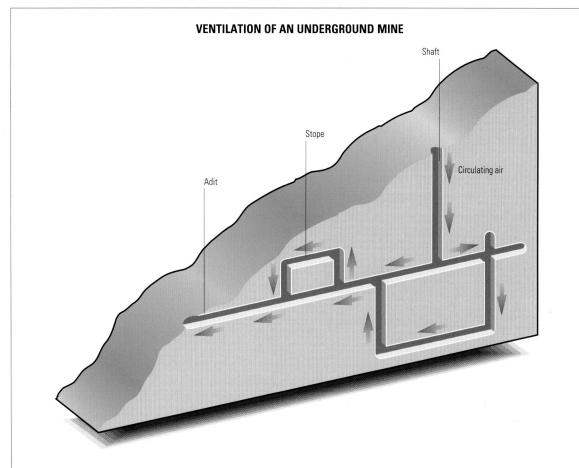

VENTILATION OF AN UNDERGROUND MINE

Shaft

Circulating air

Stope

Adit

The air in an underground mine must constantly be replaced to prevent the buildup of toxic fumes and to make it safe for miners to breathe. Ventilation is usually driven by large fans.

The basic steps used in mining then are still used today: drill the holes for explosives, blast, load the rock into a hauler, haul or hoist it to the surface. At the beginning of the 20th century, the holes were still drilled and the rock was shoveled by hand.

As mines grew in number and size, inventors and engineers developed first steam-powered drill machines, then compressed-air drills, and today hydraulic drills to quickly pound holes for the explosive. Dynamite replaced black powder and has been in turn replaced by chemical gels, each safer to handle than its predecessor.

Hand shovels have now been displaced by compressed-air powered loaders called mucking machines, or muckers. A compressed-air radial piston engine exhausts air rather than the toxic gases that would be produced by an internal combustion engine. These muckers have a small bucket that picks up the ore then rotates in a 180-degree arc to load a car behind it. Newer, larger mine openings allow the use of rubber-tired, diesel-powered loaders similar to those seen on surface construction sites. Their exhaust is "scrubbed" to keep the air clean. Small mine locomotives powered by electricity or diesel pull trains of ore cars to the shafts. In shallow underground mines or flat-lying deposits, small diesel trucks move the ore through levels connected by long ramps. When the rock is easily broken and not sharp, conveyor belts are used (see CONVEYOR).

The success of mining mostly lies in efficient material handling—efficient in terms of safety, cost, and volume. Different ore and rock types and their depositional features have created fairly standard mining methods.

Modern surface mining

Mining today is most notable for the total mechanization of the age-old operations of mineral extraction. Coal mining in particular has evolved into nearly a totally mechanized business; this is

DRAGLINES

Draglines used in surface coal mines are among the largest pieces of mobile equipment used in the United States. The draglines are used to remove the overburden that lies on the coal seams. By using a dragline, surface coal mines become a moving pit. The material from a new cut to expose coal is dumped directly into the preceding cut, and reclamation can follow immediately after that.

To dig a hole 200 ft (70 m) deep and to deposit the material 300 ft (90 m) to the side requires a big machine. One of the largest draglines weighs 800 tons (725 tonnes), and a full bucket contains 160 cubic yards (120m^3). This bucket capacity is larger than a railroad car. Draglines operate on circular flat bases and "walk" using two huge side shoes like crutches that drag the machine forward. The cables that lift the bucket are over 5 in (12.7 cm) across.

A CLOSER LOOK

QUARRYING

A view of one of the world's largest quarries, in North Wales. This quarry has been in use since 1765 and in 1999 was over 1100 ft (335m) deep.

Quarrying is normally employed to produce stone, such as marble and granite, for construction. The marble quarries of Italy have produced stone for building construction for thousands of years. A small but important product is the stone used for sculptures. Brazil produces vast quantities of marble of fine texture and in a wide range of colors.

Highly prized stone is quarried by drilling many small holes and splitting pieces off the main block. Marble or granite destined to be polished is sawed free using wire saws. These saws consist of continuous strands of wire that rub on the rock and cut through using hard grit that is fed as a paste onto the wires.

Some quarries supply aggregate for roads. These quarries drill and blast the rock, since it will be crushed to size before use. Limestone quarries supply road material, but limestone is also used to make cement. Other lime products are used to reduce acidity in soil for agricultural use.

A Closer Look

partly due to the physical weakness of coal and the fact that it lies in long, flat seams: factors that make it easier to mine than most other rocks and minerals.

The conditions in surface mines are constantly being improved by new systems and equipment. For example, surface coal mines in Wyoming have been dug through the overlying strata (overburden) of limestone, shale, and sandstone to expose coal seams that are 100 ft (30 m) thick. Rotary drill machines, which can bore 17-in- (45-cm-) diameter holes through 100 ft (30 m) of rock in less than an hour, cut into the overburden. These holes are loaded with ammonium nitrate–fuel-oil blasting agents (see EXPLOSIVE). Usually the overburden is fractured by the explosion just enough to dig through, and a dragline digs the overburden and deposits into the previous, adjacent, pit from which the coal has already been removed. A dragline is a large crane that has a bucket controlled by cables to dig the shattered overburden. A large, modern dragline has a bucket with a capacity of 160 cubic yards (120 m^3) and a boom 360 ft (110 m) long (see the box on page 877).

Another method, called cast blasting, uses immense amounts of explosives to literally cast or blow the unwanted overburden into an adjacent pit.

After the coal is exposed, it is drilled, blasted, and then loaded by electric shovels that have bucket capacities of over 50 cubic yards (38 m^3) into trucks that carry up to 350 tons (320 tonnes) per trip. The box of the truck is as big as a small house. The coal is hauled to a preparation plant and then loaded into railcars of 100-ton (90-tonne) capacity. Trains of 100 or more railcars are assembled and move as a unit train to electric power plants up to 1500 miles (2400 km) away, 10,000 tons (9070 tonnes) at once.

Although not common in the United States, some mines use even larger machines called bucket-wheel excavators. Bucket-wheel excavators are extremely large and have head and tail booms with conveyors running their length. The vertical head has a rotating hollow wheel with smaller digging buckets around its circumference. The buckets continuously dig and drop the rock onto the conveyors; they can dig over 100,000 cubic yards (76,000 m^3) each hour. Their digging ability is so fast that belt conveyors, and not slower trucks, are required to haul the overburden or coal away.

Modern underground mining

Underground coal mining can be done by conventional, continuous, or longwall mining methods. Conventional mines still drill, blast, load, and haul, but the equipment is mobile and rubber-tired. Continuous mines dispense with the drilling and blasting stages. Instead they use a huge machine with rotating arms or drums spiked with hard teeth that can bore or rip their way into the coal. They load the mined coal into four-wheel-drive vehicles that pull shuttle cars or trucks.

Longwall mines are very productive because they do not require waiting for a shuttle car. The longwall panel or section is designed to be up to 1000 ft (300 m) wide and up to 5000 ft (1500 m) long. The mechanical components are a shearing drum, a pan conveyor, and hydraulic shields. The shearing drum, again spiked with hard teeth and equipped with water sprays to suppress dust, ranges along the width of the panel. It shears off coal, which then drops onto the pan conveyor, where it is pulled to the side and a belt conveyor takes it out away from the panel. The hydraulic shields are each about 10 ft (3 m) wide and hold the roof up. As the shearer passes along the long face, the shields in sequence push the conveyor closer to the face. They then lower themselves, pull forward, and extend upward to hold the roof for the next cut. The roof behind the shield supports collapses and that reduces the load on the shields. Longwall mining is very safe and highly productive.

Underground metal mining still requires drilling and blasting because the rock is very hard. All of the equipment is on rubber tires, however, and is diesel-powered; each machine has two drills on articulated hydraulic booms. The blasting agent—a high-powered chemical gel—is loaded through hoses.

Bauxite (aluminum ore) is blasted from a surface mine in Australia's Northern Territory.

After blasting, large front-end loaders, which are designed for operation in confined spaces with low headroom, load the ore into trucks or transfer it to loading pockets by tram, where it is dropped to lower levels through ore passes bored in the rock. The ore passes converge at the bottom level, where they feed the ore into waiting trains, skips, or large trucks. Deep mines require powerful hoisting towers to lift the skips full of ore from the bottom level to the surface. Shallower underground mines use trucks or conveyors and an extensive underground ramp system to bring the ore to the surface.

Most underground hard-rock mines are refilled since, unlike coal mines, only a small portion of the rock contains marketable ore. For example, in a gold mine in Nevada, as little as half an ounce of gold may be extracted from a ton of ore. The ground and milled remains (tailings) can be mixed with water to form a slurry, which is then piped back underground, or they may be hauled back into the mine by truck. Mixing cement with the tailings creates a strong backfill and improves the strength. Some mines use this cut-and-fill method and actually mine downward, underneath the cement-filled chamber from an earlier cut.

Ore veins that are narrow but rich in a valuable ore can be mined using traditional methods and tools, including hand-held drills. The mined areas are called stopes. The ore that has been drilled is dragged from the stopes to the ore passes by a cable-hauled scraper blade. At the bottom level, the ore from the ore passes is loaded into narrow-gauge railcars for transport to the shaft. Due to the confined working conditions, this method is more labor intensive—and consequently more expensive—than mining using larger, rubber-tired equipment.

T. FINCH

See also: COAL; ENVIRONMENTAL ENGINEERING; HAZARDOUS WASTE; HYDRAULICS AND PNEUMATICS; IRON AND STEEL PRODUCTION; NONFERROUS METAL; OIL AND NATURAL GAS PRODUCTION; ORE EXTRACTION AND PROCESSING; POLLUTION AND ITS CONTROL; PROSPECTING; SURVEYING; TUNNEL.

Further reading:
Dutton, A. *Handbook on Quarrying*. Adelaide, Australia: Department of Mines and Energy, 1993.
Mining and its Environmental Impact. Edited by R. Hester and R. Harrison. Cambridge, England: Royal Society of Chemistry, 1994.
The Mining Industry. Edited by D. Banks. Philadelphia: Hanley & Belfus, 1993.
Rock Mechanics: For Underground Mining. Edited by B. Brady and E. Brown. 2nd edition. New York: Chapman & Hall, 1993.

ENVIRONMENTAL CONCERNS

Mining poses considerable environmental concerns. Modern surface coal mines reclaim the mined area by removing the topsoil before mining. After mining and recontouring, the topsoil is replaced and revegetated. A reclaimed coal mine is difficult to distinguish from its undisturbed surroundings.

Underground metal mines place the waste rock back underground to avoid affecting the surface environment. Not only does this keep the surface clean but the backfilling supports the underground structure.

Surface metal mines cannot be refilled economically; instead, their waste dumps are constructed with shallow surface angles, which helps the revegetation process. In some cases, waste from ore processing is buried and sealed in a capsule of clay. Ground water must be channeled away from the dump to prevent it from leaching (dissolving and carrying away) the buried waste.

WIDER IMPACT

MISSILE

Missiles are self-propelled, projectile weapons that are aimed or guided to their targets

A Tomahawk cruise missile flies over a cement plant in the Mojave desert.

CONNECTIONS

● The development of missiles has been closely linked to advances in **SPACE TRAVEL AND TECHNOLOGY.**

● Most modern **NUCLEAR WEAPONS** are delivered to their targets by missiles as part of **STRATEGIC DEFENSE SYSTEMS.**

Although the Chinese reputedly invented the rocket about 800 years ago, the first feasible military missiles did not appear until around the start of the 19th century. British ordnance engineer Sir William Congreve (1772–1828) developed missiles with explosive or incendiary (fire-causing) warheads. These were first used by the British navy in 1807 against French emperor Napoléon's forces at the port of Boulogne, France. Congreve's rockets were used in anger again in 1814, this time against the United States in the War of 1812: the "rockets' red glare" in the U.S. national anthem refers to the Congreve rockets that were fired from the British warship H.M.S. *Erebus* in the attack on Fort McHenry in Baltimore harbor, Maryland (see ROCKETRY).

Rockets were used in the Mexican War (1846–1848) and in the Civil War (1861–1865), though their use was limited because they were very inaccurate. By the World War I (1914–1918), U.S. engineer Robert Goddard (1882–1945) had used stronger construction and more powerful propellants to produce longer-range rockets. In 1917, U.S. inventor Elmer Sperry (1860–1930) developed an aerial torpedo—a pilotless airplane, stabilized by a gyroscope, that carried an explosive charge that could be aimed at a specific target.

A year later U.S. inventor Charles Kettering (1876–1958) produced a more sophisticated missile for the U.S. Army Signal Corps. The flight direction of the missile was again gyro-stabilized, and an aneroid barometer detected the air pressure and was used to maintain a preset height. Sharply upward-pointing biplane wings stabilized the missile, keeping it from rolling (see FLIGHT, PRINCIPLES OF). The range of the weapon would be determined by selecting a preset number of revolutions for a propeller that was turned by the airstream as the missile flew through the air. This measured the distance traveled. When the preset limit was reached, the wings would be jettisoned and the missile would plunge to earth under the weight of its warhead.

CORE FACTS

■ The first cruise missile was developed in 1917 by Elmer Sperry as an aerial torpedo, or gyro-stabilized pilotless airplane, that could be aimed at targets many miles away.

■ The Germans successfully launched missiles from submerged submarines as early as 1942.

■ Today's ballistic missiles can reach a target on the other side of the world with a flight time of just over half an hour from launch to impact.

■ MIRV (*m*ultiple *i*ndependently targeted *r*eentry *v*ehicle) missiles have a final stage that can release several warheads on different trajectories to hit completely different targets.

■ A cruise missile can hit its target with an error of less than 150 feet (46 m) after a 1500-mile (2400-km) flight.

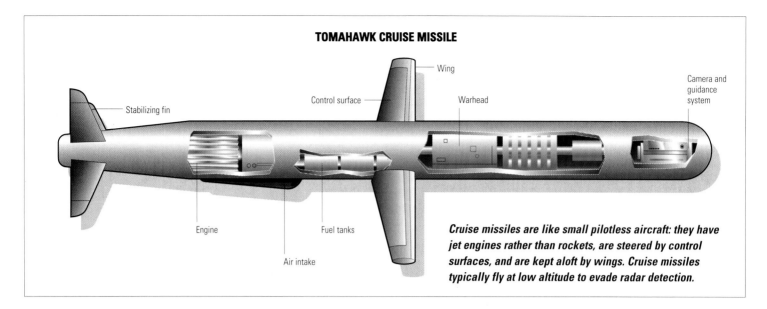

TOMAHAWK CRUISE MISSILE

Wing
Control surface
Warhead
Camera and guidance system
Stabilizing fin
Engine
Fuel tanks
Air intake

Cruise missiles are like small pilotless aircraft: they have jet engines rather than rockets, are steered by control surfaces, and are kept aloft by wings. Cruise missiles typically fly at low altitude to evade radar detection.

Types of missiles

German technology (see the box on page 883) was used after World War II (1939–1945) to develop a whole family of tactical guided missiles. These included antitank missiles, which could be carried by two soldiers and launched from their carrying cases. As the solid-fuel rocket propelled the missile toward its target, it was controlled from the ground with a joystick of the type used to steer an aircraft. Commands were relayed down a thin, long wire that unrolled behind the missile as it flew. A flare in the tail section helped keep track of the missile as it progressed toward its target.

The British, French, Soviet, and U.S. armies all had variations of this tube-launched, wire-controlled missile for use against tanks. It was guided by sight. The U.S. forces' TOW (*t*ube-launched, *o*ptically-sighted, *w*ire-guided) missile was a larger version, with greater range and destructive power. The TOW was mounted on vehicles, including helicopters, and once the gunner had the target centered in the sight, the guidance was automatic. Optical-fiber- or radio-control systems replaced wire guidance systems in later developments of this type of missile.

Air-to-surface missiles—those that are launched from aircraft to hit targets on the ground—were the descendants of wartime unguided rockets. The U.S. Bullpup missile was steered by the crew of the launching aircraft toward its target, but this attracted hostile fire to the launch aircraft. Some current air-to-surface missiles, such as the U.S. Maverick, carry an onboard television camera so that the controlling pilot sees a view of the target from the missile and the launch airplane is free to take evasive action and leave the immediate area.

Air-to-air missiles—those that are launched at airborne targets from airplanes—tend to be lighter, faster, and more maneuverable than other types, since their targets are themselves more maneuverable. Because a fast response to changes in the target position is necessary, air-to-air missiles use automatic homing systems, based on radar or infrared heat-seeking equipment, to guide them to their targets.

As their performance improved, a whole series of different types was developed with increasing ranges and improved maneuverability to counter evasive action once the target spotted the threat.

In the cold war years after World War II, the Soviet Union established an early lead in antiship missiles because of the Western allies' overreliance on carrier-borne aircraft for antiship strikes. New types

CRUISE MISSILES

Cruise missiles—unlike ballistic missiles—operate at relatively low altitude. Their flight is easier to control and they are more difficult for air defense systems to detect and destroy. Jet engines (rather than rockets) usually power cruise missiles, which reduces speed but increases range.

The heart of a modern cruise missile is a computer navigation system. This uses a digital contour map of the route to the target, created from radar and photographic images. The route is marked as a series of checkpoints, where the missile's guidance system compares the picture on its own radar with the digital image on the computer system and makes course changes to eliminate any discrepencies between the two. This allows the missile to approach its target on an indirect course to avoid known defenses. As it approaches its target, the missile's computer map focuses on a smaller area. The error at impact is typically less than 150 feet (46 m) after a flight of some 1500 miles (2400 km).

Because missiles are much smaller than a piloted aircraft, they are less obvious to enemy radar. By steering between checkpoints using inertial navigation (see page 883), it sends out no transmissions for much of the flight. Small jet engines deliver relatively little heat and are more difficult to detect with infrared equipment than rockets at higher altitudes. Nevertheless, future missiles are likely to use stealth technology to confuse or evade defense radar systems (see ELECTRONIC COUNTERMEASURES).

The other advantage of cruise missiles is their versatility. Larger cruise missiles such as the Tomahawk can be launched from surface warships or from the missile tubes of submerged submarines, while covert air-launched cruise missiles are small enough to be carried under the wing or within the bomb bay of a piloted bomber such as the B-52. They can be fitted with a wide variety of warheads, from small nuclear weapons to conventional explosive charges or clusters of individual small bombs for cratering runways. A combination of conventionally armed Tomahawks and air-launched cruise missiles was used by NATO forces in the Kosovo crisis of 1999.

A CLOSER LOOK

A U.S. destroyer launches a Tomahawk cruise missile during an exercise in the Pacific Ocean.

then dive on the target from above. This makes it more difficult for naval defense systems designed to hit sea-skimmers to ward off a Harpoon attack.

After World War II, a group of different types of surface-to-air missiles was developed that incorporated German-developed technology. These missiles included portable shoulder-launched short-range weapons, such as the U.S. Redeye and Stinger, and larger, longer-range missiles for attacking higher-flying airplanes. Most used solid-fuel rockets to provide the initial acceleration and simple jets called ramjets to power them for the rest of their flight to the target (see AIRCRAFT ENGINE).

The U.S. Hawk SAM (surface-to-air missile) system was a semimobile, radar-guided missile that had to be unloaded and set up at a launching site for firing. It was used to destroy incoming enemy missiles. SAM has now been replaced by the Patriot semimobile system, which proved very effective in the Gulf War (1990–1991) against incoming Iraqi missiles. This system is able to relay information about targets from the missile radar to the fire-control installation on the ground.

Guidance and control

Early post-World-War-II guided missiles, such as the TOW and the Bullpup, used command guidance systems. A human operator watched their flight and steered them to the target by signals down a wire or over a radio channel. A later variation was beam-riding control, where a radar beam was directed at the target, and the missile sensed that beam and followed it. With longer-range weapons, optical tracking was replaced by television tracking, whereby images from a camera mounted in the missile were relayed to a distant operator who would control the flight from a safe distance from enemy fire.

More recently, command guidance systems increasingly rely on laser beams to mark the target and provide a signpost for the missile, and on computers to track the missile and issue commands to guide it to the target. Another technique, used in the U.S. Patriot system, is called track-by-missile guidance. This uses a radar system on board the missile to track the target and transmit information on the target's bearing and range from the attacking missile back to the control post. This data is fed into a computer, which calculates the optimum route to the target and transmits control commands back to the outgoing missile.

The latest generations of missiles are controlled by active or passive systems on board the missile itself. Active system missiles have a radar system that instructs an onboard guidance computer of the path and location of the target. Passive systems track targets by detecting radiation that is emitted by the target itself. For example, heat-seeking missiles home in on infrared radiation from hot objects such as ships' funnels, vehicles' engines, or jet engines.

All these guidance systems are vulnerable to countermeasures. Radar signals can be jammed—fooled by decoy signals or clouds of chaff (strips of

have been developed by a number of different nations. These missiles skim the surface of the sea at high speed and pack sufficient explosive power to destroy or disable relatively large warships. These include the British Sea Skud—a small missile that can be launched from helicopters—and the larger, longer-range French Exocet, which has a range of up to 40 miles (64 km). The Exocet launched by Argentina that sank the British destroyer H.M.S. *Sheffield* during the Falklands war in 1982 failed to explode, but unspent fuel from the shattered missile ignited and started the fires that led to the eventual destruction of the ship.

The U.S. Harpoon antiship missile, like the Exocet missile, can be launched either from ships or from aircraft. Its versatile guidance system allows it to make surface-skimming attacks, or, if needed, it can be programmed to approach at low altitude, climb sharply when close to its intended target, and metal foil dropped in front of the target) that generate spurious echoes. Infrared heat-seeking missiles can be drawn off their targets by firing a decoy flare as the missile approaches. The heat emitted by the flare lures the missile away from the target and allows enough time for the target to make its escape.

Semiactive guidance systems have been developed to overcome this problem. A system based outside the missile illuminates the target, either by radar or laser designation. The missile's own system then detects the signal that is reflected by the target. The target-illuminating radar or laser transmitter does not even have to be located on the launch site. A long-range missile can be launched at a safe distance from a particular target that has been marked by an observer much closer to that target.

As missiles with even longer ranges are developed, inertial guidance systems (onboard systems that detect the movement of the missile) have been adopted to steer missiles to the vicinity of the target before close-range guidance systems come into action. For long-range antiship missiles and air-to-air missiles, this means that there is no radiation emitted by the missile itself or the launch vehicle to betray their positions to defense forces. Inertial guidance is also used for antiradar missiles that home in on enemy radar transmissions. If the radar stops transmitting to make the missiles miss their targets, inertial guidance enables them to continue the approach toward the target (see NAVIGATION).

All these improvements mean that more missiles can be launched on a "fire-and-forget" basis, whereby automatic systems are relied on to guide the missile to its target after launch. The more powerful fire-control computers allow ships and aircraft to engage larger numbers of hostile targets at the same time. The U.S. Navy's F-18 Hornet can take on ten different targets at once (see MILITARY AIRCRAFT).

Ballistic missiles

The term *ballistic* is derived from the Greek word *ballein*, which means "to throw." A ballistic missile follows the same kind of trajectory as a thrown stone—it climbs rapidly after launch, reaches a high altitude, and drops steeply on its target. Strategic ballistic missiles carrying nuclear warheads—direct descendants of the German V-2—were originally based at launch sites on land. However, as accuracy of the long-range missiles improved, surface sites became too vulnerable to attack by incoming enemy missiles. Launchers were therefore shifted to submarines that could travel over long distances without surfacing (and therefore could avoid easy detection) or to underground concrete silos that were strong enough to survive even a nuclear explosion.

The mechanism of deterrence depends on knowing that the launching of any nuclear strike will inevitably result in a massive counterstrike. This was central to the MAD (Mutual Assured Destruction) doctrine that was adopted by the protagonists in the cold war. More recently, with the threat of hostile missiles of still greater accuracy, other measures have

THE V-1 AND V-2

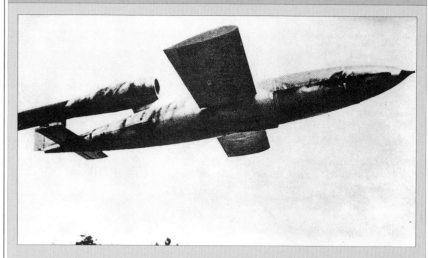

A V-1 doodlebug is launched for an attack during World War II.

Wartime Germany's *Vergeltungswaffen* (revenge weapons) included the first working cruise missile (the V-1) and the first ballistic missile (the V-2). The V-1, nicknamed the doodlebug, was a small, pilotless airplane that was catapult-launched from a ramp in order to attain the 150 mph (240 km/h) needed for its crude pulse-jet engine to function. It had a top speed of 400 mph (640 km/h) and a range of more than 150 miles (240 km).

Its course was set by magnetic compasses and gyrocompasses, and its height was controlled by an aneroid instrument. As was the case with Charles Kettering's missiles, the range covered by the V-1 was monitored and its warhead activated by the turns of a propeller. At the target, a spoiler pushed the nose down and cut the fuel supply. V-1s were fired against London in 1944, where their throaty drone led to their being called buzz bombs. Their low speed and operating height made the V-1 very vulnerable, and many were destroyed by antiaircraft fire or tipped off course by defending fighters.

The V-2 was a single-stage liquid-fueled rocket with a guidance system adapted from aircraft autopilot technology. The V-2 used control fins and vanes for steering, reached a height of approximately 50 miles (80 km), and had a horizontal range of 200 miles (320 km). Traveling much faster than sound, it gave no warning of its approach, and guns and aircraft were powerless against it. Its massive 1600-pound (725-kg) warhead caused widespread destruction. Around 4000 V-2s were fired against London, Paris, and Antwerp.

By the end of the war, the Germans had developed a whole range of experimental missiles. The smaller, shorter-range Rheinbote multistage missile was more accurate than the V-2, and 200 were fired against Antwerp in 1944. Radio-controlled glider bombs were launched from aircraft. One of these sank the new Italian battleship *Roma*, on its way to surrender to the Allies in 1943. Other German projects included air-to-air missiles, a surface-to-air missile, and the first missiles fired from a submerged submarine as early as 1942.

HISTORY OF TECHNOLOGY

been taken to guarantee the ability to deliver a devastating retaliatory strike. These include using camouflaged mobile launchers and building very large numbers of launch sites, some of which would house dummy missiles. Despite showing up clearly on satellite images, it would be impossible for an aggressor to know with certainty which sites actually contain live missiles at any time.

Early ballistic missiles, such as the V-2, were mainly run on liquid fuels. They had limited range and had to be launched relatively close to their

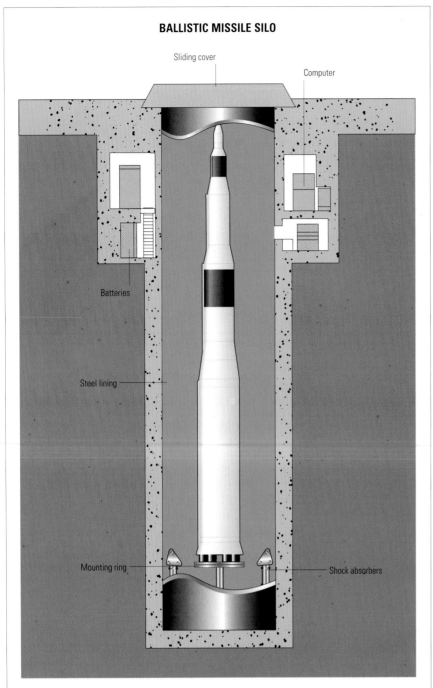

BALLISTIC MISSILE SILO

Sliding cover

Computer

Batteries

Steel lining

Mounting ring

Shock absorbers

Long-range ballistic missiles such as this Minuteman III are stored and launched from underground silos in the United States. The silos are designed to be able to protect the missile from direct attack by nuclear weapons.

minutes that a Soviet missile would take from launch to impact. However, the development of new fuels and new types of pump reduced the fueling time first to 20 minutes and finally to just one minute.

Solid-fueled missiles did not have this readiness problem. Unlike liquid-fueled missiles, solid-fueled rockets such as the U.S. Minuteman were stored with the propellant already in place. However, there were initial difficulties with guidance, since it was impossible to vary the thrust produced by the rocket engines. The submarine-launched Polaris was also solid-fueled, and because it could be fired from beneath the surface, it was possible to make optimum use of its 1700-mile (2700-km) range by patrolling close to the coastline of the potential target nation.

The next step toward ensuring MAD was to increase the number of warheads carried by each missile in order to widen coverage of a given target—the multiple reentry vehicle (MRV) concept. The MRV was further developed as the multiply targeted independent reentry vehicle (MIRV) missile, whose final stage had its own control function to release several warheads on different trajectories, hitting completely different targets. Both the land-based Minuteman III and the submarine-launched Trident are MIRV missiles, each carrying between three and eight independent warheads.

Like the rockets used to deliver payloads into orbit, most ballistic missiles consist of several stages. During the boost phase, one or more rocket engines accelerate it on to the correct trajectory to reach the intended target. This requires very precise inertial navigation and a sophisticated guidance computer to predict the gravitational forces acting on the warheads on their way to the targets. After the boost is complete, the rocket engines fall away, leaving the warheads, the guidance system, and any countermeasure equipment to continue the trajectory. At a certain point, the multiple warheads separate and begin falling toward their individual targets under the influence of gravity.

D. OWEN

See also: ELECTRONIC COUNTERMEASURES; MECHANICS; NUCLEAR WEAPONS; ROCKET ENGINE; ROCKETRY; UNPILOTED VEHICLES AND AIRCRAFT; WEAPONRY: SPECIALIZED SYSTEMS.

Further reading:
Defending Against Ballistic Missile Attacks: The Concept of Defensive Deterrence. Edited by J. Frelk and G. Tait. Washington D.C.: George C Marshall Institute, 1990.
Karp, A. *Ballistic Missile Proliferation: The Politics and Technics.* New York: Oxford University Press, 1996.
Mackenzie, D. *Inventing Accuracy: An Historical Sociology of Nuclear Missile Guidance.* Cambridge: MIT Press, 1990.
Navias, M. *Going Ballistic.* First edition. London: Brassey's, 1993.
Seth, C. *Ballistic Missiles in the Third: Threat Response.* New York: Praeger, 1990.

targets. For U.S. missiles aimed at the Soviet Union, for example, this necessitated launch bases in territories close to the Soviet Union, such as Turkey and what was then West Germany. In the case of Soviet missiles, an attempt to establish missile bases close to the U.S. coast precipitated the Cuban missile crisis of 1962—historically viewed as the closest the world has come to a nuclear war.

Liquid-fueled missiles initially suffered from lengthy fueling times: to reduce the risk of explosions, liquid fuel and oxidant are only loaded into a missile shortly before its launch (see FUELS AND PROPELLANTS). The original U.S. Titan missiles took more than an hour to load—much longer than the 35

MONEY AND BANKING TECHNOLOGY

Monetary systems encompass paper currency, coins, and a worldwide electronic exchange network

Early civilizations used a system of bartering to exchange goods and services. Every transaction required finding someone who both had the goods the prospective trader wanted and was willing to accept the goods offered in exchange. Eventually, many societies started using commodities, such as grain, salt, or beans, to help "price" goods. For example, an ass might fetch twice as many beans as a goat. However, such commodity money had drawbacks as a medium of exchange. It could be heavy and tended to be used to even out values in bartering rather than to buy something outright. Consumables were also found not to be a very good way to store value over the long term. Instead, precious metals, such as gold and silver, began to be used, each piece being carefully weighed on a balance.

The first coins were produced about 3000 years ago in what is now Turkey. By standardizing the value of a fixed weight of the metal, scales were not needed for every transaction; buyers of goods merely needed to count out the required number of coins. This provided a common medium of exchange with an agreed value, paving the way for retail markets and an expanded role for commerce in everyday life.

Following their invention of paper, the Chinese went on to invent paper money as well. Mongol emperors forced their people to use the currency and strictly enforced its value. Indeed, the government confiscated all the gold and silver and issued the paper currency in its place. Paper money made trade and administration easier across the far-flung Chinese territories, because it was much easier to carry than large quantities of coins.

In modern times, the trend toward lightweight money has been taken to its logical conclusion: today's money often weighs nothing at all but consists of information stored on computers. People write checks and use credit cards to purchase goods and may pay their bills by transferring money from a bank account. Fortunes are made and lost without coins or currency ever changing hands. However, paper and coins have not been replaced for everyday purchases, and increasingly advanced methods are used to produce them and to prevent counterfeiting.

A collection of U.S. standard issue silver and gold coins, including $20 St. Gaudens and Liberty gold pieces and a $10 Indian Head gold piece that dates from the early 19th century.

CORE FACTS

- Money is a medium of exchange used to trade and store value.
- Coins were first used around 3000 years ago.
- Modern paper money incorporates several features that prevent counterfeiting.
- Electronic funds transfer, enabled by the global telecommunications network, began to be widely used in the 1970s and has changed the ways in which the world does business.

Coinage

Each year, up to 20 billion coins are minted (made from metal) in the United States alone. Huge machines stamp coin blanks from 1500-ft- (457-m-) long strips of metal. The blanks are softened in a furnace, washed, and then dried. Next, they are mechanically sorted to insure they are the correct size and shape. A milling machine creates a raised edge on each blank (see the box on page 886). Finally, the coins are struck or pressed with the design. Before being packed for shipping to the Federal Reserve Banks, from which they make their way into the general banking system, they are carefully inspected by hand. Misshapen or misprinted coins, along with the metal left over from cutting the blanks, are recycled.

Unlike coins of the past, the value of which lay in their gold or silver content, modern U.S. coins are made of copper, zinc, and nickel and cost less than one-tenth of a cent to produce. Just as with paper money, their intrinsic value is unimportant because they are backed by the government and their worth is accepted in the marketplace.

CONNECTIONS

- **PAPER AND PAPERMAKING** and **METALWORKING** were both important technological developments in the history of money and banking.

- Many people already use the **INTERNET** for transferring money between accounts and for paying their bills.

A woman uses an automated teller machine to withdraw money from Banco Popular in San Juan, Puerto Rico.

Paper currency

Before the American Civil War (1861–1865), U.S. banks issued their own paper currency, or bank bills. The many varieties of paper money led to a great deal of confusion, and it is estimated that 30 percent of the currency in circulation was counterfeit. Several Acts of Congress during this period brought the issuing of paper money under government control. The Department of Treasury's Bureau of Engraving and Printing was established in 1862 and has printed all U.S. currency since 1877.

Advanced photocopying techniques have led to the incorporation of new features to stop the counterfeiting of bank bills. These include microprinting, the effects of which can be seen with a low-power magnifying glass. However, microprinted bills are too small to be reproduced by photocopying. Similarly, watermarks—variations in the paper density that form patterns—do not reproduce when the bills are photocopied. In addition, special color-shifting inks appear black or green, depending on the angle from which the bill is viewed. Security threads in the paper glow when held under an ultraviolet (UV) light source.

Money in cyberspace

The electronic transfer of money arose with the invention of the telegraph by U.S. artist and inventor Samuel Morse (1791–1872) in the early 19th century. Money began to be "wired" from one place to another, but this was essentially a customer service practice, speeding up the extension of a line of credit that still needed to be settled with hard currency. Electronic funds transfer between banks began in the 1970s, followed by electronic direct deposit of payroll and government checks into customer accounts. At first, this was a rather clumsy system involving vast numbers of magnetic tapes. By the 1990s, however, banking systems worldwide conducted their transactions over telephone lines. Indeed, a worldwide electronic network, based in Belgium, coordinated the international movement of funds.

Automatic teller machines (ATMs) allow account holders to access money 24 hours a day, and networks of ATMs provide service nationwide. Credit and debit cards used with ATMs and point-of-sale systems (small computer terminals in shops and other retail outlets) employ a magnetic strip containing information such as the customer's account number and bank identification. Transactions are submitted to the bank or other clearinghouse to be authorized and implemented. The expense is then charged to the user's account. However, this procedure does not lend itself to the many small purchases that people generally make with coins, for example at vending machines, pay phones, and public photocopiers. Microchips embedded in smart cards have provided a way to prepay such expenses. The chips are programmed with a preset amount of money, and expenses are deducted as they occur.

With the explosive growth of the Internet on personal computers, many customers have online access to their account information and other services. Electronic commerce and banking services will become increasingly important, and they may someday make coins and paper currency obsolete.

S. CALVO

See also: CASTING; COMMUNICATION NETWORK; INTERNET; METALWORKING; PAPER AND PAPERMAKING; PRINTING; RETAIL INDUSTRY TECHNOLOGY.

Further reading:

Galbraith, J. *Money: Whence It Came, Where It Went*. New York: Houghton Mifflin Company, 1995.
Weatherford, J. *The History of Money: From Sandstone to Cyberspace*. New York: Crown Publishers, 1997.

AROUND THE EDGES

Coins have raised edges to prevent them from wearing thin. On all U.S. coins of denomination 10 cents or higher, the edges are grooved around the sides. The purpose of the grooves was originally to make the coins more difficult to counterfeit and to prevent the gold or silver used in them from being shaved off. The grooves were not made on pennies and nickels because they did not contain precious metals and were less profitable to counterfeit.

Today, none of the coins in ordinary circulation contain gold or silver, but the grooved edges remain. They are useful to the visually impaired in distinguishing between, for example, the penny and the dime. Since 1998, paper currency has also incorporated features to assist the visually impaired in recognizing the bill. These include a larger portrait and numeral representing the denomination, and a machine-readable feature compatible with optical scanners.

A CLOSER LOOK

MONORAIL

A monorail is a railway with only one rail, which the train either rides on or hangs from

Although far less common than conventional railroads, monorails have been used for carrying both passengers and freight since the early 19th century. There are a number of different designs. The most obvious difference between existing designs is that some have cars that sit astride a single rail, while others have cars that are suspended above the ground from an overhead rail.

Advantages and disadvantages
Because monorails use only one rail, the track takes up less space than conventional railways. This makes them useful in large metropolitan areas, where space is at a premium. Using a single track also means that there is less friction between the train and the track, making the train more efficient and less costly. Systems have also been designed that allow the cars to lean to one side when the track bends, allowing corners to be taken more quickly and comfortably.

However, monorails tend to be harder to build than conventional trains. Cars that ride on the rail need a mechanism to keep them upright, while those that hang down need a supporting structure.

Saddle-shaped designs
Early monorails were pulled by horses on ropes and ran on a wooden rail that was raised up from the ground. The cars stayed upright because they hung down on either side of the rail, lowering their center of gravity. An early example of such a system was the steam-driven monorail demonstrated at the United States Centennial Exposition of 1876, which took place in Philadelphia.

Ground rails
Monorails that use a single rail on the ground or on an elevated track take up less space than saddle-shaped designs. The cars can be kept upright by using wheels that run on either side of the rail. However, this causes extra friction. Another way of keeping cars upright is to use gyroscopes. These are spinning wheels that resist any forces that would alter their axis of rotation, and so they stop any object that they are attached to from tipping over (see GYROSCOPE).

Gyroscopically-balanced monorails were in operation as early as 1907, and many existing monorails still use this system. The main disadvantage of using gyroscopes in monorail cars is that these heavy wheels require power to keep them spinning.

Suspended monorails
Cars that hang from an overhead rail, known as suspended monorails, have been in operation since 1901, when the *Wuppertaler Schwebebahn* (swinging railroad) began operation in Wuppertal, Germany. The line carries 50,000 people a day over 9.3 miles (15 km). Modern monorails, such as the French

Because of a powerful electromagnetic field, this monorail in Sydney, Australia, floats a few millimeters above the track along which it runs.

SAFEGE system, have two different sets of wheels that run inside a hollow rail. The bottom of the rail has an open slot to allow a bar to connect the wheels to the car below.

Future monorails
Many new monorails are in various stages of planning. One of the most unusual proposals is to use monorails for personal rapid transit (PRT). Drivers would board the vehicle, punch in a destination, and settle back. One such device, the monomobile, runs on rails but will also be able to disconnect from the rail and operate independently. Because monorails take up little room, they could be incorporated into existing highway systems, or run above the road while automobiles continued to run below. In the future, monorails may even be suspended by magnetic levitation. This is a means to lift the vehicle slightly off its track using opposing magnets. Such vehicles can be moved forward using linear motors. This eliminates the need for wheels, which produce friction (see LINEAR MOTOR; MAGNET).

J. TEMPLE-DENNETT / W. KRAGH

See also: CHAIRLIFTS AND GONDOLAS; MASS TRANSIT SYSTEM; MOUNTAIN RAILROAD AND FUNICULAR.

Further Reading:
Fickewirth, A. *California Railroads*. San Marino, California: Golden West Books, 1992.

CONNECTIONS

● Modern monorails are powered by an **ELECTRIC MOTOR**, a **GAS TURBINE**, or an **INTERNAL COMBUSTION ENGINE**.

MOTORCYCLE

A motorcycle is a two-wheeled motorized vehicle used for personal transportation and sport

U.S. company Harley-Davidson has a reputation for mass-producing stylish motorcycles, such as this 1994 Electra Glide Classic.

Motorcycles are popular as transportation and sport vehicles because of their performance characteristics and economical operation compared to automobiles. Some motorcycles can accelerate from 0 to 115 mph (185 km/h) in 12 seconds. Even the largest motorcycles travel 45–50 miles (72–80 km) on a gallon of gasoline. Motorcycles are highly maneuverable, and because of their small size, they can be practical vehicles for driving in heavy traffic. Unfortunately, the lack of protective metal around the rider puts them at greater risk of injury and death than drivers of automobiles. Protective gear such as helmets, gloves, goggles, boots, and leather clothing are therefore usually worn by riders. These provide some protection against wind and rain, and they can help reduce injuries in the case of falls and accidents. Helmets and eye protection are required by law in most American states.

History

Unsurprisingly, the motorcycle first developed from the bicycle. German engineer Gottlieb Daimler (1834–1900) began developing the motorcycle in 1885 by adding a gasoline engine to a wooden bicycle frame. Although Daimler subsequently went on to put his engine on a four-wheel vehicle, other experiments with two-wheel vehicles continued until the early 1900s, when motorcycles became very useful and extremely practical modes of transportation.

Early motorcycle frames quickly became heavier to make them more robust, and lower to make them more stable. As the vehicles became faster, the development of sprung suspension systems became essential for giving drivers and passengers comfortable rides. In other improvements, a transmission, clutch, and chain drive were added to improve performance. A starter pedal allowed the rider to get

the engine started with a kick (early motorcycles had to be pushed to get them started).

In 1906, Bill Harley and the brothers Arthur, Walter, and William Davidson hired their first employees in Milwaukee, Wisconsin, and built 50 duplicates of their first Harley-Davidson motorcycle. This motorcycle had a low center of gravity, and the motor was mounted on a sturdy frame. The company claimed a top speed of 45 mph (72 km/h) and a driving range of 100 miles (161 km) on its 1.5-gallon (5.7-liter) gasoline tank. By 1912, the company was producing around 13,000 motorcycles every year. Although sales were slowed by automobile mass production, the popularity of the motorcycle continued to increase.

Motorcycles were widely used to dispatch messengers in World War I (1914–1918). This use led to further improvements in speed and reliability. By the 1920s, the foot-change gear selection system had become standard on most vehicles. In World War II (1939–1945), the U.S. Army used motorcycles along with automobiles to move troops from battlefield to battlefield. Since the 1930s, the basic design of the motorcycle, although improved subtly, is basically the same.

Types of motorcycles

Today there are several general types of motorcycles.

Touring motorcycles. Touring motorcycles are designed to carry a driver and one passenger. They have windshields to protect riders from wind, debris, and rain.

Off-road motorcycles. Off-road motorcycles are lighter and are designed for driving on dirt roads and trails. They have specially designed suspension systems to absorb the shock of rough terrain.

Motor scooters. Motor scooters are small motorcycles with a flat floorboard between the front and rear wheels. The rider's feet rest on the floorboard, and the motor is over the rear wheel.

Mopeds. Mopeds, or motorized bicycles, are lightweight motorcyles with low-power engines. New designs with small engines are enjoying renewed interest because of their ease of driving and exceptional fuel mileage.

CORE FACTS

- Motorcycles have more rapid acceleration than automobiles and are more fuel efficient.
- The earliest motorcycles were adapted bicycles with gasoline engines attached to them.
- Modern variations include touring motorcycles, off-road motorcycles, motor scooters, and mopeds.
- Many motorcycle components have been adapted from the automobile industry.

Motorcycle subsystems

A motorcycle can be divided into the same subsystems as an automobile. However, the design of many of these and their arrangement can vary greatly.

Engine. The motorcycle engine is located between the two wheels, behind and beneath the rider. Motorcycle engines can have from one to six cylinders that operate on either a two-stroke or four-stroke cycle. The two-stroke engine is lubricated by oil added to the gasoline and is generally more responsive than the four-stroke engine. The four-stroke engine is lubricated with a pressurized circulating system similar to that in an automobile. The engine can be air-cooled or water-cooled. Some motorcycles are powered by rotary engines (also known as Wankel engines), which have a shaped rotor in place of a piston. These have the advantage of being smaller and lighter than piston engines, but they can be noisier (see INTERNAL COMBUSTION ENGINE; MECHANICAL TRANSMISSION).

Transmission. Most motorcycles have either four or six gears. However, some vehicles have as few as two, while racing bikes may have as many as eight. Power is usually transmitted to the rear wheel by a chain, although some vehicles use a belt or a shaft system. The equivalent of a gearshift lever in a car is located on a foot pedal (see STEERING SYSTEMS).

Frame and suspension. The frame is usually made of steel tubing with sheet metal reinforcing high stress areas. An extension of the frame helps hold the front wheel in place. The front fork has internal coil springs and light-viscosity oil forced through restricted opening, to provide damping that cushions the rider against bumps. The rear swing arm, a hinged U-shaped member, allows the back wheel to move up and down for stability over bumps.

Wheels and tires. Motorcycles for street driving usually have wheels and tires that are constructed similarly to those of automobiles. The wheels are usually made of aluminum or steel. The tread on motorcycle tires is more rounded than the tread on automobile tires, which provides traction for leaning through turns (see TIRE; WHEEL).

Brakes. Brakes are operated on the front and rear wheels, with the front brake giving most of the stopping action. Hydraulically operated disk brakes have been standard on the front wheels since the 1970s. In a disk brake, the brake pad is pushed against a rotating disk attached to the wheel. Rear wheels use disk brakes or drum brakes. In a drum brake, an arrangement of brake pads called a brake shoe pushes against a rotating drum when the brake is applied (see BRAKE SYSTEMS; HYDRAULICS AND PNEUMATICS).

Steering and other controls. Motorcycle riders use their entire body to control the vehicle. Turning is accomplished through movement of the handlebars, which turns the front wheel, and leaning the body to one side. Electric starters from the automotive industry have largely replaced kick starter pedals, so that many motorcycles are as easy to start as cars. The throttle, which regulates the speed of the engine, is a hand twist grip usually on the right

handlebar. The front brake is activated with a hand lever, also on the right handlebar. The rear brake is controlled with a foot pedal.

P. WEIS-TAYLOR

See also: AUTOMOBILE; BICYCLE; FUELS AND PROPELLANTS; MECHANICAL TRANSMISSION.

Further reading:
Wilson, H. *The Encyclopedia of the Motorcycle.* New York: Dorling Kindersley, 1995.

MOTORCYCLE RACING

Powerful engines allow motorcycles to create the accelerations needed in racing.

Although motorcycle engines are small, they produce around twice the amount of mechanical power as an automobile engine for every cubic inch that the piston displaces as it moves up and down in the cylinder. This superior power output for a given engine size, combined with their lighter weight, allows motorcycles to accelerate much more quickly than automobiles. Their quick acceleration and direct handling make motorcycles a popular vehicle for racing on paved tracks or dirt courses and cross-country events. Dirt-track races, endurance races, and cross-country races are all held frequently across the United States. Dirt-track races on flat oval tracks and motocross races, run on rugged courses with jumps, hills, and other obstacles, are also very popular.

A CLOSER LOOK

MOUNTAIN RAILROAD AND FUNICULAR

This mountain railroad in Chattanooga, Tennessee, has been preserved for use by tourists.

CONNECTIONS

● Other common forms of transportation in mountainous areas are **CHAIRLIFTS AND GONDOLAS**, which are often used to transport skiers and other tourists.

Mountain railroads and funiculars (cable-operated vehicles) are two different forms of transportation used to carry passengers and freight up steep inclines. Both forms of transportation were developed for use in the mining industry, where they were used to carry excavated material in wagons to the surface of a mine or quarry.

The use of mountain railroads and funiculars remained popular throughout the late 19th century. However, the development of the automobile and other forms of transportation led to a decline in their popularity, although in some parts of the world they remain in use because they are still the best transportation option available. Fortunately, visionaries saw the historic value and tourism potential in retired mountain railroads and funiculars and have successfully worked to keep them running.

Mountain, or rack, railroads

A rack railway is a specialized type of railway that enables specially designed locomotives to climb hills that could not be negotiated by normal adhesion (adhesion refers to the force that keeps the wheels of a train locked to the rails; see RAILROAD CONSTRUCTION AND TRACK). A steel cogged rail is laid between the running rails; pinions on the train mesh with (engage) the cogged rail and so control movement (see the diagram on page 891). The train hauls itself along by gripping these teeth with a powered gear wheel (the pinion; see GEAR). This type of railway is able to negotiate steep gradients and is used in mountainous regions only. In an emergency, the pinion provides a means of stopping the locomotive and carriage from careering down the gradient by locking into the rack. This system is backed up with sets of regular and emergency brakes on the locomotive and on each car (see BRAKE SYSTEMS).

Mountain railroads and funiculars are used to transport passengers and cargo up steep gradients

The first cog-wheel railroad was demonstrated by U.S. engineer Sylvester Marsh (1803–1884) in 1869 on Mount Washington in New Hampshire. His design became widely adopted around the world, especially in the Alps of Switzerland. In 1889, for example, the Pilatus railway opened, operating over a maximum gradient of 48 percent. This particular railroad, still in existence today, is electrified. However, the cog-wheel principle is not confined to any one source of power.

In the 19th century, for example, steam-powered locomotives were commonly used to haul passenger and freight cars up the steep inclines. However, the development of the diesel engine in 1896 by German mechanical engineer Rudolf Diesel (1858–1913) largely replaced steam power by the 1930s, and the locomotives used on mountain railroads were soon fitted with diesel engines. In a diesel engine, diesel oil is sprayed into the cylinders of the engine, where it is heated by compression until it ignites and drives the pistons. In turn, these drive a generator, which makes electricity. The generator supplies power to the traction motors that turn the locomotive's wheels. Extra electricity is stored in batteries. Diesels are more efficient and provide a smoother driving force than steam-powered locomotives, which causes less damage to the track.

In many cases a third rail is used to carry the electricity that powers the locomotive and cars. Alternatively, electricity may be supplied to the motor by means of a pantograph (sometimes called a pickup) on top of the locomotive. The lines are high-voltage for good long-distance transmission, but transformers aboard the locomotive convert it into low-voltage direct current, making the components used for the motor less expensive. Most modern mountain railroads are powered by electricity.

Cable-operated railroads and funiculars

For gradients that would be impracticable to negotiate even by rack railways, cables may be used. The cables, usually made from reinforced steel, are set either between or beneath the tracks and are able to

---

CORE FACTS

■ Mountain railroads use rack-and-pinion gear systems to haul passengers and freight up steep inclines.

■ The first mountain railroads were powered by steam engines. Today, however, most railroads are electrified.

■ Funiculars use reinforced cables to haul carriages up inclines too steep to be negotiated by normal or rack railroads.

■ The operation of both mountain railroads and funiculars is largely based on the principles first used to haul excavated material from mines and quarries.

haul railed vehicles up very steep inclines. Stopping and starting are effected by gripping and releasing the moving cable in conjunction with the vehicle's brake system. Originally, this system was one of the first attempts at propulsion without horses for routes along roads (which did not necessarily constitute abnormally steep gradients).

The idea of cable-pulled transportation came to fruition in the 18th century as a means of moving heavy loads from areas of low altitude to areas of high altitude. The system was first used in the mining industry, where cables were attached to coal wagons on tracks and passed around a rotating cable drum. Usually, the cables are wound onto the drum starting from the outer edge and working to the center. In the past, steam was the basic source of power to move the cable drum, with the steam engine housed in a separate building at the top of the incline.

The concept was adapted to everyday use in San Francisco in 1873, based on an earlier patent in 1867 by U.S. engineer and inventor Andrew S. Hallidie (1836–1900). The system soon spread throughout the world. However, the arrival of the electrical age caused the disappearance of cable traction. Cable cars are no longer used for roads, but they continue to be used for travel up steep gradients, where they are known as funicular railroads. In this instance, two vehicles of equivalent weight are linked to opposite ends of a cable, one being at the base of the incline and the other at the summit. The cable is usually looped around and powered by a pulley system at the top of the incline. The weights of the cars balance each other as they ascend and descend, with a loop in the track for passing if only one track is provided (see the diagram at right). As a result, relatively little power is needed to run the system.

Unlike cable cars, which attach themselves to start and detach themselves to stop, funiculars are stopped and started by activating and deactivating the motor that winches the cable, rather than by the car operator's use of the grip to attach to the cable. The first true funicular railway is thought to have been constructed in Naples, Italy, in 1839. The funicular railroad traversed 5 miles (8 km) from Naples to the then-royal home of Portici. Funicular railroads are still in existence today. A good example is the one used to transport local residents and the many tourists from Georgetown to the summit of Penang Hill, Malaysia. Funiculars can also be found in Pittsburgh (the Angel's Flight railroad), Hong Kong, Istanbul in Turkey, and Rio de Janeiro in Brazil. Funicular railroads are particularly common in the alpine region of western Europe.

L. GRAY

See also: ELEVATOR; MONORAIL; RAILROAD CAR; RAILROAD LOCOMOTIVE; RAILROAD OPERATION AND SIGNALING; RAILROADS, HISTORY OF; SAFETY SYSTEMS.

Further reading:

Burden, M. *Professor Lowe and His Mountain Railroad.* Los Angeles: Borden Publishing Company, 1993.

Adhesion railcar

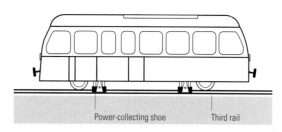

An adhesion (or regular) railcar moves when the wheels push against the rails. This system is unsuitable for steep gradients.

Funicular

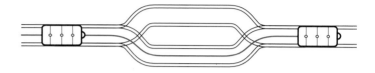

Funicular railcars are hauled up inclines by cable, rather than under their own power. There are usually two cars—one descends as the other ascends.

Rack railroad

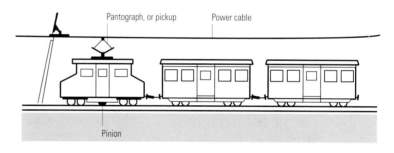

Rack railroad locomotives (see above) have pinions (gear wheels) underneath that mesh with a similarly toothed rack between the rails (see below).

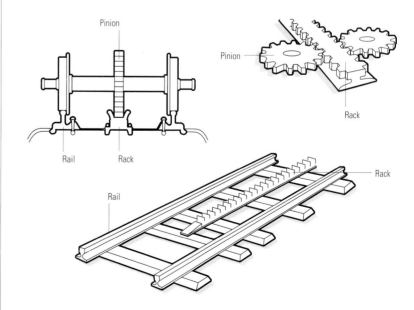

The pinion on a rack railcar is physically attached to the rack rail on the ground, either vertically (left) or horizontally (right).

MULTIMEDIA

Multimedia is an interactive computer-based technology that allows the user to digest information

CONNECTIONS

● To use a multimedia package, you would need a **COMPUTER** with a sound card, a CD-ROM or DVD-ROM drive, and a high-resolution color monitor.

● A **FLIGHT SIMULATOR** is a special kind of multimedia product that reproduces the look and feel of the inside of an airplane's cockpit in **FLIGHT**. It is used to train aircraft pilots.

Rapid improvements in computer technology, especially in the areas of processing speeds and data storage, have enabled the growth of a new market in computer-based information (see COMPUTER). By taking advantage of this new technology, publishers have been able to relaunch some of their older products and create new ones using a multimedia approach, which combines text, sound, pictures, animation, and video on a high-capacity medium such as CD-ROM (compact disc read-only memory) or a DVD-ROM (variously digital video disc or digital versatile disc read-only memory).

The principal advantage of multimedia technology is that it is possible to access all the required information on a topic from a single source. Assuming that the user's computer is up to the task, he or she can, for example, find out what a symphony is, hear the various instruments in the orchestra, follow an animated musical score, watch a video of an orchestra in action, and then travel along Internet links to further information if required (see INTERNET).

However, this is not to suggest that multimedia is the sole preserve of electronic encyclopedias, such as the *Encarta* CD-ROM produced by U.S. corporation Microsoft. Since the 1960s, flight simulators—which combine sound and a visual element—have been used extensively by the military and the aerospace industry. These were probably the first multimedia products (see FLIGHT SIMULATOR).

The various media (elements such as text, sound, and pictures) are linked using a computer language called hypertext markup language, or HTML (see the box on page 893). Essentially, this is an electronic connection between media in the product, allowing the user to cross-reference between similar articles, pictures, animations, or videos. In the case of the musical CD-ROM outlined earlier, the user could read an article on the various instruments in an orchestra and come across the word *bassoon*. If this is the first mention of the word, there may be a hypertext link to a sound file, which, if selected, will demonstrate the sound of a bassoon. The link may also take the user to a definition of that word.

The CD-ROM

Most multimedia applications are delivered on a CD-ROM (see COMPACT DISC). This is an optical device containing information stored in a digital (binary)

CORE FACTS

- Multimedia technology combines text, sound, pictures, animation, and video on a CD-ROM or DVD-ROM.
- All the multimedia elements are linked using a computer language called hypertext markup language, or HTML.
- CD-i is an interactive video format that allows the user to take part in the action on a computer monitor.

form, which can be read using a low-powered laser (see DIGITAL SIGNALS AND SYSTEMS; LASER AND MASER). A typical CD-ROM can store around 650 megabytes of information. (One megabyte is the equivalent of over 8 million binary digits, or bits.) Since most multimedia products require large amounts of storage space, and that the information in storage be accessed quickly, it is difficult to imagine how the multimedia industry could have grown without the enormous storage capacity of the CD-ROM.

The information on the CD-ROM has to be accessed using a compact-disc drive, which is now fitted to most home computers. Once this is done, the computer treats the information as it would any other piece of binary code, converting it into text, sound, pictures, animations, or video as required.

The production process for a multimedia product is similar to the publication of a book but with the added dimensions of sound, animations, and videos. While this expands the possibilities for ways in which the information in the product is presented, it also requires a greater degree of planning. First, the editorial board will decide on the content of the product, while a team of graphic designers will examine the overall look of the product. The teams then come together to decide how the product will proceed smoothly. This involves deciding which elements will be linked and which concepts might best be illustrated using animations or videos.

Rough designs for each of the screens (the multimedia equivalent of pages in a book) are drawn up and the teams will begin to assemble a prototype. All the elements in the prototype will be drawn together using a software package such as *Director*. This is an authoring application that allows the team to link each of the proposed components of the product and see how they will work together.

Simultaneously, a team of software engineers will develop the "run-time engine," a computer application that coordinates and runs all the elements of the product. When the design team and editorial board have completed their work, the screens are assembled and the interactive links added. The product is tested extensively to identify any bugs that may have crept in and to allow fine-tuning of the product. When all this work is complete, the CD-ROM is burned on to a master disc, which will serve as the template for the CD-ROMs offered for sale.

Other formats
Although CD-ROMs are the most common format for interactive multimedia products, other formats are available. The CD-i (the letter *i* stands for *interactive*) is a video format that allows the user to interact with characters on screen and determine, for example, the direction of the plot of a film.

The DVD-ROM is an optical disk that is read by laser in the same way as a CD-ROM but is double-sided and can hold up to 4.7 gigabytes of information. Just like an ordinary compact disc, it is possible to leap to any point in a movie without the need to spool through masses of videotape.

Other multimedia applications
The educational possibilities offered by multimedia technology are immense, but it is also increasingly being used in other areas, especially in the field of entertainment. The digital revolution in broadcasting has allowed users to select the songs, television programs, and even films they would like to hear or see.

Many people believe that improvements in computer hardware will soon allow users to "walk" around museums or art galleries without the need to leave their homes, by means of virtual models accessed through the Internet.

M. FLYNN

The information contained in a CD-ROM or compact disc is stored as a series of tiny pits in the surface of the disc. Interference effects between the light waves reflected from each pit cause the familiar pattern of brilliant colors.

See also: ANIMATION; SOUND RECORDING AND REPRODUCTION; TELEVISION AND COMPUTER MONITOR; VIDEOGRAPHY.

Further reading:
Reynolds, A., and Iwinski, T. *Multimedia Training: Developing Technology-Based Systems.* New York: McGraw-Hill, 1996.

MULTIMEDIA LANGUAGES

The coding language of the hypertext that links all the elements in a multimedia product is called HTML, or hypertext markup language. (This is also the language used to create World Wide Web pages on the Internet; see INTERNET.) HTML is just one example of a computer language generated using the conventions dictated by SGML (standard generalized markup language). SGML was designed so that people using different computers could share information across the Internet, despite the differences in their machines—for example, sharing information between an Apple Mac and a PC. Another language, VRML (virtual reality modeling language), is similar to HTML but is used to create virtual, three-dimensional environments in which the user can "walk" around.

A CLOSER LOOK

MUSICAL INSTRUMENT

Many musical instruments have been developed over time to provide a variety of pitch and sound qualities

Different musical instruments produce sound by causing air to vibrate. This can be done, for example, by percussion, strumming a string, or vibrating a reed.

CONNECTIONS

● Many types of musical instruments have been made in **ELECTRONIC** versions, which can be heard by connecting them to an **AMPLIFIER**.

Humans were making music long before written history began. While the human voice was undoubtedly the first musical instrument, primitive drums, rattles, horns, and whistles have been found by archaeologists in early settlements all over the world, and stringed instruments such as lyres and harps were used in the ancient Middle East about 5000 years ago.

The technology of instrument making has developed by trial and error over thousands of years and was quite advanced before the physics of acoustics was well understood (see ACOUSTICS AND SOUND).

Good vibrations

In the sixth century B.C.E., Greek philosopher and mathematician Pythagoras (c. 580–500 B.C.E.) recognized that a vibrating string could be stopped at fixed ratios of its length to yield musical octaves, fourths, and fifths—the intervals (distance between two notes) on which most early Western music was based. But it was not until the 1600s that scientists discovered the relationship between vibration, frequency (rate of sound), and pitch (the highness or lowness of a note).

Now there are tape recorders, spectrum analyzers (machines that measure musical wavelengths), and computers that help people to understand the complex vibrations they hear. This has enabled people not only to understand and improve existing musical instruments, but has also fostered the development of entirely new methods of making music.

The human ear hears sound when air is caused to vibrate and stimulate a corresponding vibration in the eardrum. A pure tones is a simple periodic vibration with a single frequency. A tuning fork—a two-pronged metal implement invented in 1799 to produce a standard pitch when struck and thereby help musicians tune their instruments—is designed to produce such a tone. But most musical instruments produce complex waveforms in which harmonics (multiples of the fundamental frequency) are superimposed to create the instrument's distinctive sound. Harmonics occur because vibrations are set up not only in the instrument as a whole, but also in its various sections. The shape of a particular instrument will cause some harmonics to be emphasized and others to be supressed.

Instrument grouping by type of vibration

Musical instruments may be classified by considering what is vibrating to create the resulting sound. Some instruments are designed to cause the vibration of air, and this group may be further divided by how the vibration is made to happen.

Instruments such as harmonicas and accordions, organs, and bagpipes all use the vibration of a thin sliver of wood or metal to produce a sound. Brass instruments, such as trumpets, cornets, and trombones, use vibrations of the air blown through their players' lips to produce a sound.

In other instruments, the air is vibrated by a stretched membrane. Percussion instruments such as drums are the major category of stretched membrane instruments, but this family also includes the kazoo, in which the membrane is made to vibrate by blowing or humming into a mouthpiece.

CORE FACTS

- Sound is generated by vibrations, and musical instruments may be classified by the way in which they create these vibrations.
- The main categories of instruments are woodwind, brass, percussion, and stringed instruments.
- Electronic synthesizers have been used in popular music since the late 1960s.

Triangles and cymbals are examples of instruments that made of materials in which the vibrations multiply to create a distinctive sound. This class of instruments includes various types of wooden blocks that are banged together or scraped, rattles, tambourines, and bells and xylophones. These are generally grouped together with drums as percussion—or struck—instruments.

The final major class of traditional instruments are those in which the sound is generated by the vibration of stretched strings. The strings were originally gut (tough cord made from animal intestines), but they are now generally nylon or wire. They can be made to vibrate by plucking or strumming (as in the harp or guitar), rubbing a bow across them (as in the violin or cello), or striking them (as in the dulcimer). Stringed instruments with keyboards include the harpsichord, in which the strings are plucked, and the piano, in which the strings are struck with small hammers (see the box on page 897).

In the past few decades, electronic instruments, or synthesizers, have been developed. These can create an enormous variety of sounds through control of their frequencies, amplitudes, and combinations (see the box on page 898). Synthesizers have become increasingly important in popular music, special effects, and commercial music for advertizing, and electronic keyboards are now often seen in homes as a compact alternative to a piano. But the musical world is unlikely ever to do away with the richness of an orchestra or the virtuosity of individuals skilled on traditional instruments.

Woodwinds

Woodwind instruments—a term that originated from the fact that most of these instruments were once made of wood—create sound by making air vibrate in a tube. The tube may be straight (like the clarinet), or curved (like the saxophone), and it may be made of wood, metal, or even plastic (like some inexpensive recorders). These attributes affect the character of the sound and the length of the tube determines the pitch. The purpose of the keying mechanism—which may be a simple set of finger holes or an elaborate collection of hinged keys and pads—is to control the effective length of the sound by letting the air out at various points. Keys allow the holes to be placed wherever they are needed on the instrument based on its acoustic properties and regardless of whether this is a convenient position for the fingers. They also make it possible to use holes larger than the fingers could cover. The keying mechanism developed in the 1840s by the German jeweler and flutist Theobald Böhm (1794–1881) is still used in woodwind instruments today.

In some woodwinds, the vibrations are started by blowing air across a sharp edge. In the flute, the instrument is held sideways and the air is blown across a hole in the mouthpiece. Recorders have a whistle-type mouthpiece in which the air is directed from the mouthpiece across a slit an inch or so farther down the tube.

Reed instruments are woodwind instruments that function in a slightly different way. Reeds are strips of cane shaved very thin so that they will vibrate when air is forced over them. In single-reed instruments, such as the clarinet and saxophone, a ligature holds the reed onto a mouthpiece of plastic or wood. The mouthpieces of the oboe, bassoon, and English horn have two reeds held tightly together at the bottom by a metal staple. Double-reed instruments are considered to be among the most difficult to play because of the breath control necessary to force air at high pressure through the small space between the reeds.

Brass instruments

Like the woodwinds, brass instruments generate sounds by the vibration of a column of air. The column is generally in the form of a narrow tube that coils one or more times and ends in a flared horn. The musician sets the air vibrating by means of blowing into a cupped mouthpiece at one end of the tube. Control of the position and tension of the lips and the

The liu sheng, *pictured above, is a mouth-blown instrument that originated in China.*

RINGING THE CHANGES

A man cleans a carillon in a church tower in Salzburg, Austria.

In the Middle Ages, when the church was the centerpiece of every village and timekeeping was based upon the prayer cycle of the liturgical day, the church bell marked the passage of the hours. Sets of bells were sometimes rung in sequences called changes, or they were used to play simple tunes.

In the 1500s, churches began to equip their towers with carillons—sets of fixed bells tuned to a musical scale. The bells were struck by hammers controlled from a keyboard. Playing the carillon was a strenuous operation, because the keys were more like levers, requiring the force of the carillonneur's entire hand, while the tune necessitated moving at considerable speed. Sometimes foot pedals were used as well.

When clockwork mechanisms became available, the bells were set to operate on their own at the appointed hours. Eventually it was found that a cylinder with pins placed at precisely the right intervals could control the hammers that struck the bells, operating the automatic carillon just as holes in paper sheets control the keys of a player piano. Large carillon mechanisms had two-ton (1.8-tonne) brass cylinders with thousands of pins. They can still be found in some churches and town halls, particularly in the Netherlands and Belgium.

In orchestral music and opera scores, fixed tubular bells are sometimes used to simulate the sound of the carillon. Modern churches often make use of carillonic bells—an amplified electronic keyboard instrument weighing a few hundred pounds and costing only a small fraction of the price of a traditional carillon.

HISTORY OF TECHNOLOGY

force of the breath is required in order to produce different notes. The pitch may also be altered by placing a hand in the horn and by the use of valves.

Valves—of which there are typically three—divert the airflow to extra lengths of tubing. When the valves are in their rest position, the air bypasses this extra tubing. But if a valve is pressed, an extra length is open, thus lowering the pitch. The valves may be used singly or in combination, allowing all the notes of the scale to be produced.

There are other ways to vary the length of the tubing in a brass instrument. Before valved instruments were developed in the 18th century, some horns had detachable lengths of tubing called crooks.

Players of these horns became practiced at quickly switching these crooks in mid-performance.

The trombone's pitch is varied by a telescopic slide. Its position determines the length of the tube. Valved trombones are available but have never been as popular as the original design, which is based on a 15th-century instrument called the sackbut.

Strings
Stringed instruments may be classified by their basic shape. Stringed bows are the simplest, with a string, or strings, attached between the ends of a curved stick. They are still common in Africa and South America. Lyres have a box or bowl-shaped resonator

PIANO HAMMERS AND PEDALS

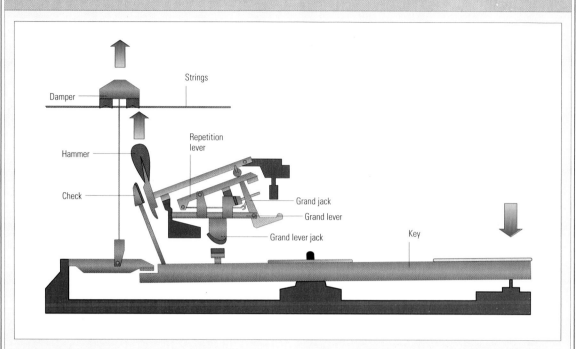

Modern piano strings are made of steel, with the bass strings copper-wound. The diameter of each string has an effect on the volume of sound that string produces. Hence, to produce an even volume across the seven-octave range, bass notes have one string, middle notes have two, and high notes have three.

When a key is pressed, it acts as a lever. Its opposite end rises, lifting a hinged assembly and resulting in throwing a hammer against the string or strings. A check keeps the hammer from immediately falling all the way back to its original position so that a note may be repeated in quick succession.

When the keys are at rest, dampers hold the strings in place and keep them from vibrating. The dampers are lifted from the strings when a key is pressed and generally return as soon as the finger has been removed from the key so that the sound stops. Depressing the right, or sustaining, pedal keeps the dampers off the strings until the foot is raised. Many pianos also have a center pedal, which sustains only those tones in the lower half of the piano's range. The left, or soft, pedal produces a quieter sound by shifting the hammers slightly to one side so that they don't make full contact with the strings.

A CLOSER LOOK

(a sound box that amplifies the sound) and a crossbar supported by two arms. The strings run between the resonator and the crossbar. Harps have strings running diagonally from the resonator to the neck, and zither strings run the length of the instrument's body, raised by a bridge. The lute family has strings running from near the base of the resonator box, over a bridge, to finally wind around attachments called tuning pegs near the top of the neck. This group includes the violin, viola, cello, and double bass, as well as the guitar, mandolin, and banjo.

Strings may be strummed, bowed, plucked, beaten with sticks, or even, as in the Aeolian harp, moved by the wind. Their pitch is affected by their thickness, tension, and length. Thicker strings produce a lower pitch. Tightening a string raises its pitch, and loosening it lowers the pitch. Therefore, most stringed instruments have screws for tuning. The effective length of a string can be changed by pressing it against the instrument's body. Instruments like the guitar provide frets—lines on the neck to guide the musician in finding the correct position.

Percussion

Drums are built in various shapes, such as cylinders, cones, and barrels with sloping sides. A kettledrum is a pot or vessel topped with a playing head, or skin. Other drums, such as the tambourine, have the skin stretched over a frame. There may be a single playing head or one on each side. The heads may be attached with glue, nails, pegs, laces, or a tight hoop around the perimeter. Drums may be struck by hand or with various types of sticks to achieve the desired sound.

Although only a few specialized drums—such as the steel drums of the Caribbean—are used to play a melody, every drum has a pitch. It can be changed by adjusting the tension of the drumhead when there is a mechanism to do so. In modern orchestras, the tunable timpani are important. These are large kettledrums that are tuned by using a pedal that both operates rods to change the skin tension and registers on a tuning gauge to indicate the pitch. Less expensive hand-screwed timpani are still available, but it can be tricky to adjust the tension evenly, and they can only be tuned to a few different pitches.

Besides drums, many percussion instruments—both tuned and untuned—are used to create special musical effects. Such instruments may be banged together or on another surface, struck with a stick or mallet, shaken, rubbed, or scraped. The xylophone is an important tuned percussion instrument often used in orchestral arrangements. Its two rows of wooden keys, comprising about four octaves, sit atop hollow metal resonator tubes.

Pianos and organs

Keyboards were first added to stringed instruments in the late Middle Ages to make them easier to play. Early examples looked like converted lutes, which is more or less what they were. The hurdy-gurdy, which survived into modern times, is an instrument of this type. By about the 15th century, keyboard instruments were starting to take the familiar shape that most people would recognize today. Among these were the harpsichord (in which the keys controlled quills, called plectrums, that were pushed up to pluck the strings), and the clavichord (in which the key mechanism caused the strings to be struck).

The modern piano is the product of almost 300 years of design innovations to make keyboard instruments more expressive, with a mechanism that controls volume, the length of the notes, and how fast they can be repeated (see the box on page 897).

Today the piano is available in a relatively compact upright version, as well as in several sizes of grand piano, in which the large horizontal body and open lid allow maximum sound projection. The piano is important in orchestral works and popular music, and it is a common feature in the home.

The organ is a much older instrument than the piano, having been invented in Alexandria in the third century B.C.E. Air was pumped manually into the instrument and exited through one or more of the pipes, as selected by moving sliding boards with holes in them. Within a few hundred years, keyboards had been added. In the Middle Ages, the organ gained widespread use as a church instrument, and ranks of pipes were built into cathedral galleries. The ranks include pipes of the same pitch but different tonal qualities. A variety of effects is obtained by using stops (valves) to divert air through different combinations of pipes to produce the desired tones.

S. CALVO

See also: ACOUSTICS AND SOUND; ELECTRONICS; SOUND RECORDING AND REPRODUCTION.

Further reading:

Baines, A. C. *The Concise Oxford Dictionary of Musical Instruments.* New York: Oxford University Press, 1992.
The Illustrated Encyclopedia of Musical Instruments. Edited by Robert Dearling. New York: Schrimer Books, 1996.
Kartomi, M. J. *On Concepts and Classifications of Musical Instruments.* Chicago: University of Chicago Press, 1990.

SYNTHESIZERS

U.S. electronic scientist Robert Moog (1934–) with a Moog synthesizer.

Synthesizers can produce almost any sound imaginable by combining the output of multiple sound-generating devices. These include electronic oscillators (which generate pure pitches) and noise sources (which produce sounds of no specific pitch to simulate such phenomena as ocean waves or thunder). Filters are used to shape the sound by letting some of its components pass through while screening out others. Amplifiers and attenuators allow the user to change the volume of the sound as well as the level of such effects as small fluctuations in pitch and volume that create the texture of the music. The synthesizer is played using a keyboard to generate the basic pitch, with pedals, joysticks, knobs, and switches to create the other effects.

The first electronic musical instrument, called an Automatic Operating Musical Instrument of the Electric Oscillation Type, was introduced in 1929 at the Paris Exposition. It used four oscillators controlled by punched holes in a paper tape. More than 25 years later, RCA introduced the first instrument to actually be called a synthesizer; it was based on similar principles and played in the same way. The first synthesizer to be mass-produced was invented by Robert Moog in 1963. Rather than using binary code similar to the paper-tape models, it was voltage controlled, so it could be operated using signals input through jacks. Control voltages to trigger various effects could thus be varied much faster than would be possible manually. In the 1970s, portable synthesizers were developed, mainly for live performances of popular music.

In the 1980s, digital synthesizers—which use streams of binary numbers to represent the signal—began to appear on the scene. This coincided with the rise of the personal computer and its use as a tool by musicians, both for composing and for controlling other sound components such as drum machines. Exchange of data between the various components was made possible by the introduction of the Musical Instrument Digital Interface (MIDI), an eight-bit code transmitted at 31, 250 bits per second. Unlike audio formats, which allow playback of recorded sounds, MIDI represents the actual notes and other musical information, allowing it to be manipulated, cataloged, and transcribed into a musical score.

HISTORY OF TECHNOLOGY

Small double-headed snare drums are used in bands and orchestras. Snares are lengths of gut, nylon, or wire stretched across the bottom head to add a distinctive rasping sound to the drum's tone. This effect is heightened by the hard wooden sticks used to play snare drums.

NANOTECHNOLOGY AND MICROMACHINES

Nanotechnology is the process of manufacturing devices and machines on the scale of clusters of atoms

Miniaturization has become one of the hallmarks of modern technology—new products that are smaller, cheaper, and more powerful than their predecessors emerge every year. The silicon chip microprocessor is the most familiar example of the drive to miniaturization to the scale of microns (millionths of a meter). Each silicon component contains billions of atoms, but there are no laws of physics to stop the creation of machines thousands of times smaller than the smallest chip components, made out of clusters of atoms. These devices are examples of nanotechnology: technology on the scale of nanometers (billionths of a meter).

Types of nanotechnology

Nanotechnology can be approached in two ways, called top-down or bottom-up. The top-down approach tries to improve on the methods already used in making microprocessors and other miniature devices, pushing the limits of techniques for cutting separate components from a bulk material such as silicon. However, the devices produced by these methods are still many hundreds or thousands of atoms across, and so are more properly called micromachines (see page 901).

True bottom-up nanotechnology involves the construction of devices from individual atoms and molecules. It mixes techniques from chemistry and biotechnology with more usual engineering methods. However, building individual nanomachines is extremely labor-intensive—no useful devices have yet been built in this way.

Multiplying machines

The great problem with mass-producing nanomachines is the scale difference between these machines and the machine-building tools that are currently available. The early supporters of nanotechnology

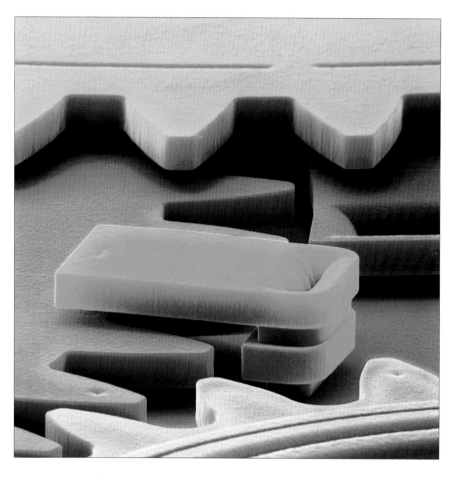

An electron micrograph of an array of micromotor gears, magnified about 1200 times.

recognized that the first nanomachines would have to be "assemblers"—all-purpose chemical machines capable of constructing a variety of other machines depending on the signals they are sent and the materials with which they are supplied. Large-scale robot assemblers were proposed by U.S. scientist John von Neumann (1903–1957), but it was not until 1959 that Richard Feynman (1918–1988) proposed the use of assemblers for nanotechnology in a speech at Caltech, the California Institute of Technology (see the box on page 900).

One possible approach to building nano-scale assemblers involves biotechnology. Natural DNA is a type of assembler that pieces together the complex molecules of life from bases, which are simple molecular building blocks. Biotechnologists already have techniques for making customized DNA strands by adding individual bases to a chain and by cutting and splicing together lengths of DNA (see BIOTECHNOLOGY; GENETIC ENGINEERING).

Synthetically formulated DNA has also been used to make artificial proteins not seen in nature, using a process that mimics the formation of natural proteins inside a living cell. These proteins could potentially act as molecular machines—enzymes and muscles, for instance, are made of protein—but there is at present only limited knowledge of how to design the molecular makeup of a protein to give it

CORE FACTS

- Nanotechnology is technology on the scale of nanometers (billionths of a meter).
- There are two basic approaches to miniaturization: top-down (starting from bulk materials) and bottom-up (starting from individual atoms). Top-down micromachines (on the scale of millionths of a meter) already exist.
- Workable nanotechnology will require the development of assemblers—nanomachines that can build other nanomachines, including copies of themselves.
- A first generation of assemblers may be created using protein engineering techniques developed in biotechnology.
- Nanotechnology cannot use electronics—nanomachines will have to work chemically or mechanically.

CONNECTIONS

- Nanotechnology could make use of **CLONING** procedures to produce many identical molecular components.

- For a long time nanomachines have been touted to be important in **MEDICAL TECHNOLOGY**, especially for use in **SURGERY**.

the required mechanical properties. Nevertheless, it is likely that the first generation of assemblers for nanotechnology will be custom-made proteins.

The possibilities

As complex organic molecules, the first assemblers are likely to be prone to chemical change and will only be able to work in the same controlled conditions as natural proteins and enzymes. But once technology has reached the nanometer scale, the assemblers themselves will be able to produce a vast array of smaller, simpler, and stronger second-generation nanomachines.

FEYNMAN'S CHALLENGES

The eminent physicist Richard Feynman explains his ground-breaking theory.

The race for nanotechnology began with a 1959 speech by U.S. physicist Richard Feynman (1918–1988) to the American Physical Society, entitled *There's Plenty of Room at the Bottom*. In his lecture, Feynman pointed out the vast possibilities of the microscopic scale, beginning with the relative simplicity of writing the entire *Encyclopedia Britannica* on the head of a pin (each letter would still contain hundreds of thousands of atoms).

Feynman went on to consider the possibilities of using assemblers to build machines on ever-diminishing scales or of using evaporation techniques to manufacture tiny machine parts—the technique that is currently used to etch circuits on silicon chips.

The speech closed with two challenges: a prize of $1,000 to the first scientist who could make an operating electric motor just 1/64 inch (0.39 mm) wide, and a similar prize for the first person to reduce the size of writing by 25,000 times. The electric motor prize was claimed within a few months—by a Caltech physicist using traditional watchmaking techniques—but the prize for writing on such a small scale went unclaimed until 1985, following the invention of the atomic force microscope (see page 901).

Today, there is a new Feynman prize, promoted by the Foresight Institute. The first group to manufacture two important nanotechnology devices—a robot arm capable of working on the nanometer scale and a nanocomputer circuit capable of adding two eight-bit binary numbers—will receive $250,000.

PEOPLE

Second-generation nanomachines will consist of very few atoms and will be built with very strong chemical bonds so that they will still function in extreme conditions. These nanomachines will form the basis of new technologies that could affect all our lives. Supporters of nanotechnology have already suggested nanomachines that could repair damage to Earth's environment or terraform other planets—change their environments to make them suitable for lifeforms found on Earth. Another popular suggestion is that nanomachines could be injected into living organisms—including human bodies—to repair damaged tissues, act as a secondary immune system to fight off infections, or even prolong human life. Nanomachines would also be able to manufacture large-scale structures according to instructions from a nanocomputer, so that it might be possible to "grow" complex machines such as automobiles.

All nanotechnology will operate in one of two ways—chemically or mechanically. Ironically, the great modern science of electronics, which relies on the flow of large numbers of charged electrons through a bulk material, will not work with the limited number of electrons present in nano-scale objects. However, finely controlled chemistry and mechanics can be used to do many of the tasks that currently use electronics (see box on page 901).

Chemical nanomachines will operate in the same way as natural molecules inside organisms, and are unlikely to be very complex. It might be possible to design a molecule that binds onto chlorofluorocarbon chemicals and prevents them from attacking the ozone layer. Since nanomachines are themselves just molecules, they could be released high in the atmosphere and remain suspended there for years, repairing the damage caused in the past fifty years.

Mechanical nanomachines will be far more complex and will more likely be used in controlled factory conditions. This type of nanomachine would work like a miniature robot, but without electronics. It would rely on a series of chemically operated pistons and other moving mechanical parts to control its position and functions. A nanomachine like this could well be driven by the molecular equivalent of a punched-card system (see COMPUTER). Holes in an instruction tape would allow certain rods to move through them in a complex preprogrammed sequence, triggering a series of actions inside the structure of the nanomachine.

Progress and problems

Although many scientists are confident that nanotechnology will revolutionize our lives in the next few decades, the same opinion has existed since the 1960s. While nanotechnology is now a familiar concept, progress toward making it a reality has been slower than expected, partly because the necessary tools have not been available. Before the current boom in biotechnology, most physicists approached the problem as one of basic engineering—there was no obvious alternative to building the first assembler atom by atom.

The basic tool of this type of nanotechnology is the atomic force microscope (AFM), a probe sharpened to a single atom at its tip so that it can detect the bumps of individual atoms on an object's surface. Movement of the probe can be converted into an electronic signal and fed back to a monitor as pictures of the atoms. The AFM is an astounding imaging device, but it can also act as a tool—it can be used to push atoms around and rearrange them. In 1989, an IBM researcher used an AFM to write the company name on a nickel surface using only 35 xenon atoms. However, creating an assembler with hundreds of thousands of atoms in this way would be an immense task and would take a huge amount of design time. The biotechnological approach, on the other hand, uses procedures that are already becoming well established. However, the design of the assembler remains a major problem.

There are also some physical problems that arise when working on the nano-scale. At the atomic level, heat (in the form of rapid vibrations in atoms and molecules) can cause errors. Borrowing from the natural world again, nanofactories will require template molecules that can be used to check whether individual nanomachines have been assembled according to the required specifications.

Micromachines

While bottom-up nanotechnology remains a dream for the future, machines that can be measured in just microns (millionths of a meter) are already becoming widespread. Microengineering is an extension of the technology currently used to create microelectronic circuits. Circuits are etched onto a silicon chip using materials that are burned away using a beam of ultraviolet light that passes through a computer-designed photographic mask (see INTEGRATED CIRCUIT). The same technique can be used to create miniature mechanical components that are subsequently separated from their substrate before assembling them to form tiny machines.

Micromachines have applications in a variety of situations. Tiny and extremely sensitive accelerometers are used to trigger the release of vehicular air bags by detecting the forces of a car crash (see AIR BAG). A possible future application could improve aircraft fuel efficiency by using microsensors to detect tiny pockets of turbulence on the wing surfaces and microactuators to raise or lower miniature flaps and improve the aircraft's aerodynamics (see FLIGHT, PRINCIPLES OF). In information technology, microactuators may also be used to control the position of reading heads as data storage devices such as magnetic disks become more and more tightly packed (see MAGNETIC STORAGE MEDIA).

The miniaturization of machines and circuits is now reaching the point where X-ray beams are replacing ultraviolet light for etching. X rays have shorter wavelengths than ultraviolet light and can be used to etch much smaller details. However, X-ray-etched components are still thousands of atoms across, and the limits of top-down miniaturization

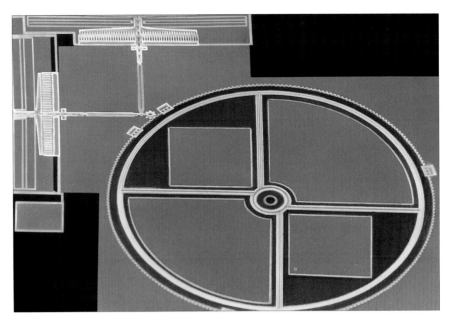

The rotor of a tiny electric motor (shown here magnified 28 times) in a micromachine was fabricated using silicon-chip technology.

are fast being approached. Nevertheless, if the problems can be overcome, nanotechnology has the potential to change our world as much as the industrial and electronic revolutions before it.

G. SPARROW

See also: CHEMICAL INDUSTRY, INORGANIC; CHEMICAL INDUSTRY, ORGANIC; ELECTROMAGNETIC RADIATION; ELECTROMECHANICAL DEVICES; MECHATRONICS; ROBOTICS.

Further reading:

Drexler, K. *Engines of Creation*. London: 4th Estate, 1996.
Drexler, K. *Unbounding the Future*. New York: Morrow, 1991.

NANOCOMPUTERS

Nanotechnology cannot use electronics, but the precision engineering it offers can be used to make mechanical equivalents of electronic circuits—even complex computers.

The original computers built by Charles Babbage (see COMPUTER) were mechanical devices consisting of gear wheels and metal rods, so there is no fundamental link between electronics and computing. For most of this century, however, electronics has been the most precise way of creating the logic gates at the heart of a computer. Electronic signals are also extremely fast.

A logic gate works by comparing two inputs and producing an output that changes depending on the input values. In one theoretical nanocomputer, this is done by attaching large molecules, called probes and blocks, onto a network of carbon filaments. Normally the filaments run freely past each other, but when a probe and a block intersect, they lock together and cannot move. Careful arrangement of probes and blocks on just four filaments (two inputs, an output, and the gate itself) can copy the action of any electronic logic gate.

Nanocomputers could compress millions of logic gates into the space occupied by single element on a silicon chip. The tiny distances that the filaments in a nanocomputer would move would also compensate for their slower speed as compared to electronic computers.

A CLOSER LOOK

NAVIGATION

A modern compass, consisting of a fluid-damped magnetized needle fixed to a plastic ruler, is placed on top of a map to locate directions. The needle, which rotates on a pivot, is aligned to Earth's magnetic field and rests north to south on the compass. From this, true north can be calculated and points on the map can be oriented.

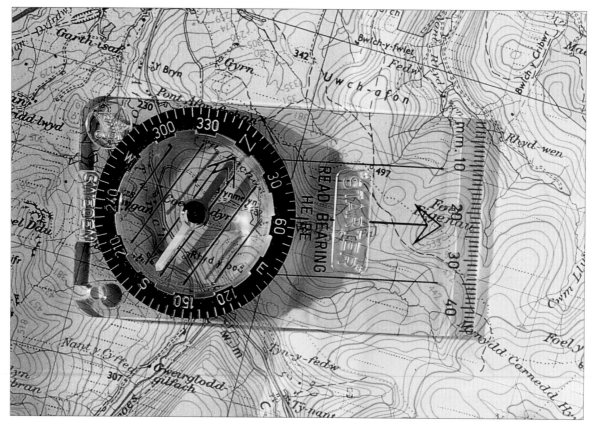

CONNECTIONS

● The **RADIO RECEIVER** and **ANTENNA AND TRANSMITTER** are devices used in **MARITIME COMMUNICATION** to aid the captains of **SHIPS AND BOATS** in their navigation.

While *navigation* historically refers to location- and direction-finding aboard ships, it is also essential for both air and space flight. Each of these forms of transportation poses its own unique challenges for navigators.

Fundamentals of navigation

To find a position on Earth's surface, a system of coordinates is needed. Today the system used universally consists of latitude and longitude.

Latitude is measured in degrees north or south of the equator, with the equator defined as 0 degrees, and the poles as 90 degrees north and 90 degrees south. Longitude is measured on lines running from north to south called meridians and is given in degrees east or west of a prime meridian, which runs through Greenwich in London, England.

Greenwich is located at 0 degrees, and lines of longitude run from 0 degrees to 180 degrees east and west. These longitudunal lines all meet up at the International Date Line on the other side of Earth from the Greenwich meridian. For increased accuracy in measurement, each degree is split into 60 minutes, and each minute into 60 seconds.

The equator and lines of longitude travel around the entire circumference of Earth because their centers coincide within the center of Earth; they are called great circles. The shortest distance between two points on Earth's surface is always along the great circle that contains these points.

TRADITIONAL NAVIGATION

A wide variety of navigational techniques were developed by ancient and medieval seafarers. Even today, it is a good idea for a sailor to understand these basic principles and be able to use them in an emergency.

Coastal navigation

The simplest form of navigation is simply to follow the coastline, but coastal waters can also be some of the most dangerous. Before the introduction of modern buoys and beacon systems, a coastal navigator (called a pilot) would have to navigate by landmarks.

CORE FACTS

■ Navigation involves the measurement of position on Earth's surface in terms of latitude and longitude.

■ Latitude can be found easily from the stars, but longitude requires an accurate clock, which did not become available until the 18th century.

■ Magnetic compasses indicate magnetic, not true, north. They have been replaced in many applications by gyroscopic compasses.

■ Radio signals can be used in many different ways for navigation, such as in range finding—measuring the speed for two signals to reach a receiver.

■ Satellite navigation now allows a person to know his or her position on Earth's surface, or even in orbit, to within a few meters.

At first, this involved looking for a recognizable natural or artificial structure that might indicate the way into a harbor, but as artificial harbors were created and chart-making techniques developed, marine navigation became much more dependable.

It became possible to establish a vessel's position accurately by measuring the bearing (angle from true north) of two landmarks. The first bearing establishes a line on which the vessel is positioned, and the second marks the position along that line, giving a "fix." An accurate fix can only be found, however, if the two bearings are taken simultaneously or if the vessel's movement is taken into account. Bearings can be taken with several different instruments.

Many ancient peoples were skilled coastal pilots, particularly the Mediterranean Phoenician traders whose descendants may have traveled as far north as Iceland around 340 B.C.E. Yet even on their longest journeys they rarely strayed from the coasts.

A few seafaring peoples did dare to go farther out to sea, most notably the Vikings of Scandinavia and the Polynesians of the South Pacific (see the box below right). Out of sight of the coast, the sea is a flat gray-green expanse with no landmarks by which to navigate. However, these early voyagers understood the sea in a way few modern navigators do. They noted changes in currents in particular areas of the sea—often caused by islands many miles away—and they realized that, even in midocean, there was always one fixed point of reference: the sky.

Latitude from the heavens

It is fairly easy to find one's latitude from the sky, and various methods of doing this were used by navigators for centuries. At nighttime in the Northern Hemisphere, the simplest method is to measure the angle of elevation of the star Polaris, which happens to lie very near the north celestial pole (NCP). Because the NCP is a projection of Earth's North Pole, it will lie overhead (elevation 90 degrees) at the pole, and on the horizon (elevation 0 degrees) at the equator. The elevation of the NCP is always equal to the observer's latitude. Navigators also compiled tables which they used to correct for the fact that Polaris does not lie exactly on the NCP. In the Southern Hemisphere, where there is no conveniently bright pole star, the Polynesian navigators developed other methods of stellar navigation (see the box to the right).

In daytime, the Sun can be used for navigation. Its elevation as it crosses the meridian at noon also varies with latitude. Yet the Sun's seasonal cycle of movement complicates matters—it slowly moves from the sky's northern to southern hemispheres and back again over the year. In order to calculate latitude accurately, a navigator needed to carry an accurate almanac (an astronomical catalog that listed the changing position of the Sun from day to day).

A variety of instruments can be used to measure the elevation of celestial objects. The earliest, the astrolabe, was originally an astronomical instrument. This device consisted of a brass disk with a pointer

from which the elevation of a star could be measured. The quadrant, a simplified version of the astrolabe, had only one quarter of the disk. Yet both instruments were inaccurate on a swaying ship since they had to be hung vertically to work.

A much simpler instrument, the cross staff, was introduced in the mid-15th century (see the illustration above). Designed specifically for use at sea, it consisted of a long horizontal stick and a shorter vertical one. The navigator looked along the horizontal stick and kept it in line with the horizon, then moved the vertical cross staff in or out until its top lined up with the object to be measured. A scale on the horizontal stick then gave the precise angle of elevation.

The cross staff remained popular for many years but was still far from perfect. A great leap forward came in the mid-17th century with the invention of the mirror sextant by English scientist John Hadley (1682–1744) and American scientist Thomas Godfrey (1704–1749). Both of these instruments

This German illustration of a 15th-century cross staff shows the long horizontal stick, which is aligned with the horizon, and the short vertical stick, which is moved up and down to measure an object. When the top of the vertical stick is aligned with the top of the object, its angle of elevation can then be read on the long stick.

POLYNESIAN EXPLORERS

Probably the greatest of all the ancient seafarers were the people who settled the Polynesian islands of the South Pacific. Spreading out from Samoa and Tonga, they colonized all the tiny island groups—even the far distant Easter Island—in the first millennium C.E.

The Polynesians are believed to have become aware of the distant islands in the first place by studying the migration patterns of birds. However, they had to develop sophisticated navigation methods to move between these islands. In the Southern Hemisphere they had no pole star to guide them, so they developed a system of "on-top stars," memorizing in poems and chants the stars that passed overhead at the latitudes of particular islands, then sailing along these lines of latitude in their boats. They also had a unique understanding of sea patterns and currents and how these were affected by landmasses hundreds of miles away.

HISTORY OF TECHNOLOGY

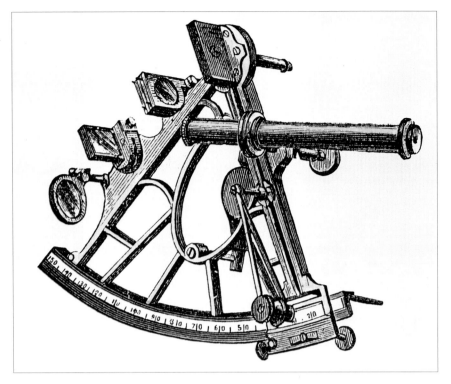

This is an early 18th-century illustration of a sextant, which was invented c.1730 and used in both navigation and astronomy to measure celestial bodies. By looking through the eyepiece on the right, the user can see a reflected image of the celestial body. By aligning this image with the horizon, the angle between the horizon and the celestial body can be measured. The navigator can then calculate his location, because the position of celestial bodies depends on the observer's location.

work on the same principle, reflecting the light from the object to be measured so that it appears to lie on the horizon. The observer can look in the same direction at both objects and make fine adjustments to the tilt of the sextant's mirror before reading the measurement. Dark glass filters were also made to reduce the glare of the Sun.

The compass

As early as the first century, the Chinese discovered that natural magnets would point to the north when allowed to rotate freely. However, the compass as an instrument did not become important to navigation until it reached Europe around the 12th century.

The compass revolutionized navigation because, for the first time, it was possible to establish direction without reference to the sky. Yet the magnetic compass has some problems—it actually points toward the magnetic pole, so it shows a variation called declination from true north. Metal parts in a ship's hull can also cause deviation in the compass.

By the 19th century the compass had become a far more accurate navigational instrument. Charts were compiled that showed lines of equal magnetic declination, called isogonic lines, which enabled the compass reading to be corrected. The compass needle pivoted above the center of a circular card, which was marked with the compass points and a circle of 360 degrees so that readings could be taken easily. The entire apparatus was immersed in a sealed bowl of water for stability and mounted on a pivoting mechanism called a compensating binnacle, which pivoted in all directions to keep the compass horizontal and used a series of magnets to cancel out the magnetic field produced by metal parts in the ship.

During the 20th century, the magnetic compass was replaced on large ships and aircraft by the gyrocompass. This uses the principle of the gyroscope—a

spinning device that maintains its vertical orientation even when the ship in which it is mounted is pitching and rolling (see GYROSCOPE). The gyrocompass is particularly useful in navigation because it points to true north (see the box on page 907).

The establishment of longitude

By the 18th century, navigators could find their latitude with great accuracy, checking the measured positions of the Sun or stars against tables published by observatories around the world. They could use the compass to sail along lines of latitude or chart a new course at a set bearing (allowing for compass error). But there was still no accurate way of finding longitude—and without this, errors in the other measurements accumulated dangerously.

Longitude could easily be calculated if the time at a ship's home port was known accurately—local time (easily measured at noon) was four minutes later for every degree west of home. Unfortunately, the only clocks available then were driven by pendulums and incapable of working at sea.

The longitude problem reached a crisis point in 1707 when an English fleet was wrecked in thick fog off the Scilly Islands, southwest of the British mainland. The admiral in command of the fleet had been convinced they were safely in the mid-Atlantic—and had hanged a man who dared to suggest otherwise only the day before.

The wreck of the English fleet was just one in a long line of disasters. By 1714, the British government had created a special body, the Board of Longitude, to look into the problem. They also offered a prize of £20,000—the equivalent in present-day value of several million dollars—for anyone who could find a method of determining longitude at sea to within a fraction of a degree.

Many people took up the challenge, and it was finally met by English clockmaker John Harrison (1693–1776; see the box on page 905). He devised a series of marine chronometers that permitted the accurate measurement of time on long journeys (see TIME MEASUREMENT). Longitude could then easily be calculated by comparing local celestial measurements with those in an almanac compiled for a specific meridian of longitude at a specific time of day. For some time, the Royal Observatory at Greenwich became the most important source of this information, and to this day longitude is measured east or west of Greenwich.

Measuring speed

With accurate methods for measuring position and direction, setting a course became a simple matter of geometry. Because Earth is spherical, the shortest distance between two points is along a great circle that contains them. However, although the path is curved, the course must be transferred to a flat sea chart and is best followed in a series of short straight lines (see the box on page 906). In order to change course at the right position without constantly having to repeat the laborious calculation of position, a

JOHN HARRISON

John Harrison, the man who finally solved the longitude problem, was the self-educated son of a Yorkshire carpenter. Fascinated by clocks from an early age, he was determined to win the longitude prize of £20,000 (a vast fortune at the time) and began work on the problem in the 1720s.

Harrison presented the H-1 marine chronometer to the Royal Society in 1735, and sea tests proved its accuracy. Yet the Board of Longitude, convinced that astronomy, not engineering, would provide the answer, constantly changed their conditions for awarding the prize.

Over the next three decades Harrison developed three further chronometers. The last of these, the H-4, was not much larger than a pocket watch. The chronometers were proved accurate again and again, but still the Board of Longitude refused to hand over the prize money. Finally, in 1773, the British government stepped in and handed over the money itself.

John Harrison's H-1 marine chronometer

PEOPLE

navigator could use "dead reckoning," a method of estimating the ship's position based on its earlier location, direction of travel, and speed.

The earliest way of measuring a ship's speed was to throw a floating object such as a wooden log into the sea ahead of the vessel and record the time it took for it to pass the length of the ship. An alternative, the hand log, was tied to a long rope with knots at even intervals. The operator threw it overboard and counted the rate at which the knots ran out. Ship's "logs" still measure speed in "knots"; 1 knot is roughly equivalent to about 1.15 mph (1.85 km/h).

In the 19th century, speed measurement became more accurate. The patent log, introduced in 1802, used a float with a spinning propeller drawn behind the ship and linked to a mechanical recorder on board. Other alternatives used today include a small propeller or a diaphragm for measuring changes in water pressure attached to the vessel's hull.

MODERN NAVIGATION

With accurate methods established for finding latitude, longitude, direction, and speed, navigation had become a more precise if tedious procedure, which changed very little until the early 20th century. At that time, new technologies appeared that could make the task of navigating much simpler; meanwhile the development of aircraft and flying put people in an environment where traditional navigation techniques were far more difficult to use.

Radio navigation

One of the earliest uses of radio was to improve navigation. It was clear that it was possible to transmit a standard time signal to receivers on a ship, and thereby correct errors in the vessel's chronometer. Radio also offered a way of overcoming the navigator's traditional enemy—poor weather conditions.

Radio direction-finding (D/F) systems use a special antenna containing a wire loop. The loop receives the strongest signal when it is oriented edge-on to incoming radio waves, and it detects no signal at all when its open face is pointing directly at them. This makes it easy to adapt it into a direction-finding device. The navigator only needs to tune the D/F system into the signals from two distant radio beacons, find their directions, and plot where the two lines overlap. Automatic direction finders (radio compasses) use a motor to keep the loop constantly aligned on a pretuned beacon.

Unfortunately, the low-frequency signals used in early radio navigation could be affected by the movement of air in the atmosphere. As the technology improved, however, it was soon possible to generate higher frequencies, so that radio offered another important advantage: it could be used in the air.

Navigation above the ground

The first aircraft had limited ranges, rarely flew over large expanses of water, and could be navigated using little more than a map and a compass. By the 1920s,

PORTOLAN AND SEA CHARTS

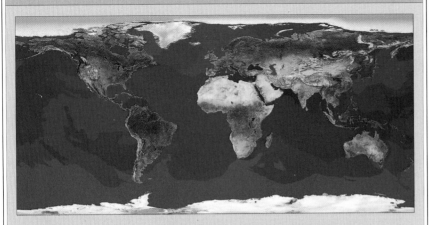

A satellite image of Earth in Mercator projection shows distortion at the poles.

From the earliest times, maps and charts were vital to navigation. The earliest surviving sea charts—medieval Italian portolans—may be the descendants of classical charts, but most early maps contained serious, even dangerous, errors.

One of the greatest problems mapmakers encountered was how to transfer the spherical shape of Earth onto flat maps. The first person to come up with a solution to this problem was Belgian mapmaker Gerardus Mercator (1512–1594), whose Mercator projection is still the most popular type of chart used today.

The Mercator projection has many drawbacks, however. The closer it gets to the poles, the more distorted the map becomes. A side effect of this is that straight paths across Earth's surface become curved courses on the chart. The best way to follow a straight path, such as the line of a great circle, is to set a series of short, straight-line courses following a curve.

Mapmaking was revolutionized in the 18th century as accurate methods for finding longitude were established. Britain, France, and Holland charted great expanses of the ocean in the 18th and 19th centuries, and not even the satellite surveys of the past few decades have had such a major impact on the world map.

HISTORY OF TECHNOLOGY

however, as commercial flight became more popular and aircraft flew longer distances, new navigational instruments and techniques had to be developed.

Many of these instruments relied on gyroscopes to control the direction of a compass and to provide an artificial horizon. When a gyroscope is set spinning horizontally before takeoff, it will maintain this alignment and the pilot can use it to find a straight and level course. Modern airliners are equipped with an inertial navigation system (a system of accelerometers mounted on a gyroscopic platform). These accelerometers give accurate information about the aircraft's movements, which is used by a computer for dead reckoning of the aircraft's position. A similar inertial guidance system is used in spacecraft.

The radio range is another navigation technology widely used in aircraft. A range station consists of four antennas that broadcast signals into four quadrants. The signals are designed so that they interlock on the border between two quadrants and produce a continuous beam that can be used for navigation.

Omnirange works on the same principle of interlocking signals but can be used to calculate a bearing at any angle (rather than just on the beam). An omnirange station has four range antennas and a single reference antenna. The reference antenna broadcasts one half of the signal, while the four range antennas broadcast a varying signal in a rapidly rotating beam designed to interlock with the reference signal when due north but be out of phase with it at other angles. Instruments on the aircraft then measure the phase difference and convert it into a bearing.

Radar and loran

Radar systems work by measuring the time it takes for a radio signal to bounce back from a distant object. Because radio waves travel at a fixed speed (186,000 miles per second, or 300,000 km/s), the time it takes to receive a radar reflection is a direct measurement of the distance of a particular object from the radar's source (see RADAR).

Although some scientists experimented with radio range finding in the 1930s, the radar systems used today (which rely on sending out pulses of high-energy radio waves) did not become practical until World War II (1939–1945).

At the same time, the principle of range finding was used to develop the loran (long-range navigation) system. A loran station consists of a master and a slave station. The master transmitter broadcasts a series of short pulses at precise intervals; the pulses are received and rebroadcast at the slave transmitter. A loran receiver tuned to the frequency of the station picks up both sets of signals, displaying them on a cathode-ray tube. The small time delay between the master and slave signal pulses corresponds to a curve of possible positions on a loran chart. By retuning to another loran station, the navigator can get a fix at the point where two curves intersect.

Another important application of radio range finding in aircraft is the radar altimeter. It bounces a signal off the ground below the aircraft and therefore gets an accurate measure of altitude. This system is far more efficient and reliable than earlier altimeters that were based on the measurement of air pressure.

Ground control

The most dangerous part of any flight is the landing, and airliners use two electronic systems that can ensure safety, even in the most hazardous conditions. One of these is ground-controlled approach (GCA), a high-precision radar system operated from air traffic control, which is used to stack aircraft (line them up above each other) prior to landing and guide them in to the final approach (see AIR TRAFFIC CONTROL). In extremely poor visibility, the aircraft can land using the instrument landing system (ILS). Receivers on board the aircraft pick up radio signals that guide the craft horizontally and vertically onto the runway. The horizontal bearing is given by a radio range with only two antennas, designed to produce a beam down the middle of the runway, while the vertical glide path is provided by a very narrow radio beam angled on a slope of 2.5 degrees. The ILS system locks onto both of these signals and provides the pilot with information to keep on the correct approach.

An artist's conception of one of the 24 NAVSTAR satellites in orbit around Earth. The first of the worldwide NAVSTAR Global Positioning System (GPS) satellites was launched by the U.S. government in 1978, the last NAVSTAR satellite was launched in 1993, and the system was in full operation by 1995.

Satellite navigation

The exploitation of space and the development of smaller, more powerful computers in the 1980s resulted in the ultimate navigational aid: satellite navigation. The most advanced satellite navigation system is the Global Positioning System (GPS). Initially, GPS was developed by the U.S. Air Force, but today the NAVSTAR satellites it uses are available to everyone. GPS consists of 24 NAVSTAR satellites orbiting at an average height of 12,500 miles (nearly 20,000 km). From any point on Earth at least four of these satellites are visible at one time. Each one carries a very accurate atomic clock on board, which it uses to generate a time signal that is beamed down to Earth. Because the time signal is limited by the speed of light, there is a short delay in the time it takes to reach the ground, and this time delay increases as the distance from the point directly below the satellite increases.

A GPS receiver consists of a tunable radio unit with a built-in computer and database that carries information about each satellite's position and orbit. When the receiver picks up a time signal, it compares it to its own built-in clock. From the time delay, it works out the distance to the satellite and calculates the curve on which the receiver itself could be located. It then locks on to two more satellite signals, repeating the calculation until it places itself at the intersection of three curves. For an airborne system, the receiver locks onto the fourth available satellite and uses this signal to calculate its altitude. Because most satellites and spacecraft orbit below the altitude of the NAVSTAR system, they can also use GPS for navigation and survey work.

In order to correct for satellite orbit variations, and to keep the receiver's clock in step with the satellite atomic clocks, a new database is uploaded daily to the satellites. From the satellites this information is transmitted to the receiver unit, which automatically adjusts its calculations accordingly.

GPS units are very compact and are now standard equipment on many aircraft and ships. They are also used as in-car or even handheld units—for locating specific fishing spots in the ocean, for example. With the ability to find their position to within a few meters anywhere on Earth, they have brought an end to the historical search for accurate navigation.

G. SPARROW

See also: COMMUNICATION NETWORK; COMPUTER; GROUND STATION; SATELLITE; SPACE FLIGHT.

Further reading:

Blanchard, A. *Navigation: A Three-dimensional Exploration.* New York: Orchard Books, 1992.

AUTOPILOTS

The introduction of gyrocompasses and artificial horizons on board ships and in aircraft, along with the development of sophisticated and compact computers, has allowed the introduction of automatic pilots. Autopilot systems on aircraft, for example, consist of gyroscopes to measure the angle of the aircraft and its direction, a barometric altimeter to measure altitude, and accelerometers to measure the rate of change in each direction. Changes in the behavior of the aircraft create forces in these instruments, which can easily be converted into electronic signals. These are fed into the autopilot computer.

The autopilot then creates a picture of the overall behavior of the aircraft and compares it to the programmed course instructions, producing a series of electrical signals that are transmitted to servomotors operating each of the control surfaces—the rudder, flaps, and ailerons (see FLIGHT, PRINCIPLES OF).

The first autopilots were simple devices used only for straight and level flight or straight courses through open sea. Today they are far more advanced. The pilot can program them to execute complex maneuvers or even to analyze navigational data from radio signals or GPS and follow a preset path. However, all autopilots are designed to be fail-safe so that a failure will not put the vessel or aircraft in danger. They can be easily overridden by the pilot in an emergency.

A CLOSER LOOK

NONFERROUS METAL

Nonferrous metals are metals and alloys that do not contain significant amounts of iron

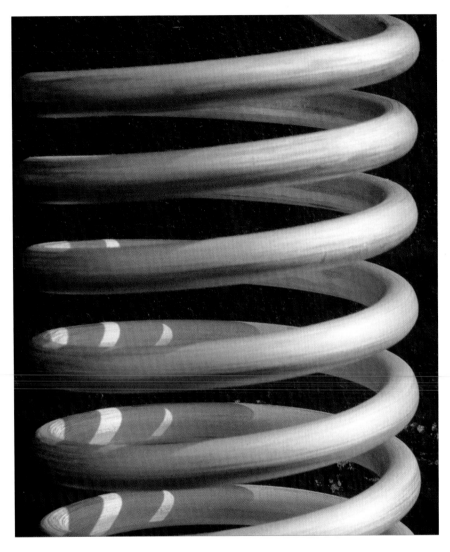

A coil of aluminum—the most common metal on Earth.

Although iron and steel are the most widely used metals as a consequence of their cheapness and versatility, nonferrous metals are important in specialized uses because of their distinctive properties. Nonferrous metals are often used in alloys (see ALLOY), but they also have a number of uses in their pure, chemically uncombined forms.

The nonferrous metals are divided into various classes. The light metals—all with relative densities less than 5.0 on a scale where water has a density of 1.0—include aluminum, magnesium, titanium, and beryllium. The low-melting metals are lead, tin, zinc, and mercury. Zinc has the highest melting point in this group, at 788°F (420°C) compared to iron with a melting point of 2800°F (1536°C); mercury is a liquid at room temperature, melting at −38°F (−39°C). Gold, silver, and platinum, the main precious metals, are prized for their rarity and inertness. Other metals are classified according to their atomic structure and chemical reactivity. For example, the group of metals that includes sodium and potassium is known as the alkali metal group, since all of the members form alkalis when they react with water.

Aluminum

Compounds of aluminum were used as medicines and for dyeing textiles in ancient and medieval times. However, the metal itself was not isolated until 1825, when Danish chemist Hans Christian Ørsted (1777–1851) extracted the metal from its ore by electrolysis (see ORE EXTRACTION AND PROCESSING). For decades, aluminum had the status of a precious metal: French emperor Napoléon III (1808–1873), used knives and forks of aluminum for his most prestigious banquets. Once a commercial electrolytic method of obtaining aluminum from its ore was discovered in the late 19th century, the use of the metal became widespread.

Aluminum has a low relative density (2.8) and excellent thermal and electrical conductivity, particularly when compared weight-for-weight with other good conductors of heat and electricity, such as copper. These properties make aluminum an ideal material for a wide range of domestic and industrial applications, including cooking foil, kitchen utensils, beverage cans, aircraft construction, and overhead power lines. Its main drawback is its relatively low melting point of 1220°F (660°C), which limits its use in high-temperature situations.

Pure aluminum is very reactive chemically. However, when it is exposed to air, it rapidly forms a thin film of aluminum oxide on its surface that protects the underlying metal from further reaction (see CORROSION). Compared to articles made from iron and many other metals, aluminum items are very resistant to atmospheric corrosion. Furthermore, its natural resistance to corrosion can be enhanced by a process known as anodizing, which thickens the oxide coating by an electrolytic process. In the anodizing process, aluminum articles—door frames or kitchenware, for example—are dipped in a bath of sulfuric acid. The article is connected as the anode (positively charged electrode), and the positive charge stimulates the reaction that thickens the oxide coating. A feature of this process is that articles such as kitchenware can be colored permanently by including a dye in the anodizing solution—the dye becomes trapped in the hard oxide layer.

Surprisingly, aluminum is the most abundant metal on Earth, accounting for more than 8 percent of the mass of Earth's crust. However, it is three

CORE FACTS

■ Aluminum is the most common and most used of the nonferrous metals.

■ Many pure metals are limited in their use because of their relatively low strength and melting points.

■ Titanium is valued for its combination of strength, lightness, and tolerance to heat and chemicals.

times more expensive than iron because of the high cost of extracting it from its ore. Current global production is 19 million metric tons annually.

Copper

The first use of copper dates from around 8000 B.C.E. Native deposits (naturally occurring deposits of pure, uncombined metal) were made into tools and weapons. Copper was valued for its beauty and its ability to be made into different shapes. Over the next few millennia, its use became widespread in Europe, the Americas, and Asia.

Copper is highly malleable (formable by hammering) and ductile (easily drawn into wires) and is a good conductor of electricity and heat. It is also fairly resistant to corrosion. Its main uses are as electrically conducting wire and cable and in piping and radiators for central heating systems. However, copper is too soft to shape by machining when pure, so it is used as an alloy with zinc (brass) or with tin (bronze)—both alloys are harder than pure copper.

Tin

Tin, like copper, has been in use for thousands of years. Archaeological evidence suggests that bronze articles containing up to 10 percent tin were being used as long ago as 3500 B.C.E. by civilizations in the Middle East. The Romans were the first to make use of the low melting point of tin—450°F (232°C)—to add a protective coating of tin to copper cooking vessels by dipping them in liquid tin. Tin-plating was developed in central Europe in the 14th and 15th centuries and used for a wide variety of household objects such as plates and cups.

Tin is a relatively soft and weak metal. It is fairly resistant to atmospheric corrosion, and it is used in pewter and solder alloys. The main use of the pure metal is in tin cans, where a thin layer of tin coats the surfaces of carbon-steel cans for food. The tin prevents corrosion of the outside of the can and protects the food from any reaction between the steel and the food in the can.

Zinc

Although brass—a zinc-containing alloy—was first used by the Romans around 200 B.C.E., pure zinc was not isolated until the 14th century in India. Zinc is relatively soft, has a relatively low melting point of 788°F (420°C), and is fairly reactive. The main use of zinc is as a protective coating for steel objects. The objects are galvanized (coated with zinc) by dipping them into the molten metal. If the surface is scratched, the zinc (which is much more reactive than steel) corrodes first, filling in the scratch with oxide and leaving the underlying metal intact. Galvanized steel is used for making fences, sheet metal, and small objects such as screws.

A block of zinc can be electrically connected to large steel objects designed for use in water, such as ships, bridges, and pipelines, where it provides protection of the entire object by reacting preferentially with salt water and air.

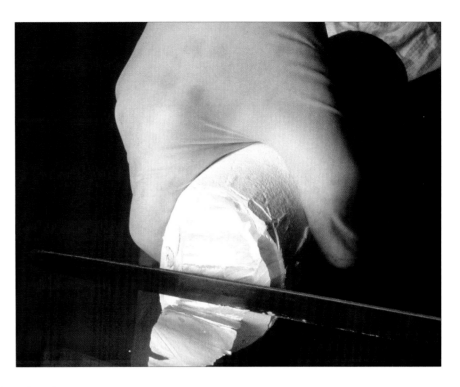

Titanium

Titanium ore was first discovered in 1791, when British clergyman William Gregor (1761–1817) discovered it in rocks on a beach in Cornwall, England. The pure metal was not extracted until early in the 20th century. The U.S. Air Force became interested in titanium in the 1940s because engineers thought that it could perform better than either steel or aluminum in jet engine parts.

Titanium possesses a special combination of properties: lightness, strength, good resistance to corrosion, and a high melting point of 3034°F (1668°C). These properties make titanium and its alloys invaluable for components in the aerospace and gas turbine industries.

Magnesium

Magnesium is the lightest of the metals that are used for structural purposes (relative density: 1.7). The pure metal is soft and chemically reactive, which makes it prone to corrosion and a potential fire hazard. However, if alloyed (most often with small

Sodium is so soft it can be cut with a knife. It is also very chemically active, reacting easily with water and air. Therefore it is usually stored in oil.

TITANIUM AND HIP REPLACEMENTS

If a part of the body becomes worn or damaged, it may be possible to replace it with an artificial implant, or prosthesis. However, the materials used to make the prosthesis must be biocompatible—the material should not be corroded by body fluids, such as blood, and it should not be rejected by the immune system.

Although it does not occur naturally in the human body, titanium has a high biocompatibility. It is also light and strong. It is therefore used widely in hip replacements to restore mobility to people whose hip joints have worn down from arthritis. Pure titanium is not strong enough to make an ideal prosthesis, so it is alloyed with 6 percent aluminum and 4 percent vanadium. The search is under way for more durable hip replacements made from new alloys.

WIDER IMPACT

Oxides of uranium—a radioactive nonferrous metal—give this bowl its eerie green-yellow glow.

amounts of zinc, aluminum, or manganese), the resulting material combines a lightness approaching that of magnesium with increased strength and reduced reactivity. Magnesium alloys are used to make components for aircraft, automobiles, luggage, and lawn mowers.

Alkali metals
Sodium, lithium, and potassium are three of the alkali metals. They are extremely reactive and produce alkaline solutions when they react with water (see ACID AND ALKALI). They are soft and have very low melting points—sodium melts at 208°F (98°C), which is below the boiling point of water. The softness, reactivity, and low melting points of the alkali metals severely limits the uses of the pure metals to extremely specialized uses. Sodium vapor is used in streetlights, and liquid sodium is used to transfer heat from nuclear reactor cores to the steam-generating system (see NUCLEAR POWER).

Precious metals
The precious metals are silver, gold, platinum, palladium, rhodium, ruthenium, iridium, and osmium. They are all soft, ductile, and heat resistant. The first three are common and are widely used in jewelry. Gold is also used for making electrical contacts in integrated circuits. Platinum gauze is used as a catalyst, particularly in motor vehicle catalytic converters, which convert pollutant exhaust gases into less harmful substances.

Lanthanides and actinides
The lanthanides, formerly known as the rare earth metals, are a group of 15 metals with very similar properties. Their ores tend to occur together, and the metals are so similar in physical and chemical properties that they are difficult to separate. In fact, they are often used as the mixture of metals, known as misch metal, that is obtained from the mixed metal ores. Lighter flints frequently contain misch metal, which itself contains around 25 percent lanthanum by weight. Other uses for the lanthanides have been developed only recently. Yttrium, gadolinium, and europium are used (as mixtures of their oxides) in red phosphors for color televisions.

The actinides are a group of metals with higher atomic masses than the lanthanides but similar chemical properties. The actinides are all radioactive, and some of them, americium, fermium, and curium included, do not occur naturally but can be synthesized in nuclear reactors. They are mainly used in the nuclear power industry and in radiotherapy for treating cancerous tumors.

S. ALDRIDGE

See also: AIRCRAFT DESIGN AND CONSTRUCTION; AIRCRAFT ENGINE; ALLOY; ARMOR; ELECTRICITY AND MAGNETISM; IRON AND STEEL PRODUCTION; MAGNET; MATERIALS SCIENCE; METALS; METALWORKING.

Further reading:
Fahey, J. *A Century of Western Mining.* Seattle: University of Washington Press, 1990.
Neely, J. *Practical Metallurgy and the Materials of Industry.* New York: Prentice Hall, 1994.
Resources of the Earth: Origins, Use and Environmental Impact. Edited by J. Craig, B. Skinner, and D. Vaughan. New York: Prentice Hall, 1996.
Santos, F. *The Impact of Financial Risk on the U.S. Nonferrous Metals Industry.* Washington, D.C.: U.S. Department of Interior, Bureau of Mines, 1995.

NUCLEAR ENERGY

Nuclear energy is released by the radioactive decay of atomic nuclei

Nuclear energy, sometimes referred to as atomic energy, is energy that is created when changes in the nuclei of atoms destroy minute quantities of matter. Although the most familiar forms of this energy are found in nuclear power stations and nuclear weapons, energy from atomic nuclei can be used in many other ways, with applications in medicine, scientific research, and food preparation.

PRINCIPLES OF NUCLEAR ENERGY

Natural radioactivity

All nuclear physics is based on knowledge developed from studying naturally radioactive elements such as uranium and radium. Radioactivity was discovered by French scientist Henri Becquerel (1852–1908) in 1896, when he found that the samples of uranium salts he was investigating were giving out some form of invisible radiation that clouded a photographic plate (see PHOTOGRAPHY).

Becquerel's discovery inspired the work of Polish scientist Marie Curie (1867–1934) and her husband French scientist Pierre Curie (1859–1906), who discovered the radioactive elements radium and polonium in 1898 and worked to refine some of the first pure sources of radioactivity.

British physicist Ernest Rutherford (1871–1937) conducted pioneering work into the nature of radioactivity (see box on page 912). In 1898, he announced that two different particles were being emitted: a heavy, positively charged alpha particle, and a light, negatively charged beta particle (which was identical to the electron, discovered in 1897). In 1900, he added a third type of emission: gamma rays. Unlike alpha and beta particles, gamma rays are a form of high-energy electromagnetic radiation (see ELECTROMAGNETIC RADIATION).

Properties of different types of radiation

Alpha and beta particles and gamma rays are together known as ionizing radiation because they can ionize materials they pass through, stripping away some

An alpha particle (yellow), present in the nucleus of all atoms, scatters a proton (red) in the hydrogen gas filling the cloud chamber. The proton shoots off to the right, while the heavier alpha particle is deflected only slightly.

of the negatively charged electrons of an atom to create an ion (an electrically charged atom). Ionization requires an input of energy to an atom, and the more energy a particle or gamma ray has, the larger the number of atoms it can ionize. The most powerful ionizing agents are alpha particles, but because of their large size they collide frequently with other particles such as air molecules and lose their energy after very short distances. Beta particles are smaller, so they have less ionizing energy, but they travel over longer distances (several yards or meters) before losing all their energy. Gamma rays have the least ionizing energy but the longest range; nothing short of heavy lead shielding can block them. As Rutherford continued his work on radioactivity, he found that radiation was emitted by disintegrating atoms and that heavier elements were transformed into lighter ones during decay.

The discovery of protons and the nucleus

Around 1900, radioactivity was just one part of a greater mystery—the internal structure of the atom. Scientists knew that atoms contained negatively charged electrons and that a neutral atom therefore must contain an equal amount of positive charges, but little else besides this.

In 1909, two of Rutherford's students used a beam of alpha particles to probe the structure of gold. They discovered that the gold atom's positive

CORE FACTS

- The nucleus of an atom is made up of protons and neutrons. Too many neutrons make the nucleus unstable and radioactive.
- Natural radioactivity involves the release of an alpha or beta particle, with gamma radiation, in order to reduce the number of neutrons in the nucleus.
- Changes to the nucleus cause energy to be released because of slight changes in mass between the initial atoms and their products.
- Nuclear energy is used in medicine, warfare, power generation, and scientific research.

CONNECTIONS

● Radiation is used in techniques for **FOOD PRESERVATION**.

● Radiotherapy is a form of **CANCER TREATMENT** that uses radiation to destroy cancer cells.

ERNEST RUTHERFORD

British physicist Ernest Rutherford was born in New Zealand but did most of his work in Britain after moving there in 1895. Rutherford and his team of talented students did more than anyone to solve the mysteries of the atom and radioactivity. As well as establishing the three different types of ionizing radiation and the nature of the particles in the nucleus, he confirmed that radioactivity was due to a transformation of atoms from one element to another and coined the term *half-life* as a measure of the speed of this transformation. With Bertram Boltwood he worked out the basic sequences of radioactive transformations and made the first measurements of the half-lives that enabled Boltwood to date rocks by examining the proportions of radioactive elements they contained. In 1934, Rutherford also played a key role in the discovery of nuclear fusion.

PEOPLE

THE STRUCTURE OF AN ATOM

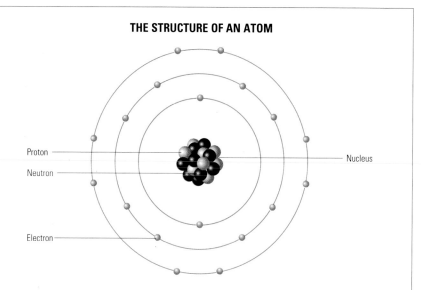

The atom is the smallest particle that characterizes an element. An atom has a dense core—the nucleus—that consists of protons and neutrons. Under normal conditions, the nucleus is surrounded by a cloud of electrons that are in constant motion.

ALPHA PARTICLE EMISSION

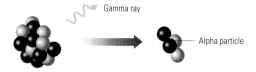

A radioactive nucleus can get rid of its surplus neutrons by the release of an alpha particle.

BETA PARTICLE EMISSION

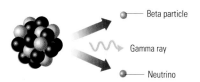

When a neutron in the nucleus changes into a proton, a beta particle is emitted along with a neutrino.

charge was concentrated in a tiny area at its center. This concentrated positive charge was enough to deflect the alpha particles through large angles. It soon became clear that this central atomic area, which was called the nucleus, occupied less than a 100,000th of the atom's radius but contained nearly all of the atom's mass.

The next breakthrough came in 1920, when another of Rutherford's students, English physicist James Chadwick (1891–1974), established that atomic nuclei contained positively charged particles, each equivalent to the nucleus of the smallest atom, hydrogen. Rutherford called these new particles protons. The charge on the nucleus was equal to the number of protons present. This number of protons, or atomic number, also determines the number of electrons in an atom.

Matter and energy

Meanwhile in Switzerland, German physicist Albert Einstein (1879–1955) was developing his theory of relativity, which included the famous statement of the relationship between energy (E) and mass (m): $E=mc^2$ (where c is the speed of light).

The mass of all the products of any radioactive decay was found to be slightly less than that of the atom that produced them. Somewhere, a small amount of mass was lost during radioactive decay. Once Einstein had shown that energy and matter were equivalent, it was realized that this mass was being transformed into pure energy.

The discovery of the neutron

Despite these new insights into the nature of the atom, one problem still puzzled scientists. While the atomic number increased by one with each step along the periodic table of elements, the mass number (a measurement of mass in multiples of the mass of hydrogen) frequently jumped in larger steps. Furthermore, some elements were found in two different forms, called isotopes, that had different masses but the same number of protons and electrons. As early as 1920, these problems led Rutherford to propose a third subatomic particle. It would have the same mass as a proton but no charge, and he called it the neutron.

When Chadwick finally confirmed the existence of the neutron in 1932, all the pieces of the atomic puzzle were in place. The atom was made up of negatively charged electrons with a negligible mass, and these orbited a central, positively charged nucleus made up of protons and neutrons (see the diagram at left). All atoms of one element had the same atomic number (number of protons in the nucleus), but the mass number (the number of protons and neutrons) could vary, producing different isotopes.

The nature of radioactive decay

In general, neutrons balance or outnumber protons in the nucleus, and the heavier isotopes, with the largest quantities of neutrons, are more likely to be radioactive. This knowledge finally allowed the equations of radioactivity to make sense. Rutherford had found that alpha particles were identical to helium nuclei in that they contained two neutrons and two protons.

Beta decay involves the emission of an electron or its positive equivalent, a positron, by the nucleus. The beta particle is created by the transformation of a neutron into a proton or vice versa. Beta decay also produces a particle called a neutrino. In both types of decay, excess energy is released as gamma rays (see the diagram on page 912).

Artificial radioactivity, fusion, and fission
Within just a few years of these breakthroughs, two new discoveries were made that finally showed how the atomic nucleus could be controlled and used as a power source. The first of these was once again inspired by Rutherford. The vastly improved understanding of atomic structures had led to the discovery of many new isotopes, including deuterium, a heavy form of hydrogen containing a neutron as well as a proton. Working with a team of U.S. physicists, Rutherford bombarded deuterium with deuterons (deuterium nuclei), producing a new hydrogen isotope, tritium (containing two neutrons and a proton) and releasing energy. This combination of smaller atoms to make a heavier one is now called nuclear fusion (see the diagram above right).

Then in 1938, Austrian-born Swedish scientist Lise Meitner (1878–1968) discovered another new type of nuclear reaction (see the box on page 914). At the time, she was working with a team of scientists attempting to create new heavy elements by bombarding uranium with neutrons. If uranium was bombarded with extra neutrons, and some of these then transformed into protons and electrons, a different element with a larger number of protons would be formed.

When Meitner and her colleagues analyzed the results of this experiment, however, they discovered that its products were much lighter than expected. They had in fact split the uranium atoms into two equal chunks, producing several new radioactive isotopes of barium. Meitner's nephew Otto Frisch named the process fission (see the diagram at right).

At first, it was a mystery how both these processes could generate energy, but it soon became clear that in both cases some mass was being converted to energy; the products always had a slightly lower mass than the initial atoms. The reason for these mass defects is the energy change needed to bind together the protons and neutrons in the nucleus. This energy has to come from somewhere, and so, according to Einstein's equation, it affects the mass of the atom. The proportions of protons and neutrons affects the binding energy required. The most stable elements with the lowest binding energy per nucleon are those around the mass of iron (atomic mass 56). Elements lighter than iron are more likely to undergo fusion, forming heavier elements. Those heavier than iron are more likely to undergo fission, forming lighter elements.

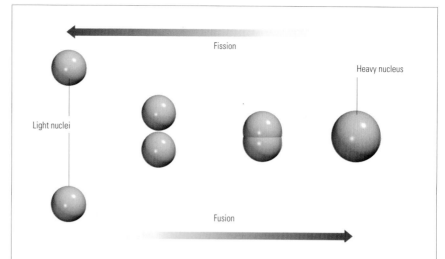

Fission and fusion are opposites: fusion is the joining of two light nuclei to make a heavy nucleus. Fission is the splitting of a heavy nucleus into two lighter nuclei.

APPLICATIONS OF NUCLEAR ENERGY
In the century since the discovery of radioactivity, this phenomenon, nuclear energy, has been used in a variety of applications, from medical to military—the latter with devastating consequences.

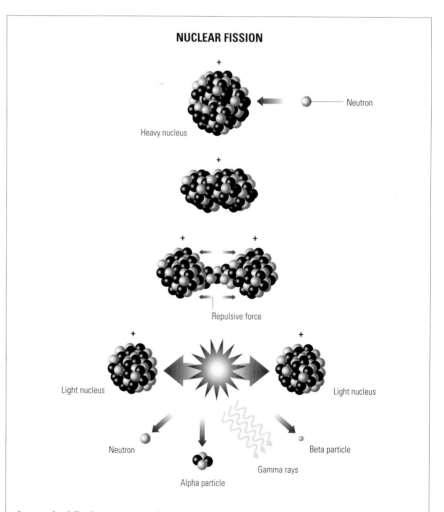

In a typical fission process, a heavy nucleus such as uranium-235 absorbs a neutron. The nucleus becomes elongated, and repulsive electrical forces between the two positively charged sides pull the nucleus apart into two equal halves. Alpha, beta, and gamma radiation can all be emitted, along with neutrons.

LISE MEITNER

Lise Meitner (1878–1968) perhaps made one of the most important breakthroughs in the development of nuclear physics. Born in Vienna, Austria, she became only the second woman to gain a Ph.D. from the University of Vienna in 1905. She then moved to Berlin to work with Otto Hahn (1879–1968) at the Kaiser-Wilhelm Institute for Chemistry, but their supervisor would not allow a woman in his laboratory. Nevertheless, she and Hahn made many discoveries about the nature of radioactive decay, and by 1917 Meitner was the institute's joint director.

In the 1930s, Meitner, Hahn, and Meitner's nephew Otto Frisch began to work on the possibility of producing new elements by bombarding uranium with neutrons to create a heavier element. However, their work was interrupted by the Nazi invasion of Austria. Hahn continued his work with Fritz Strassman (1902–1980). Meitner, who was Jewish, fled to Sweden with the help of other physicists. There she analyzed the results of new tests conducted by Hahn and realized that, far from being heavier than uranium, the "new" elements were isotopes of the much lighter element barium. Meitner and her colleagues had actually discovered nuclear fission.

PEOPLE

Medical applications

Medicine was the first field to make widespread use of radiation sources, but many people were slow to realize the dangers associated with overexposure. As high-energy particles and rays pass through living tissue, they can ionize those atoms and molecules, killing cells or causing them to mutate.

Becquerel had made his first discoveries while investigating X rays (another electromagnetic wave produced by some radioactive elements), and radioactive materials were soon being widely used as X-ray sources for medical imaging. In 1906, Becquerel burned himself by carrying a radiation source in his pocket, and many of the early radiation pioneers began to fall ill with cancer. However, this did not stop the craze for radioactivity in the early 20th century, such as radioactive bath salts, that were sold for spurious medical benefits.

RADIOISOTOPE ENRICHMENT

Before they can be used in many applications, the radioactive isotopes of a material need to be concentrated in a small source. Natural deposits of uranium contain a natural mixture of the isotopes uranium-235 and uranium-238, but only uranium-235 is fissionable in nuclear reactors. Normal chemical reactions cannot separate the two isotopes, but there are several methods by which the uranium-235 can be enriched.

The two most common methods both rely on converting the uranium into uranium hexafluoride, which becomes a gas when heated. Once the molecules are moving freely in a gas, they can be more easily separated. One technique for doing this is to use a gas centrifuge—a rapidly spinning drum in which the heavier molecules (containing uranium-238) move to the edge and can be filtered off. The other common technique is gaseous diffusion, in which the gas is forced through a series of membranes with microscopic pores that separate out the heavier molecules.

A CLOSER LOOK

More useful medical applications include the use of radioisotopes to image soft tissues in the body, or to trace the path of materials through the body (see MEDICAL TECHNOLOGY).

Scientific uses

Radioactive sources have also found many uses in science. One of the most important has been in geological and archaeological dating. In 1907, Rutherford's colleague Bertram Boltwood (1870–1927) used the decay of uranium to measure the age of Earth, revolutionizing geology.

In archaeology, similar processes are used. The best known, radiocarbon dating, measures the proportions of radioactive carbon-14 and nonradioactive carbon-12 isotopes in once-living things.

Another scientific application is irradiation. Exposing some substances to gamma rays can trigger chemical changes. In some complex polymer materials composed of long-chain molecules, exposure to radiation helps cross-links form between neighboring chains, hardening the material's surface. Tire rubber, paints, and plastics can be processed in this way (see CHEMICAL INDUSTRY, ORGANIC).

Military uses

Nuclear weapons were the first devices that did not just make use of radioactive decay, but instead triggered it artificially. The earliest nuclear bombs triggered a fission chain reaction by detonating a mass of suitable material, such as uranium. In a large enough mass of radioactive material, a single random radioactive decay by one atom can trigger further decays, spreading rapidly as a chain reaction and releasing energy.

However, the fission bomb is almost puny compared to the fusion, or hydrogen, bomb. This device is triggered by a small fission bomb at its heart; the energy from this explosion is used to heat and compress a hydrogen-rich shell to the point where it will undergo nuclear fusion (see NUCLEAR WEAPONS).

Nuclear power

Tapping nuclear reactions to provide a controlled source of power is far more difficult than releasing them in a weapon. Today's nuclear power stations are based on fission. They generate power in a carefully controlled chain reaction of uranium-235 fission (see NUCLEAR POWER). Meanwhile, scientists around the world are trying to develop controlled nuclear fusion—a process that uses only hydrogen isotopes and creates no radioactive by-products.

G. SPARROW

See also: HAZARDOUS WASTE; MEDICAL IMAGING; NUCLEAR FUSION; PARTICLE ACCELERATOR; POWER STATION; RADIATION DETECTION.

Further reading:
Bodansky, D. Nuclear Energy: Principles, Practices, and Prospects. Woodbury, New York: American Institute of Physics, 1996.

NUCLEAR FUSION

Nuclear fusion is a process that generates energy by joining two atomic nuclei together

Nuclear fusion is the power source that lights the stars and is considered a potentially pollution-free alternative to current nuclear power technology, which is based on a different nuclear process called fission. The theory of fusion is well understood, but the conditions needed to trigger it are so extreme that controlled fusion has remained confined to laboratories and experimental reactors. So far, the most spectacular form of fusion reaction created by humanity is the hydrogen bomb. However, the prospect of controlled commercial fusion power is gradually getting closer.

What is fusion?

Nuclear fusion is a process by which the tiny central nuclei of atoms are fused together to form heavier elements. As physicists in the 1920s and 1930s unlocked the secrets of the atom, they discovered that the masses of nuclei were actually slightly less than the separate masses of their component neutrons and protons. This was because some of the nuclei's energy is tied up as binding energy, holding the atomic nucleus together. According to German-born scientist Albert Einstein (1879–1955), mass and energy are interchangeable. (This was stated in his famous equation $E=mc^2$.) The energy of the nuclei that is taken up by the binding energy shows itself as a slight reduction in mass of the nucleus, called the mass defect. Although the mass defect is tiny, the actual binding energy related to it is huge.

When two light nuclei combine, the mass of the resulting nucleus is slightly less than the combined masses of the lighter nuclei; the difference is released as energy. The simplest form of fusion takes place in the Sun, where hydrogen nuclei combine to produce helium. This reaction is the source of sunlight.

The greatest problems with fusion are caused by the extreme conditions it requires. Because all atomic nuclei are positively charged, and because like charges always repel, nuclei repel each other when they come too close together, and this creates a huge

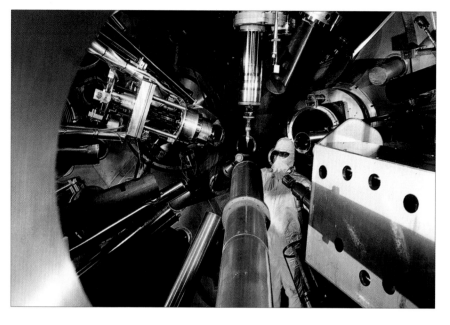

energy barrier that prevents fusion from occurring. Nuclei will only fuse if they are forced together by great pressure and temperature or if they collide at high impact speed.

Practical fusion

The earliest artificial fusion reactions were produced by British physicist Ernest Rutherford (1871–1937), working in the United States in 1934. He created high-speed collisions between deuterium atoms. Deuterium is a heavy version of the simplest element, hydrogen. It contains a neutron in addition to the single proton of ordinary hydrogen. By colliding deuterium nuclei, Rutherford was able to create tritium, a form of hydrogen with two neutrons in its nucleus. Although the fusion itself released energy, it was insignificant compared to the large amounts of power required to trigger fusion in the first place.

In order to release large amounts of energy, fusion has to take place in large amounts of material. Although Rutherford's technique of firing atoms at each other at high speed has been widely used for studying fundamental particles, it will not work for bulk matter (see PARTICLE ACCELERATOR). Instead, all the atoms within the fusion material have to be boosted to high speeds and they have to be contained so that their nuclei will be forced together.

The only way of doing this is to copy conditions in the Sun, raising the temperature of the fusion material to millions of degrees and trapping it at high pressure. Within the Sun's core, fusion takes place simply by the combination of four hydrogen nuclei. However, the long time it takes for these four nuclei to collide at random makes this reaction impractical on Earth, because extremely high energies would have to be maintained for long periods. Instead, fusion is carried out in the laboratory between

Nuclear fusion is initiated in the Nova laser fusion test chamber. To achieve this, a pinhead-sized pellet of fuel is placed in the chamber, and then a powerful laser burst lasting 50 picoseconds (trillionths of a second) is fired into the chamber.

CORE FACTS

- Nuclear fusion generates energy by combining, or fusing, the central nuclei of atoms to form new elements.
- The energy released by fusion comes from the mass defect—a slight difference between the mass of the fusing particles and the mass of the product.
- Magnetic confinement fusion traps gases in a powerful electromagnetic field, heating and compressing them to reach their ignition temperature.
- Inertial confinement fusion uses powerful lasers to compress a fuel pellet to ignition temperature, triggering a miniature fusion explosion.

CONNECTIONS

- Nuclear fusion offers the possibility of a cheap, nonpolluting **ENERGY RESOURCE** for the future.

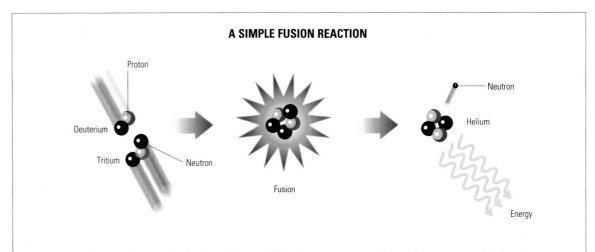

A SIMPLE FUSION REACTION

Proton

Deuterium

Tritium

Neutron

Fusion

Neutron

Helium

Energy

When a deuterium nucleus and a tritium nucleus collide, they can fuse together to form a mass of their component neutrons and protons. One neutron is ejected from the mass, leaving a helium nucleus and releasing energy.

deuterium and tritium nuclei, which makes a helium nuclei in a single collision, within a much shorter time span and with a lower energy requirement. Huge amounts of energy are still needed to raise the fusion material to its ignition temperature. However, once fusion is under way, the energy released supplies enough energy to produce further fusion.

Because of the extreme conditions needed, the first use of fusion—the hydrogen bomb—was the most destructive known. Energy released by a less powerful fission bomb heated a layer of deuterium-rich material to ignition temperature, releasing vast amounts of energy in a fraction of a second (see NUCLEAR WEAPONS). Harnessing fusion for peaceful uses has proved more difficult due to the high temperatures required and the need for confinement.

Magnetic confinement

Because the nuclei of deuterium and tritium used in nuclear fusion have their surrounding negatively charged electrons stripped away at relatively low temperatures, the bare atomic nuclei are positively charged. This allows them to form a plasma, which is an electrically charged gas. Because electrical charges and magnetic fields can interact, the plasma can be affected by magnetic fields, and this is one way in which fusion material can be controlled (see ELECTRICITY AND MAGNETISM). In a reactor called a tokamak, plasma is injected into a torus—a vacuum chamber shaped like a ring doughnut. A strong magnetic field is generated by cables in the chamber's walls, and a powerful electric current is made to flow through the plasma. The result is that the plasma is confined in a loop around the torus away from its walls, and it is heated to millions of degrees.

Tokamaks are operated by many countries around the world, and new records for energy production are set every few months. The crucial break-even point, where the reactor produces as much energy as it uses, has still not been reached.

Inertial confinement

Another area of fusion research uses lasers (see LASER AND MASER). Inertial confinement involves dropping tiny pellets of deuterium-rich material into a fusion chamber and compressing them with powerful laser beams fired from around the chamber. The pressure of the laser beams confines and compresses the fusion material in the reactor until ignition is reached. In theory, lasers can produce much higher temperatures and pressures than magnetic confinement, so the fuel is used up more rapidly and must be replaced by another pellet. A laser fusion power station would, in effect, be powered by a series of tiny hydrogen bomb explosions. This is one reason why the United States is planning a huge test reactor, the National Ignition Facility: inertial confinement offers a way to develop fusion weapons without large-scale nuclear tests.

G. SPARROW

See also: NUCLEAR POWER.

Further reading:
Fowler, K. *The Fusion Quest*. Baltimore: Johns Hopkins University Press, 1997.

MUON-CATALYZED FUSION

Both magnetic and inertial confinement fusion require enormous amounts of energy, and even when the break-even point is reached, the prototype reactors will have to be scaled up enormously to reach a point where they can act as power stations. However, there is another type of fusion that might offer an easier way forward.

A rare type of subatomic particle called the muon is known to trigger fusion reactions in a mixture of hydrogen, deuterium, and tritium at much lower temperatures and pressures than other types of fusion. The muons act as a catalyst in the reaction—a substance that causes or speeds up a reaction without taking part in it (see CATALYST, INDUSTRIAL). Although muons can be manufactured in particle accelerators, at present the energy required to make them is less than the energy they can generate in fusion. If a way of producing muons using less energy were to be found, this would open the way for a very simple fusion method with much lower temperatures needed for ignition.

A CLOSER LOOK

NUCLEAR POWER

Nuclear power is energy that is generated using the heat released by nuclear reactions

This nuclear power station is situated on the banks of the Hudson River in New York State. The domes house two pressurized-water reactors.

The same nuclear reactions that release enormous amounts of energy in a nuclear explosion can be used to provide a sustained release of energy for a long period. This energy, in the form of heat, can be used to produce steam to drive a turbogenerator in much the same way that the heat produced by burning coal or oil is used (see POWER STATION). In fact, specialists in the field of nuclear power often talk of "burning" nuclear fuel, even though the process that provides the heat is very different from the combustion process.

Although the most widespread use of nuclear energy is in nuclear-power reactors for large-scale electricity generation, nuclear reactors are also used to propel submarines and spacecraft and to provide energy for installations in remote locations. A great advantage of nuclear power is that a relatively small amount of fuel can provide large quantities of energy

without consuming oxygen (there is no combustion reaction). For these reasons, nuclear-powered submarines and spacecraft can travel farther than fossil-fueled vehicles before the fuel and air (or oxidant) run out (see FUELS AND PROPELLANTS).

Dependence on nuclear power

As of January 1999, the number of countries operating nuclear-power reactors was 32, involving a total of about 450 reactors generating nearly 360 gigawatts (GW). The country with the greatest dependence on nuclear power was Lithuania, where 82 percent of the total energy demand was supplied by two reactors, generating about 2.4 GW. The next most dependent countries were France (80 percent of electricity provided by 59 reactors, generating about 63 GW) and Belgium (60 percent from seven reactors, generating 5.7 GW). The United States generates about 100 GW by nuclear power.

Very few new nuclear reactors are being planned for construction in Western industrialized countries. In fact, the main nuclear activity at the beginning of the 21st century is likely to be concentrated in Asian countries, and particularly in China, India, South Korea, North Korea, Pakistan, and Taiwan. (For a detailed account of the types of environmental and technical problems that arise from nuclear waste disposal see HAZARDOUS WASTE.)

HEAT FROM NUCLEAR FISSION

The atomic nuclei of certain elements have a tendency to split into smaller nuclei and release subatomic particles, such as neutrons. This is known as a fission (splitting) reaction (see NUCLEAR ENERGY). When fission occurs, the mass of the products is found to be a tiny amount less than the mass of the

---

CORE FACTS

- At the beginning of 1999, 32 countries were operating nuclear-power reactors, generating nearly 360 gigawatts (billions of watts) of electricity in approximately 450 reactors.
- The complete reaction of one pound of nuclear fuel can produce as much thermal energy as burning 1250 tons (1136 tonnes) of coal.
- Since the discovery of plutonium in 1940, the worldwide nuclear industry has produced a total of about 1500 tons (1400 tonnes) of plutonium.
- Nuclear reactors are used to provide electrical power and propulsion for submarines and surface ships—mainly warships. There is approximately the same number of reactors at sea as there is on land.

CONNECTIONS

- Nuclear power stations are just one type of **POWER STATION**. Others use **COAL**, oil, or natural gas as their **ENERGY RESOURCES**. Increasingly, electricity is being generated using **SOLAR POWER, WIND POWER, GEOTHERMAL ENERGY**, and **WAVE POWER**.

NUCLEAR FISSION REACTION

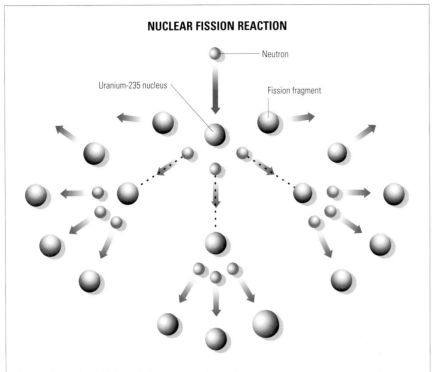

In uranium, the splitting of the atom (nuclear fission) occurs when a neutron is absorbed by the nucleus of a uranium isotope known as U^{235}. The nucleus splits into two parts and releases three more neutrons that each in turn produce fission.

starting materials. The mass (m) that "disappears" is converted to energy (E) according to the equation $E = mc^2$, where c is the speed of light.

The fission reaction

The energy released by the fission reaction is produced in the form of the kinetic energy of the fast-moving fission products—the nuclei and subatomic particles produced by the fission reaction. This kinetic energy is converted into heat when these particles collide with other matter.

Compared with combustion (burning) reactions, the energy released by a fission reaction is huge. The complete burning of one pound (0.45 kg) of a typical nuclear fuel can produce as much thermal energy as the burning of 1250 tons (1136 tonnes) of coal—a weight ratio of about 1:2,500,000. A typical nuclear power station generates about 1000 MW of electricity—enough power to supply the domestic and industrial demand for a city of a million people. Such a reactor uses about 30 tons (27 tonnes) of uranium in a year. A fossil-fuel plant of the same size uses about 2.6 million tons (2.4 million tonnes) of coal or 2 million tons (1.8 million tonnes) of oil.

REACTOR TYPES

There are several types of nuclear reactors, but only two are commonly used to generate power: thermal reactors and fast breeder reactors.

Thermal reactors

Thermal reactors are designed and operated for the production of heat. The fuel is normally uranium. The main isotopes (different atomic forms of the same element) in naturally occurring uranium are U^{235} and U^{238}. The nuclei of both isotopes of uranium contain 92 protons, but a U^{235} nucleus contains 143 neutrons, whereas a U^{238} nucleus contains 146.

A difference between the two types of uranium atoms is that U^{235} is radioactive—it undergoes spontaneous fission reactions. Furthermore, an atom of U^{235} will undergo fission when any neutron, even one moving slowly, collides with and is absorbed by it. In fact, slow-moving neutrons have a better chance of inducing a fission reaction than fast-moving neutrons—a fact that is central to the operation of a thermal reactor. By contrast, only fast-moving neutrons can cause a U^{238} nucleus to undergo fission. Consequently, U^{235} is of greater importance to the heat-producing nuclear reaction.

When a U^{235} atom is hit by a neutron and undergoes fission, it produces two smaller nuclei (various combinations are possible) and two or three fast-moving neutrons that have a chance of causing further fissions if they hit other U^{235} atoms. Under the right conditions, the fission reaction can become a self-sustaining chain reaction, which means a sufficient proportion of the fission-product neutrons is successful in starting other fission reactions and the chain reaction keeps going. If too many fission-product neutrons start fission reactions, the chain reaction accelerates and a nuclear explosion results.

Uranium from mined ores typically contains only 0.72 percent U^{235}; the majority is U^{238}. A trace (0.05 percent) of U^{234} is also present. Some nuclear reactors use natural uranium and its compounds as fuel, but most use uranium in which the concentration of U^{235} has been increased to about 2 to 4 percent. This is done by a chemical process called uranium enrichment. Because of the low concentration of U^{235}, a very large amount of uranium is needed to produce the number of fission-product neutrons necessary for a chain reaction.

Moderators in the reactor core slow down fast-moving neutrons that bump into them. The slower-moving neutrons have better chances of initiating fission reactions, and the quantity of fissile material necessary to establish a chain reaction is reduced. Moderators contain light atoms— often hydrogen, deuterium (a heavy isotope of hydrogen), or carbon; in the form of water, heavy water (deuterium oxide), or graphite, respectively. The reactor core is also surrounded by a reflector of moderator that bounces stray neutrons back into the core.

Despite their name, moderators promote the chain reaction. Control rods have the opposite effect—they slow the chain reaction according to power requirements. Control rods are made of materials such as boron that absorb neutrons.

The heat from the fission reactions must be removed from the core by a coolant to avoid thermal damage within the reactor and to provide steam for the generators. The most widely used coolants are carbon dioxide, water, and heavy water.

Magnox reactors—so named for the magnesium alloy that encases the fuel rods—were among the

MAIN THERMAL REACTOR TYPES

The main types of thermal reactors used for the commercial production of electricity are characterized by the type of fuel used, the degree of enrichment, the materials used to moderate them, and the type of cooling system used.

Reactor	Fuel	Enrichment	Moderator	Coolant
AGR (advanced gas-cooled reactor)	uranium oxide pellets	2.3% U^{235}	graphite	carbon dioxide
BWR (boiling-water reactor)	uranium oxide pellets	2.2% U^{235}	water	water
CANDU (Canadian deuterium-uranium)	uranium oxide pellets	natural (0.72% U^{235})	heavy water	heavy water
LWGR (light-water graphite reactor)	uranium oxide pellets	1–2% U^{235}	graphite	water
Magnox	uranium metal rods	natural (0.72% U^{235})	graphite	carbon dioxide
PWR (pressurized-water reactor)	uranium oxide pellets	3% U^{235}	water	water

earliest gas-cooled reactors. The most popular reactor types now use light water (normal H_2O) as both coolant and moderator. There are two types of light water reactors (LWRs): boiling water reactors and pressurized-water reactors. In boiling water reactors, the water is boiled and the steam passed to the turbines. In pressurized-water reactors, the coolant water kept is under extremely high pressure to prevent the water from boiling. The high-pressure water is then passed through a heat exchanger to produce steam, which turns the turbines.

Fission products accumulate in the fuel rods as the uranium is used up. Some fission products are good neutron absorbers and would eventually kill the chain reaction. To keep the reactor running, the used rods have to be removed and replaced with fresh ones every two to four years. Typically, a LWR will have a third of its fuel rods changed each year.

The amount of thermal energy extracted from the fuel rods is known as the burn up and is expressed as megawatt-days (MWd) per ton of uranium. The degree of burn up is 30,000–50,000 MWd/ton for an LWR. About one third of the thermal energy output of a reactor can be converted to electrical energy; the rest of the heat is lost.

An important characteristic of a nuclear-power reactor is the load factor—the fraction of time the reactor is in operation. A modern reactor has to be shut for reloading and repairs four months per year, making the average load factor about 65 percent.

Fast breeder reactors

Fast breeder reactors (FBRs) differ from thermal reactors in that they rely on highly enriched fuel to sustain the chain reaction. No moderator is used and the neutrons in the core move at or near the speed

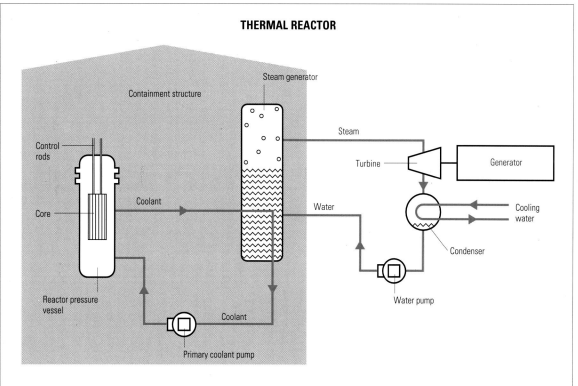

THERMAL REACTOR

A coolant transfers heat from the reactor core to a steam generator, where it turns water into pressurized steam to drive the turbines to make electricity, before being pumped back to the reactor.

THE CHERNOBYL DISASTER

The accident at the Chernobyl nuclear-power reactor (Unit 4) on April 26, 1986, dramatically brought home the fact that the major source of risk in any nuclear reactor is the huge amount of radioactive materials present in the reactor core. The release of even a small fraction of the radioactive inventory of a nuclear reactor into the biosphere presents a threat to human health and the environment.

Such a release occurred at Chernobyl, the scene of the world's worst nuclear accident. The reactor was an RBMK (from the Russian for "high-power-channel boiling-water reactor"). The core of the reactor consisted of an assembly of graphite blocks that formed the main moderator. The total weight of graphite was about 1700 tons (1540 tonnes). The fuel elements were uranium oxide fuel pellets.

Boiling water, acting as a coolant, flowed up over the fuel rods, generating steam at the top of the core. The reactor was divided into two sections, each linked to a turbogenerator; steam was fed directly to one of the turbogenerators, then it was condensed and recycled. The core was enclosed in a steel vessel, a leakproof but non-pressurized shell.

The Chernobyl accident occurred during an experiment. The engineers wanted to discover what would happen if, when the reactor was at low power or shut down so that it could not supply its own electricity to operate the pumps, an external grid failure should occur. Normally, electricity would be supplied in such an emergency by diesel generators at the reactor. The engineers wanted to find out how long the turbogenerators, when isolated from their steam supply, could be used to supply electricity as they slowed to a stop.

The experiment began by shutting the emergency regulating valves of the second turbogenerator; the first turbogenerator was already idle. Four of the eight pumps were electrically connected to the tripped turbogenerator for the experiment. As the power to the pumps went down, the disaster sequence began.

Thirty-six seconds into the experiment, the operators pressed the Scram button, but this did not shut the reactor down: nearly all the neutron-absorbing control rods were in the upper part of the reactor core.

The accident involved two explosions. The first explosion occurred because the operators shut down four of the eight main coolant pumps. As the pressure fell, the water in the core boiled vigorously. The steam that replaced the water absorbed neutrons to a lesser extent than did the water. Because most of the control rods that stabilized the power of the reactor were withdrawn, the increase in the neutron flux increased the heat produced, which produced more steam and a large power boost. The control rods could not be inserted quickly enough to check the initial power boost, and a steam or hydrogen explosion resulted. The second explosion was nuclear, caused by fission in the reactor core, and released 1000 gigajoules (GJ) of energy. The total energy released by the explosions was about 1200 GJ. The reactor and the reactor building roof were totally destroyed, and radioactive material was released into the atmosphere.

Radioactivity from the Chernobyl accident spread far and wide: about one third of the radioactive cesium released (Cs^{134} and Cs^{137}) landed in the former Soviet Union; most of the remainder was deposited in Europe and Scandinavia. Estimates suggest that the Chernobyl accident exposed people in the Northern Hemisphere to a total radiation dose of about 600,000 person-sieverts (the sievert is the unit of radiation dose), sufficient to cause 30,000 potentially fatal cancers. By way of comparison, the worst accident before Chernobyl—at Three Mile Island, Pennsylvania, in 1979—exposed the local population to a total radiation dose of 40 person-sieverts. The Windscale fire of October 10, 1957, which took place at the Windscale (new Sellafield) nuclear power plant in Cumbria, northern England, involved the first significant release of radioactive material from a reactor, including iodine-131.

WIDER IMPACT

they have when produced by the fission reaction. As previously stated, fast-moving neutrons have less chance of causing fission in U^{235} nuclei than slow-moving ones, which is why a higher flux (concentration) of neutrons is necessary to maintain the chain reaction. Another important feature is the particular choice of coolant: water and carbon dioxide (both moderators) would slow down the neutrons and cannot be used. Liquid sodium or helium gas is used instead.

Fast neutrons do have sufficient energy to react with U^{238} nuclei. However, the result is not a fission reaction. Instead, U^{238} is converted to plutonium-239 (Pu^{239}), which is also a useful nuclear fuel. Since each fission reaction (which destroys one fuel nucleus) produces more than one neutron that can convert U^{238} (nonfuel) to Pu^{239} (fuel), the reactor

can be set up to produce more fuel than it consumes. The ratio of fuel produced to fuel consumed is known as the conversion ratio. When the conversion ratio is greater than one, the reactor is said to be breeding fuel. (The *fast* in the name refers to the fast-moving neutrons in the core.)

Surrounding the core with U^{238} further increases the yield of Pu^{239} by capturing fast neutrons that are escaping the core. In this way, 50 to 60 times more fuel can be obtained from uranium ore than would be obtained by burning U^{235} alone.

A number of developmental FBRs have been built and operated in Britain, France, Germany, Japan, Russia, and the United States. However, FBRs are expensive to run because their coolants are expensive to purchase and require special handling (sodium is highly reactive). Since there is no foreseeable shortage of uranium ore, it is unlikely that FBRs will be able to compete with the more common thermal nuclear reactors in the near future.

Nuclear reactors for special purposes

In addition to reactors for the commercial generation of electricity in power stations, a number of other types have been developed. Reactors, mainly PWRs fueled with highly enriched uranium, are used, for example, to power surface warships, submarines, and icebreakers. In fact, there are about the same number of reactors generating power at sea as there are on land. Reactors are also used by the military as power sources for remote ground equipment, such as radar stations. Small reactors have also been developed to power satellite instruments.

FUEL AND WASTE PROCESSING

The main reserves of uranium ore are in situated in North America, South Africa, and Australia. The ore can be purified and converted to the uncombined metal or its oxide. Natural uranium contains only 0.72 percent of the isotope U^{235}, which is the fuel for thermal reactors. Reactor sizes and efficiencies can be improved by increasing the proportion of U^{235} in the fuel. In order to do this, the purified ore is converted to uranium hexafluoride (UF_6), which is easily vaporized by heating. Since the hexafluoride of U^{235} is slightly lighter than that of U^{238}, a centrifuge can be used to separate the two isotopes: centrifugal force drives the heavier $U^{238}F_6$ to the edge of the centrifuge while $U^{235}F_6$ collects at the center of the centrifuge. The enriched uranium hexafluoride is drawn off and subsequently converted to fuel.

The uranium fuel in a nuclear reactor is normally in the form of uranium dioxide (UO_2), which can withstand considerably higher temperatures than uranium metal. The UO_2 is manufactured into small ceramic pellets that are then assembled in cylindrical rods, typically 0.4 inch (1 cm) in diameter and 13 feet (4 m) long. A fuel element is made up from about 200 rods. The core of a modern reactor will normally contain about 200 fuel elements, also called fuel assemblies. The core of a typical nuclear-power reactor generating 1,000 MW contains about 100 tons (91 tonnes) of uranium.

Reprocessing spent thermal reactor fuel

When spent fuel elements are removed from a thermal reactor, they are highly radioactive. Therefore elements are transferred from the reactor core to a water-filled cooling pond by remote handling equipment. After about four years, when the elements are somewhat safer to handle, they may be sent to a reprocessing plant for chemical separation of the unused uranium, plutonium, and fission products.

The first operation at the reprocessing plant is the removal of the fuel rod cladding. The elements are chopped up and put into nitric acid, which dissolves spent fuel and fission products as nitrates but leaves the cladding as a solid.

The circular reactor core in a French nuclear power station. The core is being loaded (charged) with its first batch of nuclear fuel before being sealed up completely by a dome.

In a typical process called PUREX (plutonium uranium extraction), the nitrate solution is washed with tributyl phosphate (TBP) and kerosene. TBP attaches itself to the uranium and plutonium in the solution, allowing them to dissolve in the kerosene. The fission products remain in the water-based nitrate solution, which does not mix with kerosene. The uranium is then converted to uranium hexafluoride and enriched for use in new fuel rods. The plutonium is converted to plutonium oxide. From the time the element was first produced in 1940 to the end of the 20th century, military and civilian reactors have produced about 1400 tons (1270 tonnes) of plutonium, 300 tons (272 tonnes) of which is stored at reprocessing plants. The rate of

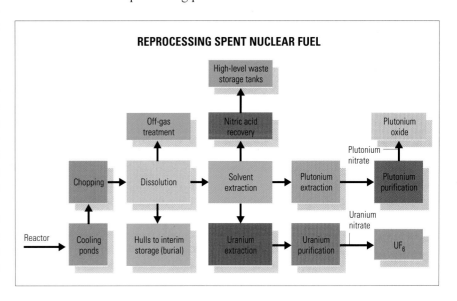

REPROCESSING SPENT NUCLEAR FUEL

Inside the containment building of a nuclear power station in Oregon. The reactor core is the circular object under the water. Beside the core are four steam generators that make steam to drive the turbines situated in an adjacent building.

result of its radioactivity; the heat generation has to be taken into account in designing storage and disposal facilities. Low-level waste (LLW) contains radioactivity not exceeding 4 gigabecquerels per ton of alpha or 12 gigabecquerels per ton of beta and gamma radioactivity. (The becquerel is the unit of quantity of a radioactive material.) Intermediate-level waste (ILW) is more radioactive than LLW but does not generate heat at a rate that requires special storage-design considerations.

Most of the ILW from the nuclear power industry consists of cladding removed from spent nuclear reactor fuel elements, filters and other wastes from effluent treatments, and decommissioned or worn-out plant and equipment. The safest place for the permanent disposal of ILW is thought to be in geologic depositories—chambers deep in underground rock. The waste may, for example, be immobilized in cement in stainlesssteel drums. Swedish and Finnish authorities have begun burying ILW in this way under their decommissioned reactors.

Reprocessing plants produce the bulk of HLW. These wastes leave the reprocessing plant as a liquid, which is stored in tanks. The liquid gets extremely hot because of the heat of radioactive decay, so the tanks must be cooled. For long-term disposal, HLW can be immobilized in glass (borosilicate) cylinders that can then be permanently disposed of in geologic depositories. Spent reactor fuel elements could also be permanently disposed of in geologic depositories.

The protection of the population and the environment from the harmful effects of radioactive material is extremely important, and the containment of radioactive waste is a major challenge. So far, no solution that is politically and socially acceptable has been found for the permanent disposal of HLW. The problem is so severe because of the huge amounts of radioactivity accumulated by our use of the nuclear fission process; the durations, which can be thousands and even millions of years, that the wastes remain a potential hazard to life; and the consequent need to isolate radioactive materials from the environment.

F. BARNABY

production of plutonium in 1999 was 70 tons (63 tonnes) per year, with 25 tons (22.6 tonnes) of this total being separated from other reactor products in reprocessing plants.

Six reprocessing plants were operating in 1999: B205 and THORP at Sellafield, England; UP2 and UP3 at La Hague, France; RT1 at Chelyabinsk, Russia; and a plant at Tokai-mura, Japan.

Mixed-oxide (MOX) fuels

Some nuclear reactors use mixed-oxide (MOX) fuel, in which plutonium oxide is mixed with uranium oxide. This fuel was developed to use up the plutonium that is recovered from fuel rods by reprocessing, but it can also be used to burn plutonium oxide that is fabricated from decommissioned nuclear weapons. Mixed-oxide fuel elements produce heat at a much faster rate than fuel elements that contain only uranium oxide. For this reason, a maximum of three in ten uranium elements can be replaced with MOX elements in reactors that are designed for uranium-oxide fuel—a greater proportion than 30 percent however, pose the threat of overheating the reactor core.

Only Belgium, France, Germany, and Switzerland use MOX fuel to a significant extent; Japan had planned to start doing so in 1999.

Radioactive waste disposal

The main sources of radioactive wastes are the nuclear power industry (fuel manufacture, maintenance, and reprocessing), and medical, industrial, and military users of radioactive materials.

Radioactive wastes are divided into categories. High-level waste (HLW) is radioactive waste in which the temperature may rise significantly as a

See also: AIRCRAFT CARRIER; FUELS AND PROPELLANTS; HAZARDOUS WASTE; HEAT EXCHANGER; NUCLEAR ENERGY; NUCLEAR FUSION; NUCLEAR WEAPONS; ORE EXTRACTION AND PROCESSING; POWER STATION; RADIATION DETECTION; STEAM TURBINE; SUBMARINE; TURBINE; WARSHIP.

Further reading:
Albright, D. *Plutonium and Highly Enriched Uranium World Inventories, Capabilities and Policies.* Oxford: Oxford University Press for Stockholm International Peace Research Institute, 1997.
Makhijani, A. *High-Level Dollars, Low-Level Sense; A Critique of Present Policy for the Management of Long-Lived Radioactive Waste and Discussion of an Alternative Approach.* New York: The Apex Press, 1992.

NUCLEAR WEAPONS

A nuclear weapon is an explosive device in which the energy is released by nuclear fission or fusion

The first nuclear weapons were successfully developed during World War II (1939–1945) by a group of U.S. and European scientists as part of the U.S. Army's top-secret Manhattan Project. The race to develop the atomic bomb ahead of Nazi Germany involved the application of various discoveries, notably that of nuclear fission in 1938 by German physicists Otto Hahn (1879–1968) and Fritz Strassmann (1902–1980). The first nuclear fission chain reaction was accomplished by a team led by Italian refugee scientist Enrico Fermi (1901–1954) on December 2, 1942, in a squash court under a college football field at the University of Chicago.

The Manhattan Project

The Manhattan Project, which began in 1942, was a massive $2 billion effort involving several thousand nuclear physicists, chemists, and engineers under the leadership of U.S. physicist J. Robert Oppenheimer (1904–1967). The first atomic bombs were designed and built at a remote mountaintop location at Los Alamos, New Mexico. Remarkable progress was made, and huge technical problems were overcome. On July 16, 1945, the world's first nuclear weapon was exploded near Alamogordo in the New Mexico desert. By the end of World War II, in August 1945, two nuclear weapons had been dropped on Hiroshima and Nagasaki in Japan.

Hiroshima and Nagasaki

The Hiroshima atomic bomb contained about 132 lb (60 kg) of highly enriched uranium and had an explosive power of 12.5 kilotons—equivalent to that of 12,500 tons of trinitrotoluene (TNT) and 5000 times more powerful than any previous bomb. The Nagasaki bomb contained about 13.6 lb (6.2 kg) of plutonium and had an explosive yield of 20 kilotons.

An aerial view of an American nuclear test explosion on an atoll in the Pacific Ocean in 1956. This bomb had an explosive yield of 13.7 kilotons.

When the atomic bomb exploded over Hiroshima, there were about 350,000 people in the city; by the end of 1945, 140,000 of them had died. At least 280,000 people were in Nagasaki when the atomic bomb exploded, and some 74,000 of them had died before the end of 1945. The people killed immediately by the bombs were either crushed or burned to death. An area of 5 sq miles (13 sq km) in Hiroshima and 2.7 sq miles (7 sq km) in Nagasaki was reduced to rubble by blast and then to ashes by fire. At Hiroshima, the bomb produced a blast of more than 3.3 tons (3 tonnes) per square yard.

Half the energy produced by the bombs was blast; the shock wave traveled almost 7 miles (11 km) in 30 seconds. The shock wave was followed by a hurricane-force wind. However, as the shock wave traveled outward, the pressure behind it fell and air flowed inward. In effect, a shock wave traveling faster than the speed of sound was followed by a hurricane and then, after an instant of silence, another violent wind blew in the opposite direction.

About one-third of the energy of the bombs was given off as heat. The fireballs produced by the nuclear explosions rapidly reached temperatures of several million degrees centigrade—similar to temperatures in the Sun. The heat was enough to burn exposed skin at distances of up to 2.4 miles (4 km) from the blast site. People in the open within about three-quarters of a mile (1.2 km) of the blast were burned to death; many were simply vaporized.

About one-seventh of the bombs' energy was given off as ionizing radiation. About one-third of this radiation was emitted in the first minute after the explosion. The residual radiation was emitted as radioactive fallout. If they were not killed instantly, half the people within two-thirds of a mile (1 km) of the bomb would have received fatal radiation doses.

CORE FACTS

- In a nuclear explosion very high temperatures—as hot as the Sun—build up in less than a millionth of a second. At the same time, pressures that are millions of times normal atmospheric pressure develop.

- The total number of nuclear warheads in the world's nuclear arsenals was about 36,000 in 1998. By the year 2008, the total may be about 22,500.

- As of 1999, there had been some 2060 nuclear explosions, of which 1030 were detonated by the United States. After 1963, atmospheric tests were banned and tests were conducted underground.

- The atomic bombs that were dropped on Hiroshima and Nagasaki in Japan toward the end of World War II killed an estimated total of 214,000 people, which represents a death rate of about one in three of those in the bombed areas.

CONNECTIONS

● Controlled fission chain reactions are used to generate energy in **NUCLEAR POWER** plants.

● Since the first nuclear weapons were developed, effective **RADIATION DETECTION** has become important not only on the battlefield, but also in power plants and hospitals.

The nuclear weapon used on Hiroshima, Japan, devastated the city center and killed hundreds of thousands of people.

plutonium-239 (Pu^{239}) captures a neutron, it undergoes fission (see NUCLEAR ENERGY). When fission occurs, the fissioned nucleus splits into two nuclei. These are called fission products, which are radioactive and contribute to the fallout from nuclear explosions. During the fission process, two or three neutrons are also emitted. If at least one of these neutrons causes another nucleus to undergo fission, a fission chain reaction is initiated. In a nuclear explosion, the chain reaction must be long and fast enough to produce an explosion. The minimum amount of a fissile material that can sustain a nuclear fission chain reaction is called the critical mass.

If a mass of Pu^{239} or U^{235} is increased above the critical level, the number of neutrons produced by fission builds up and considerably more fissions occur in each successive generation of fission. When the rate of production of fissile neutrons exceeds all neutron losses, a supercritical mass is created, and a rapid and uncontrollable increase in the number of neutrons within the mass of fissile material occurs. A nuclear explosion then takes place.

Making nuclear weapons work

Nuclear weapon designers use two techniques to produce a supercritical mass of highly enriched uranium or plutonium. One is the gun method; the other is implosion.

The gun method. The gun method was used to detonate the uranium bomb that was dropped on Hiroshima. In this design, a mass of uranium less than the critical mass is fired using high explosive into a hole in another larger yet still subcritical mass of uranium. The united mass of uranium exceeds the critical mass. When a neutron-reflecting material, such as a layer of beryllium, is used to surround the larger mass of uranium, all neutrons produced by fission are reflected back into the mass to sustain the chain reaction. Therefore, the critical mass can be as low as about 35 lb (16 kg).

The implosion method. The implosion method assembles a critical mass of fissile material more rapidly than the gun method. It is used for plutonium weapons, for which the gun method is too slow to create an explosion. In such a weapon, a sphere of fissile material (plutonium or highly-enriched uranium) is surrounded by conventional high explosives. When exploded, the high explosive uniformly and rapidly compresses the sphere of fissile material and increases its density. Since the critical mass is inversely proportional to the square of the density, the compressed fissile material then becomes supercritical and an explosion results.

To guarantee an effective detonation, very high quality conventional high explosives and reliable detonators must be used (see DETONATOR AND FUSE; EXPLOSIVE). Electronic circuits fire the detonators in a precise time sequence to cause the fissile material to implode evenly.

The fissile material in the spherical core of the weapon is surrounded by a shell of a neutron-reflecting material, such as beryllium, that directs some of

Those far enough away from the blast to survive the high temperatures still received doses of radiation that rapidly incapacitated them; many suffered from nausea, vomiting blood, and a high fever: all symptoms of radiation sickness. The majority died within ten days. Many of those who were still alive at the end of 1945 seemed at first to be healthy. However, a variety of serious illnesses—eye diseases, blood disorders, and cancers—soon started to appear. Leukemia among survivors increased rapidly for about 10 years after 1945. The incidence of other cancers is also significantly higher among survivors.

Nuclear explosions

Atomic bombs exploit the fission (splitting) of nuclei of uranium or plutonium atoms. When a nucleus of a heavy element such as uranium-235 (U^{235}) or

NUCLEAR TEST LOCATIONS

Country	Site
United States	Nevada test site
	Johnston Atoll, Enewetak, Bikini, and Christmas Islands (Pacific Ocean)
Former Soviet Union	Kazakhstan; Novaya Zemlya
Britain	Montebello Islands, Emu, and Maralinga (Australia); Christmas Islands (Indian Ocean)
France	Algeria; Moruroa and Fangataufa (French Polynesia)
China	Lop Nur
India	Rajasthan desert, near the Pakistan border
Pakistan	Baluchistan, near the Afghanistan border

Atmospheric nuclear tests have polluted Earth with radioactive isotopes. Even though most of these sites are now out of use, radioactivity that has spread around the globe will persist for thousands of years. Near the test sites, intense radioactive fallout has seriously harmed the environment and the health of local populations. In one such test, conducted by the United States on March 1, 1954, radioactive fallout from the cloud was carried eastward and contaminated a Japanese fishing boat, the *Lucky Dragon*, irradiating its crew. One of the fishermen died. The explosion also contaminated the atolls of Rongelap and Rongerik so extensively that their residents had to be evacuated.

the escaping fission neutrons back into the core. The use of a neutron reflector significantly reduces the amount of fissile material needed. In the case of plutonium, this ranges from the size of a grapefruit to the size of an orange.

The fissile material in the core of the weapon expands at very high speeds when the weapon explodes, initially at 620 miles (1000 km) per second. In less than a millionth of a second, the size and density of the fissile material change so that it becomes less than critical and the fission chain reaction stops. The task of the designer is to keep the fissioning material together against its tendency to fly apart, and long enough to produce a nuclear explosion with a high enough explosive yield. This is the function of the tamper—a shell of a heavy material, such as natural or depleted uranium, that surrounds the core and the neutron-reflecting shell. When the high explosives around the tamper are detonated, the shock wave causes the tamper to collapse. The tamper helps keep the fissile core together at the start of the explosion. This maintains a critical mass for longer and produces a more powerful explosion.

For maximum efficiency, the fission chain reaction in a nuclear weapon must be initiated at precisely the moment of maximum supercriticality; that is, the moment of maximum compression. The initiation is achieved by a burst of neutrons. In a modern weapon, the neutrons are produced by a small electronic device called a neutron gun, which is placed outside the conventional high explosives.

In a neutron gun, a high voltage is used to accelerate small amounts of deuterium down a cylindrical tube. A zirconium-tritide (a mixture of zirconium and tritium) target is placed at the bottom of the tube. When deuterium nuclei collide with tritium nuclei in the target, they fuse together and produce high-energy fusion neutrons. A shower of neutrons penetrates into the compressed plutonium core and initiates the fission chain reaction.

A typical modern nuclear fission weapon would use about 7.7 lb (3.5 kg) of plutonium surrounded by an efficient neutron reflector and tamper and about 220 lb (100 kg) of high explosive. The entire volume of the device would be about that of a soccer ball and its total weight about 440 lb (200 kg). It would have an explosive yield of about 25 kilotons.

Thermonuclear weapons

If nuclear explosions with yields greater than a few hundred kilotons are required, extra energy must come from nuclear fusion—light nuclei being fused into heavier ones. In a thermonuclear weapon, or hydrogen bomb (H-bomb), a significant fraction of the explosive yield comes from nuclear fusion.

Thermonuclear weapons use a fission explosion to provide the high temperature needed to initiate nuclear fusion. Typically, tritium and deuterium are fused together to form helium. The former Soviet Union exploded a thermonuclear weapon in 1961 with an explosive yield of 58 megatons—equivalent to about 4600 Hiroshima bombs.

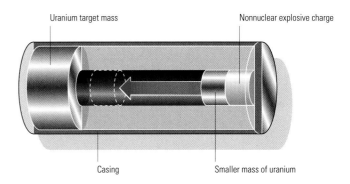

GUN-TYPE FISSION WEAPON

Uranium target mass — Nonnuclear explosive charge — Casing — Smaller mass of uranium

The gun-type weapon creates a critical mass of fissile material by firing a small mass inside a larger one. Only uranium weapons can be detonated in this way.

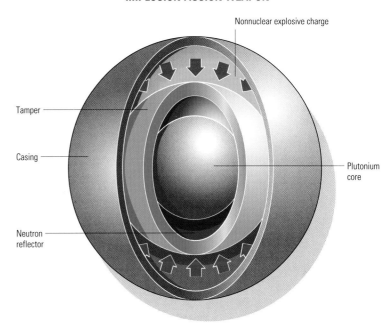

IMPLOSION FISSION WEAPON

Nonnuclear explosive charge — Tamper — Casing — Neutron reflector — Plutonium core

Implosion weapons use explosives to compress the core until it reaches supercritical mass. A layer of a neutron reflector reduces the amount of the fissile material needed.

NUCLEAR TESTING

Between 1945 and 1999 there were 2056 confirmed nuclear explosions. Of these, 1030 were detonated by the United States; 715 by the then Soviet Union; 210 by France; 45 by Britain; 45 by China; 5 by India; and 6 by Pakistan. South Africa, possibly in collaboration with Israel, may have tested a nuclear device over the Indian Ocean in September 1979, but the evidence is inconclusive.

The total explosive power of the nuclear test explosions is estimated to be equivalent of that of about 510 megatons, equivalent to 40,000 Hiroshima bombs. Five hundred of these nuclear explosions, with a total explosive power equivalent to some 30,000 Hiroshima bombs, were detonated above ground. After the 1963 Limited Test Ban Treaty, tests were done underground. A worldwide nuclear test ban—the Nuclear Proliferation Prevention Act—was signed in 1994. It was violated by India's underground test near the Pakistani border on May 11, 1998.

WIDER IMPACT

CRITICAL MASS

The critical mass of a fissile material depends on the nuclear properties of the material used—whether it is plutonium or highly enriched uranium—and on the shape of the material. A sphere is the optimum shape because for a given mass the surface area is minimized, which minimizes the number of neutrons that migrate through the surface per unit time and are thereby lost to the fission process. Critical mass also depends on the density of the fissile material. The higher the density, the shorter the average distance traveled by a neutron before it causes another fission and, therefore, the smaller the critical mass.

Further factors in determining the critical mass are the purity of the fissile material and the physical surroundings of the material. If materials other than the one used for fission are present, some neutrons may be captured by their nuclei and removed from the chain reaction. If the fissile material is surrounded by a medium that efficiently reflects neutrons back into the fissile material, such as beryllium, some of the reflected neutrons may cause fission. These neutrons would otherwise have been lost. Consequently, the use of a neutron reflector reduces the amount of fissile material needed to achieve supercriticality.

A CLOSER LOOK

Types of nuclear weapons

Strategic nuclear weapons and delivery systems are designed to attack long-range strategic targets, such as cities and missile bases. They are high-yield weapons that are intended to provide active deterrence against nuclear attack, based on the idea that destruction will be as devastating for the attacker as for the country being attacked.

Tactical nuclear weapons are shorter-range weapons designed for use by land, sea, or air forces against equivalent enemy forces. They are intended to support military operations and deliver much lower explosive yields than strategic weapons.

BOOSTED NUCLEAR-FISSION WEAPONS

The maximum explosive power of a militarily usable nuclear fission weapon is about 50 kilotons. The explosive yield of a fission weapon can be enhanced by nuclear fusion, as is the case in a hydrogen bomb, but the increased explosive yield of a boosted weapon comes from improved nuclear fission. Nuclear fusion is used to produce more neutrons for the fission reaction. The fusion process itself contributes little to the explosive yield.

In a boosted weapon, a mixture of tritium and deuterium gases are injected into the center of the plutonium sphere in a nuclear fission weapon. When the fission weapon explodes, the temperature and pressure at the center are high enough for nuclear fusion to take place. The neutrons released during the fusion process produce additional fissions in the plutonium before the weapon disintegrates, increasing its efficiency.

In an unboosted fission weapon, the rate of production of fissions is about 100 per microsecond; in a boosted one, it is about 1000 per microsecond. Boosted weapons are, therefore, about ten times more efficient than unboosted ones. Militarily usable boosted weapons have explosive yields of up to roughly 500 kilotons. In a boosted weapon, about 5 g of pressurized tritium-deuterium mixture is injected from a reservoir placed outside the main core of the weapon into the center just after the fission process has begun.

A CLOSER LOOK

The global nuclear arsenals

Nuclear explosions have been detonated to test new nuclear weapon designs; to establish the continuing reliability of existing nuclear warheads; and to test new measures developed to improve the safety of existing nuclear weapon types. The United States began testing nuclear weapons in 1945; the former Soviet Union in 1949; Britain followed in 1952; France in 1960; China in 1964; India in 1974. Pakistan detonated its first bomb in 1998, soon after India had performed an underground test near their joint border (see the box on page 924).

The number of nuclear weapons in the world's arsenals is vast, despite recent arms reduction treaties. As of the end of 1998, the United States had an operational nuclear stockpile of 8750 warheads, 7250 of which were strategic (long-range), and about 1500 of which were tactical (short- or medium-range). If the nuclear weapons in reserve and those waiting for dismantlement are added, the total comes to about 12,500. The Russian nuclear arsenal contains 7250 strategic nuclear warheads, about 4500 tactical weapons, and about 10,000 with uncertain status (a total of about 22,000 nuclear weapons). The nuclear arsenals of the other five nuclear powers are small in comparison. Estimated numbers are: Britain 400; China, 400; France, 500; India, 100; Israel, 200; Pakistan, 10. The total of nuclear warheads in the world's nuclear arsenals is, therefore, approximately 36,000.

Assuming that the Strategic Arms Reduction Talks (START) I (1991) and II (1992) are implemented, the American nuclear arsenal by the end of the year 2007 will contain about 10,000 nuclear warheads, of which 3500 will be strategic, 1000 will be tactical, and 5500 will be in reserve. By the end of 2007, the Russian arsenal should contain about 11,000 nuclear warheads: 3500 of them strategic, 2500 tactical, and about 5000 in reserve. This means that 13,500 nuclear weapons will have been removed from the operational arsenals. Many will be dismantled, which is a relatively straightforward task. The fissile cores and fusion stages can be easily removed. The plutonium and highly enriched uranium can be stored until permanently disposed of or used as fuel in civil nuclear-power reactors.

F. BARNABY

See also: MILITARY AIRCRAFT; MISSILE; NUCLEAR FUSION; STRATEGIC DEFENSE SYSTEMS; SUBMARINE; WEAPONRY: SPECIALIZED SYSTEMS.

Further reading:

Barnaby, C. *How Nuclear Weapons Spread: Nuclear-Weapon Proliferation in the 1990s.* New York: Routledge, 1993.
Bethe, H. *The Road from Los Alamos.* New York: American Institute of Physics, 1991.
Rhodes, R. *The Making of the Atomic Bomb.* London: Simon & Schuster, 1986.
Shroyer, J. *Secret Mesa: Inside Los Alamos National Laboratory.* New York, John Wiley & Sons, 1998.

OBSTETRICS AND GYNECOLOGY

Obstetrics and gynecology are medical disciplines dedicated to women's reproductive and general health

Throughout most of history, a woman in labor would summon a midwife—a woman living in the community who had a practical knowledge of childbirth gained through apprenticeship. During the 19th century, women (urban and wealthy women in particular) began turning to physicians to deliver their babies, regarding the physicians as more "modern" and "civilized." However, the physician often came straight from the bedside of a patient with an infectious disease, and he had neither antiseptics to prevent infections nor antibiotics to control them. As a result many women died of puerperal fever—a type of blood poisoning that was popularly known as "childbed fever".

In more recent times, midwifery has experienced a resurgence; many women appreciate the personal attention midwives can provide. Often they are certified as nurses and work in cooperation with a medical practice, attending births either at home or in hospital delivery rooms. Obstetricians (physicians who specialize in the care of women during pregnancy and childbirth) and gynecologists (whose practice also deals with diseases and other health concerns of women) employ a variety of medical and surgical techniques to assist women in conceiving, carrying, and bearing a healthy child.

Surgical procedures

Infertility has increased in recent decades due to a variety of factors, such as more women postponing childbirth past the time of their peak fertility. However, there are many techniques available to pinpoint the problem and repair or bypass it (see ARTIFICIAL INSEMINATION AND FERTILITY TREATMENT). If surgery is required—to open blocked fallopian tubes between the ovaries and uterus, for example—it can generally be accomplished without making a large incision in the abdomen, through the use of endo-

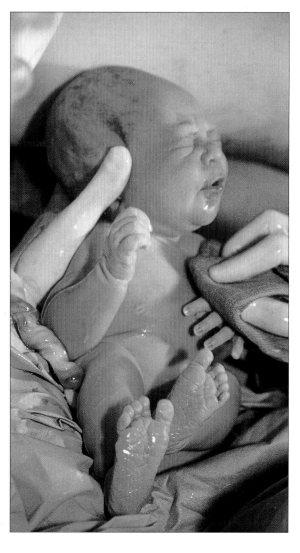

A newborn baby is cleaned by an obstetrician after birth. The obstetrician also monitors the progress of a developing fetus throughout its gestation.

scopic techniques. An endoscope is a fiber-optic tube that is inserted into the body through a natural orifice or a small incision (see ENDOSCOPE). The tube may be equipped with a tiny blade that the surgeon can control while watching his or her progress on a screen.

Laparoscopy is a procedure in which an endoscope is inserted into a small incision near the navel. Carbon dioxide or nitrous oxide gas is pumped into the abdomen to lift the intestines away from the pelvic organs. This enables the surgeon to view the uterus, ovaries, and fallopian tubes. In addition to surgery to correct infertility, laparoscopy is used for other gynecological procedures such as surgical sterilization or the treatment of endometriosis, a condition in which tissue similar to the uterine lining grows in other parts of the pelvis.

Pregnancy tests

Techniques of pregnancy testing have been improved so that a positive result may be diagnosed around the first day of a missed period. Early pregnancy testing is desirable because a woman may begin prenatal care sooner: seeing a physician, modifying her diet if nec-

---

CORE FACTS

- An obstetrician is a physician who specializes in the care of women during pregnancy and childbirth.
- A gynecologist is a physician who deals with the health and physical care of the female reproductive system.
- A midwife, who is usually a woman and often a certified nurse, assists women in childbirth.
- Pregnancy tests work by detecting a hormone called human chorionic gonadotropin (hCG) in the mother's urine or blood.
- Fetuses can be tested during pregnancy for genetic defects and other serious medical problems.
- Some fetal conditions can be corrected with fiber optics and tiny surgical instruments inserted into the uterus.
- Almost one-quarter of the babies in the United States are born by cesarean section.

CONNECTIONS

● Hospitals were particularly dangerous places for women in childbirth until **ANTISEPTICS AND STERILIZATION** were established in the 19th century.

● In the future, **GENETIC ENGINEERING** techniques could be used to eliminate many diseases and defects of the unborn child.

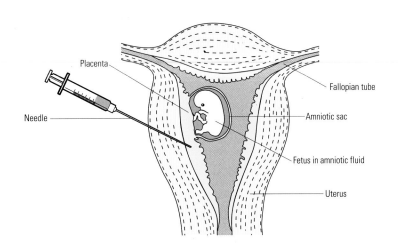

INVASIVE FETAL TESTING

Uterus

Placenta

Umbilical cord

Needle

Fetus

Amniotic fluid

Cervix

Vagina

Amniocentesis involves removing a small amount of the amniotic fluid, which surrounds the fetus, through a needle or catheter inserted through the mother's abdominal skin. This test is used to check for genetic and neural abnormalities.

Placenta

Fallopian tube

Needle

Amniotic sac

Fetus in amniotic fluid

Uterus

Chorionic villus sampling (CVS) involves collecting a few cells from a developing placenta. These cells show up genetic abnormalities in the fetus.

essary, taking vitamins, and avoiding smoking, alcohol, and certain other drugs. If the woman is considering terminating the pregnancy, early abortion options are less risky, less expensive, and, for many people, present fewer ethical problems than an abortion at a later stage. Pregnancy tests may be done in a doctor's office or clinic, and many home pregnancy tests are also available.

Pregnancy tests detect the presence of a hormone called human chorionic gonadotropin (hCG), which is produced in elevated quantities during pregnancy. The hormone is excreted in a woman's urine and is also found in her blood. Either fluid (urine is generally used for easy noninvasive testing) is exposed to a test solution containing antibodies to the hormone. A positive result is indicated by a change in color of a ring at the bottom of the test tube or a similar color change on another testing device.

Fetal testing

Once the pregnancy is confirmed, tests may be done at various stages to detect fetal abnormalities. The alpha-fetoprotein (AFP) test, done between the 16th and 18th weeks of pregnancy, detects a hormone produced in the liver of the fetus. Elevated levels indicate a potential problem with the neural tube, the structure from which the brain and spine are formed. If the neural tube fails to close properly, the spinal cord may be exposed (a condition called spina bifida), with effects that may include paralysis, retardation, or death. The brain may also fail to develop altogether—a condition called anencephaly. Decreased AFP levels may indicate chromosomal abnormalities such as Down's syndrome, characterized by mental retardation, heart trouble, and physical features such as slanted eyes and a broad, flat nose. Since these defects are so serious, and the AFP test requires only a blood sample from the mother, it is offered as a routine screening procedure. Sometimes it is done in combination with the measurement of two other hormones in a triple marker test in order to improve reliability.

Ultrasound imaging is also used routinely during pregnancy to monitor the health and development of the fetus. The abdomen is coated with oil or jelly to improve the transmission of high-frequency sound waves, which are generated by a handheld transducer passed over the body. These waves bounce harmlessly off the fetus, forming a pattern rendered as an image, or sonogram, on a video screen (see MEDICAL IMAGING). Ultrasound imaging can indicate the size of the fetus, reveal some anatomical features, and detect multiple pregnancies. It is sometimes used to determine the sex of the fetus.

Ultrasound is also useful in providing guidance during amniocentesis and chorionic villus sampling (CVS). These invasive tests are generally done only if there is some reason to suspect a problem with the fetus. In amniocentesis, a small sample of the amniotic fluid is withdrawn through a needle inserted through the abdominal wall. The fluid contains fetal cells, which are analyzed for chromosomal abnormalities. Such defects are more common if the mother is older than 35, and some physicians use the test routinely in these women. Younger women may undergo amniocentesis as a follow-up to an elevated AFP result. Although it may be done as early as the 10th week of pregnancy, this procedure is generally performed between the 16th and 20th weeks. It is sometimes used later to determine the lung maturity of fetuses that are likely to be born prematurely.

CVS may be performed as early as nine weeks into the pregnancy. A catheter is inserted either via the cervix or directly through the abdomen and used to extract cells from the outermost membrane of the fertilized egg, which will develop into the placenta. These cells, which have the same genetic makeup as the fetus, are tested. CVS can detect chromosomal problems—such as Down's syndrome, which is caused by an extra copy of chromosome 21—but not neural defects such as spina bifida.

Fetal surgery

Until recently, when ultrasound or other tests indicated problems, in most cases the only options were to terminate the pregnancy or do nothing. But now surgeons can help some tiny patients while they are still in the womb. The first fetal operation was performed in the late 1980s to correct a malformation of the urinary tract. It was done as open surgery, with the fetus partially removed from the uterus through an incision in the mother's abdomen. Some procedures are still performed in this way, but most innovative work is concentrated on surgery that can be done endoscopically, with the fetus in place in the uterus. The fetus, weighing only ounces, is operated on using tiny instruments and lasers, viewed through fiber optics the diameter of a pencil lead.

Because a fetus's organs are still forming, it is a great advantage to be able to fix problems as soon as possible. This prevents other structures from growing incorrectly. For example, if a fetus has a particular type of hernia (rupture), the intestines may migrate into the chest cavity, leaving the lungs no room to develop properly. Early intervention can make the difference between a healthy baby and a stillborn one.

Childbirth

Women have more options in childbirth now than ever before. Some move from a hospital labor room to a delivery room when the baby is about to be born; others use a more homelike birthing room throughout the entire process. A home birth attended by a midwife is also a possibility. A woman may be accompanied into the delivery room by her husband, mother, sister, or friend.

General anesthesia is no longer used during childbirth, but epidural analgesia (pain-relieving medication dripped through a catheter into the area around the spinal cord) is often used to numb the lower body (see ANESTHETICS). Other pain control techniques include breathing and relaxation exercises such as the Lamaze method. Many hospitals offer prenatal training classes in preparation for childbirth.

Labor may be induced or speeded up by administering oxytocin, a hormone that stimulates uterine contractions. The labor process puts stress on the baby, so it is important to monitor its heart rate. This may be done with external sensors on the mother's abdomen. Small probes are sometimes placed on the baby's scalp for a more reliable reading.

Metal forceps may be used if the baby's passage through the birth canal proves to be unusually difficult. These are placed on the head of the baby to protect it from the pressure of the canal and to accelerate delivery, particularly if the mother is too exhausted to push. A more recent innovation that serves the same purpose is the vacuum extractor, a pump attached via a hose to a suction cup that fits on the baby's head.

If extended labor is putting too much stress on the mother or child, or the baby is positioned in such a way that it cannot proceed down the birth canal, a

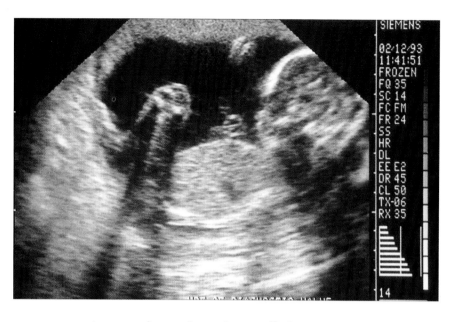

cesarean section may be performed (so called because Roman leader Julius Caesar is thought to have been born in this way). This operation involves the removal of the baby from the uterus through an abdominal incision. Cesarean section has saved the lives of countless mothers and babies who would previously have died in childbirth. At present, almost one-quarter of births in the United States are by cesarean section.

S. CALVO

An ultrasound scan of a fetus 20 weeks after conception. Ultrasound does not harm the fetus or the mother and so is widely used to monitor a fetus's progress. Imaging unborn babies with X rays was once common. However, it is now known that this has caused childhood cancers.

See also: MEDICAL MONITORING EQUIPMENT; MEDICAL TECHNOLOGY; SURGERY.

Further reading:

Benson, R., Pernoll, M. *Benson and Pernoll's Handbook of Obstetrics and Gynecology.* New York: McGraw-Hill, 1994.

DESIGNER BABIES

Reproductive technologies now allow conception to occur outside the body, embryos to be frozen for later implantation, and parents to make decisions about whether to continue a pregnancy based on the genetic traits of the fetus. A child may be the product of an egg and sperm from anonymous donors, carried in the womb of a surrogate mother, and raised by another couple altogether. Clearly, the potential for ethical dilemmas, not to mention litigation, is enormous in some cases, since the definition of *parent* is no longer straightforward.

The option of terminating a pregnancy if the fetus tests positive for a serious defect has been important to many couples. But with genetic testing available for increasing numbers of traits, some fear that parents will accept nothing less than a "perfect" baby who meets all their specifications.

Genetic engineering techniques (see GENETIC ENGINEERING) are likely to make this less of a hit-or-miss procedure. The thought of eliminating dreaded congenital defects is certainly appealing, and many ethical issues remain to be debated and solved. These include the possibility of intentionally breeding children that could be super intelligent, extra strong, resistant to disease, or conforming to the prevailing standards of beauty. However, there are already safeguards and rules being put in place by many countries' medical ethics bodies.

WIDER IMPACT

OFF-ROAD AND AMPHIBIOUS VEHICLES

Off-road and amphibious vehicles are designed for terrain that cannot be reached by ordinary vehicles

This DUKW amphibious vehicle was once a World War II military vehicle. It is now being used to ferry tourists over the beaches and waters of Table Rock Lake in Branson, Missouri—an indication of how versatile these vehicles can be.

There are many places where people, equipment, and supplies must be transported, including places with no paved roads. Standard cars and trucks do not operate well over snow, in mud, or over the branches and rocks that cover the ground in wilderness areas. Their wheels sink down and get stuck or their undercarriages get hung up on obstructions. Moving parts that are insufficiently protected may become too wet or dirty to function. Many types of vehicles have been designed to overcome these problems, facilitating work and recreation in forests, fields, swamps, deserts, and arctic areas.

Spreading the load

Vehicles that are used on soft surfaces such as mud, sand, or snow need a way of spreading out their weight so that they do not sink down and get stuck. This means that the area that contacts the surface must be much larger than that of a standard tire. The simplest way of accomplishing this is simply to widen the tires, and so large tires are used on many off-road vehicles. Increasing the number of tires serves the same purpose; six or eight wheels are often used.

For heavy equipment or very soft terrain even the widest tires cannot distribute the vehicle's weight enough to allow easy movement. In snow, which is smooth and generates little friction, vehicles often have skis or sled surfaces. But for dragging heavy weights through mud, tracks are unbeatable.

Tracks are similar to conveyor belts that have many traction devices placed on them, such as rubber ridges and metal studs driven by a sprocket. A three-ton truck with a 90-in (2.3-m) wheelbase and a 20-in (51-cm) track width exerts a ground pressure of only 1.5 pounds per square inch (4.4 kilograms per square meter), only about a quarter of that exerted by a standing adult.

Fully tracked vehicles give the best performance in deep mud and snow, but they are not the only options for a multipurpose vehicle. Half-tracks have wheels at the front and tracks at the back, which reduces costs by allowing the use of more standard drive-train components. They also simplify driver training, because they can be steered like ordinary trucks. A few companies sell removable track units for four-wheel-drive vehicles; they can be carried in the vehicle and bolted on when needed. The units weigh about 150 pounds (68 kg) and can be attached by one person in about an hour with the assistance of a heavy-duty jack (see TRACKED VEHICLE).

CONNECTIONS

● Off-road and amphibious vehicles are used in many different environments, from the **MILITARY VEHICLES** used on the battlefield, such as the **TANK** and **TRACKED VEHICLE**, to the **UNPILOTED VEHICLES AND AIRCRAFT** used in **SPACE TRAVEL AND TECHNOLOGY**.

CORE FACTS

- Off-road and amphibious vehicles are used for exploration, logging, search and rescue, construction, agriculture, recreation, and in the military.
- Large tires, tracks, or skis are used to spread out the weight of the vehicle over a larger area. This allows the vehicle to traverse soft ground or snow.
- High ground clearance is important in avoiding many obstacles in a vehicle's path.
- Off-road and amphibious vehicles are used in rugged environments where it is important to protect the engine from dirt and water and to limit the damage caused by corrosion.

Military operations

Tanks (tracked armored vehicles) were developed during World War I (1914–1918) and became an essential part of ground forces during World War II (1939–1945). Tanks and armored personnel carriers are now used by armed forces all over the world. Tracks are indispensable for moving such heavy vehicles over sand or muddy fields (see TANK).

Another military vehicle built for off-road travel is the U.S. Army jeep. Several automobile manufacturers have been commissioned to build the light four-wheel-drive vehicle, which got its name from the initials *G.P.* for "general purpose" (see MILITARY VEHICLES). About 700,000 jeeps were built during World War II, and several variants were tried, including an amphibious model, which unfortunately tended to sink in rough water. In 1950, however, two people did manage to go around the world in a highly modified amphibious jeep. Today, civilian Jeeps are manufactured by DaimlerChrysler AG and are widely marketed for recreational and other nonmilitary transportation needs.

It is often a great advantage to be able to accomplish military objectives from a distance, in order to minimize risks to personnel. For this reason, unmanned or remotely piloted vehicles have been developed for use in adverse conditions such as minefields. These include video and possibly audio links back to the operator, and they can be directed with joysticks or other controls. Unpiloted rovers (vehicles that explore uninhabitable surfaces) are used in the exploration of volcanoes and other planets (see UNPILOTED VEHICLES AND AIRCRAFT).

On land and sea

Vehicles that travel on land and sea are called amphibious vehicles. They fall into two main categories. The first is a hybrid between a boat and a car or truck. In some cases, such as the amphibious jeep, an existing vehicle was modified with a wraparound hull and an add-on propeller. Others were designed from the ground up, including the Amphiranger—an amphibious four-wheel-drive light truck built in small numbers by German company Rheinhauer Maschinen und Armaturenbau GmbH. The only amphibious car put into production was the German Amphicar (see the box on page 932). More than 3000 of these were manufactured in the 1960s. However, amphibious cars can still be built from kits, such as the British Dutton Mariner, which is made by adding a glass-reinforced plastic hull to a Ford Fiesta.

The second major category of amphibious vehicles is the hovercraft, which was developed in the 1950s (see HOVERCRAFT). Also called air-cushion vehicles or ground-effect machines, hovercraft use large fans that create air pressure for lift and are then propelled forward on a cushion of air. They are generally used for marine transport, because they provide passengers with a speedy trip and a smooth ride. Although they can operate on land, they require smooth and flat terrain, which limits their usefulness for general land travel. However, they are very

This U.S. Army Humvee four-wheel-drive vehicle is being used in assault training by soldiers at an army base in Fort Jackson, South Carolina.

useful as amphibious transportation, as well as for security and rescue operations around beaches and marshes where traditional boats would run aground. They are also well adapted to thin ice rescue and can travel river routes that vary in depth or even run dry.

Tractors and utility vehicles

Farms use many different types of equipment in the fields. The tractor, for example, is an all-purpose farm vehicle used to move about the fields and pull various types of farming implements and attachments (see TRACTOR). In the 1930s, a three-point hitch with hydraulic lift was developed, which made it much easier to switch the heavy implements (see HYDRAULICS AND PNEUMATICS).

Off-road vehicles—both wheeled and tracked—are used as work vehicles in many civilian operations besides agriculture. Construction, logging, hauling cargo, extending utility service to new areas, conservation, law enforcement, and rescue work all require vehicles that can travel where roads do not go (see CONSTRUCTION AND EARTHMOVING MACHINERY).

Bikes and buggies

Many people enjoy off-road recreational activities—so much so that the term *all-terrain vehicle* (*ATV*) has come to be generally understood as referring to a particular type of off-road recreational vehicle. ATVs have seats and handlebars resembling those on motorcycles, but they can traverse wilderness on their four wide wheels with high enough ground clearance to ride over many obstacles. With their wide tires, they are capable of traveling through mud and shallow pools of water.

Dune buggies are recreational vehicles that can accommodate a passenger as well as a driver. Often they are kit-built vehicles or production cars, such as the Volkswagen Beetle, that have been modified for traveling on sand and other off-road terrain, and sometimes even through shallow water. Tracked ATVs are also available that can handle heavier snow and mud. Dirt bikes are motorcycles designed for

A rider jumps his ATV at Pismo Beach in California. Riding ATVs has become a big recreational sport on many beaches in the United States.

off-road use: they have heavily treaded tires and a strengthened suspension. Racing is a popular recreational activity with these vehicles.

Off-road recreational vehicle enthusiasts often come into conflict with environmentalists, property owners, and others over the use of land for these activities. Recreational vehicles tend to be noisy and introduce their engine emissions and often leaked gas or oil into areas far removed from roads (see POLLUTION AND ITS CONTROL). Dune buggies and ATVs can damage delicate dune ecosystems, causing beach erosion. Recreational vehicle users defend themselves by saying that they have the right to use public lands and that they have no interest in damaging the wilderness areas they enjoy. Some participate in programs that encourage a responsible attitude toward the environment. Individuals, organizations, legislative bodies, and regulatory agencies will continue to be involved in striking a balance between conservation and recreational land use.

Over ice and snow

Snowmobiles are used both for recreation and for general transportation in snow-covered regions where dogsleds were once the only means of getting around. Early snowmobiles included the "motor toboggans" developed by U.S. inventor Carl Eliason in Wisconsin in 1927. They had a wooden sliding surface like a sled and a track consisting of cleated chain links. Today's snowmobiles have rear tracks but skis in front for steering; they range from small low-powered models for children to powerful versions for racing or carrying passengers.

For construction, hauling, or other applications in arctic areas, low-ground-pressure utility trucks are used, which are often also designed for some amphibious use. They can be fitted with a variety of attachments, such as cranes, backhoes, drill rigs, and winches (see SNOW AND ICE TRAVEL).

S. CALVO

See also: MOTORCYCLE; STEERING SYSTEMS.

Further reading:
DeLong, B. *Four-Wheel Freedom: The Art of Off-Road Driving.* Boulder, Colorado: Paladin Press, 1996.
Green, M., and J. Petersen. *Amphibious Vehicles.* Minneapolis, Minnesota: Capstone Press, 1997.
Jackson, J. *The Off-Road Four-Wheel-Drive Book: Choosing, Using and Maintaining Go-Anywhere Vehicles.* Newbury Park, California: Haynes Publications, 1995.

THE AMPHICAR

From 1962 through 1967, the German Amphicar Corporation manufactured the only amphibious car ever put into production, despite the fact that neither rustproof automobile bodies nor a market for recreational vehicles yet existed.

The Amphicar was built using parts from many European car manufacturers, including Porsche, Mercedes, Triumph, and BMW. It was completely watertight, with a flat bottom and rubber seals around the doors. A specially designed transmission system drove both the rear wheels and the propellers. The front wheels were used for steering in the water as on land. The body was made of steel, however, which tended to rust.

Most of the Amphicars built were sold in the United States. They were too expensive at the time to become widely popular, and present-day legislation controlling the level of pollutants in vehicle exhaust gases probably preclude their revival. But approximately 500 are still in regular use, their lives extended with modern anticorrosive paints and waxes. Others may be seen in automobile museums, and some make occasional appearances in movies and music videos.

A CLOSER LOOK

OIL AND NATURAL GAS PRODUCTION

Oil and natural gas production extracts petroleum and gas from underground reserves

Much of Earth's oil and gas reserves are under the seabed. Therefore huge constructions, such as this collection of drilling rigs, are used to extract and distribute these products.

Petroleum takes its name from the Latin words *petra* (rock) and *oleum* (oil), reflecting its origin in rocks and its oil-like consistency. It is also called crude oil, or simply *oil*. In certain parts of the world—notably Egypt, Venezuela, and Pennsylvania—petroleum seeped to the surface through faults in surface rocks and was used by local populations for a variety of applications, including as an adhesive, a sealant, and a medicine for camel mange. However, the use of petroleum was limited until the mid-19th century by the small volume of oil available and the absence of refining technology.

CORE FACTS

- The decomposition of dead organisms by bacteria creates a substance called kerogen. When squeezed and heated underground for several million years, kerogen gradually transforms into oil and natural gas.
- Oil and gas deposits can be located by looking for characteristic geological formations and by looking for changes in Earth's gravitational and magnetic fields.
- To extract oil, holes are drilled into Earth's crust to let the petroleum and gas escape. Sometimes various forms of pumping, using water, steam, detergents, and even fire, are used to extract the oil.

THE FORMATION OF PETROLEUM

Geologists, biologists, and chemists agree that most deposits of petroleum were formed from the remains of marine organisms—tiny plants and animals that lived in the oceans. Some deposits were formed from vegetation and animals that lived in rivers and inland lakes, but the formation processes are the same.

Marine organisms gradually sink to the ocean floor when they die. Their remains mix with the fine silt that is produced by erosion and are washed around by the underwater currents until piles of sediment start to form in areas where the currents are weak. This effect can be illustrated by stirring fine sand in a glass of water—when the stirring stops, the sand forms a heap in the middle of the glass where the water is moving more slowly. Underwater areas where deposition of fine solids occurs are known as sedimentation basins.

As time progresses, the layers of silt and organic matter (the remains of the organisms) become deeper. The lower layers are subjected to high pressures and temperatures as a result of the weight of the layers above. Bacteria that are trapped in the sedimentary mud start to digest the organic material, producing kerogen—a pitchlike substance. Kerogen is a complex hydrocarbon material (see CHEMICAL INDUSTRY, ORGANIC) that also contains small amounts

CONNECTIONS

- Crude oil is the single most important source of **GASOLINE**.

- Oil and natural gas are important starting materials for the **ORGANIC CHEMICAL INDUSTRY**.

- Oil and natural gas are vital **ENERGY RESOURCES**.

GEOLOGIC TRAPS

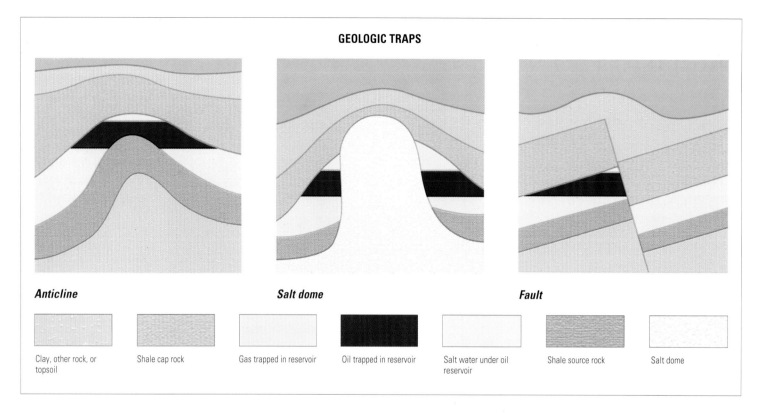

Anticline   *Salt dome*   *Fault*

Clay, other rock, or topsoil	Gas trapped in reservoir	Salt water under oil reservoir
Shale cap rock	Oil trapped in reservoir	Shale source rock
		Salt dome

of sulfur, nitrogen, and oxygen. The proportions of the elements in kerogen depend on the organisms from which it is formed and the conditions under which it is formed (see box on page 936).

In certain regions, the combined effect of further sedimentation and buckling in Earth's surface result in the oil-producing kerogen deposits being located thousands of feet below the seabed or the surface. As depth increases, the pressure and temperature become much higher than at the surface, and a chemical reaction similar to the cracking reaction used in oil refineries starts to occur (see OIL REFINING). Over millions of years, these reactions turn kerogen into liquid petroleum and natural gas (methane, ethane, propane, and butane). The exact compositions of the petroleum and the associated gases depend on the composition of the original kerogen and the conditions under which the petroleum formation occurs. At the same time as the petroleum forms, the inorganic material with which the kerogen is mixed—typically silt, sand, and bones—hardens into rock.

Characteristics of an oil field

An oil field is a geographical area where petroleum has accumulated in an underground reservoir. There are three prerequisites for an oil field to occur: a source rock in which the petroleum is formed, a reservoir rock in which the petroleum and natural gas accumulate, and a geologic trap that seals the petroleum and gas inside the reservoir rock.

The most common source rock is black shale. The reservoir rock is normally sandstone or limestone and must be permeated with cracks and pores to allow the oil and water to move around and accumulate. The reservoir rock can be thought of as a hard sponge that contains water (normally salt

water), petroleum, and often some natural gas. Petroleum and water are immiscible (they separate into two almost pure layers) and, since petroleum is typically less dense than water, the petroleum percolates upward in the reservoir rock while the water percolates down. Any natural gas that is present is much less dense than either oil or water and sits above both the other layers.

The geologic trap can form in a number of ways. Since the petroleum deposit sits on top of the salt water in the reservoir rock, the reservoir only needs to be sealed on the sides and from above. The rock layer that prevents the petroleum and gas from leaking out of the reservoir is known as the cap rock and is typically salt or a dense, impermeable shale. In one trap system—the anticline—the oil-bearing rock is buckled upward and the gas and petroleum collect in a dome under the cap rock (see the diagram above). In another type of rock formation, petroleum collects around the edge of a salt dome—a deposit of rock salt that has perforated the rock strata and created an elevated pocket of porous rock from the reservoir layer. Alternatively, a reservoir can form alongside a geologic fault where the sequence of rock layers has been interrupted and a capped ridge has formed.

EXPLORATION

Geologists have some knowledge of the parts of Earth's surface that were once underwater and therefore potential sedimentation basins—the presence of marine fossils is one sign. This knowledge helps in choosing areas for further exploration. The next step is to identify locations where there are suitable rock structures for petroleum traps to occur; if the target area is inland, rises and falls on the surface give a good indication of the underlying rock structures.

Locating potential oil fields

Aerial photographs and land surveys provide further information about the location of outcrops—protruding, hard rocks that indicate the abrupt ending of a hard-rock stratum (layer)—and therefore the location of a fault. After the preliminary survey, further information can be obtained for focused areas of particular interest by drilling into the ground and taking rock samples at various depths. By drilling several such holes in the study area, a three-dimensional map of the underground rock structure can gradually be pieced together to identify the locations of potential petroleum traps with more certainty.

Geophysical techniques

A number of techniques exist whereby the underground rock structure is investigated by measuring the physical properties of different types of rock. These techniques are particularly useful for offshore locations, where conventional surveying would be difficult and aerial photography pointless, but are also useful for inland exploration. By performing a careful geophysical analysis, the probability of finding oil when the first well is drilled is increased to around 30 percent. If oil has already been found nearby, the probability of drilling a successful well can be as high as 80 percent when geophysical techniques are used.

Seismic exploration. Sound is reflected by the boundaries between different types of rock, and this effect is exploited for seismological studies of underground rock structures. The source of the sound waves can be an explosive charge or a mobile sound generator, known as a vibroseis or thumper truck. The signals reflected by the rock boundaries are picked up by an array of geophones—microphone-like devices for measuring ground vibrations—and fed to a computer. The computer processes the results and gives an image of the underground boundaries that is similar to a sonar image.

Gravimetric exploration. Different types of rock have different densities. Those that are more dense produce a minutely stronger gravitational force than those that are less dense. Hence, high-precision measurements of the gravitational field at various points on the surface can be used to give a picture of the underlying rock structures.

Magnetometric exploration. Magnetometric studies are similar to gravimetric studies. As the name suggests, magnetometric exploration measures for the minute variations in the Earth's magnetic field that are caused by the different magnetic properties of different types of rock.

DRILLING

Conventional drilling rigs use a rotary system. A motor on the surface turns a shaft with a drill bit mounted at its lower end.

The drill string. The shaft that rotates inside the well and performs the cutting operation is known as the drill string. The drill bit is at the lower end of the drill string and is typically a tri-cone design: it has

three conical cutting heads protruding from the shaft. The drill bit is mounted securely on a hollow, cylindrical pipe that transmits the turning force from the rotary motor at the surface. The top of this pipe is clamped into a grief stern, or kelly—a shaft with a square cross section that fits the rotary system.

The rotary system. A diesel or electric motor is used to turn the rotary table, which is a circular mounting that sits on the drilling platform. At the center of the rotary table is a square cross-sectioned guide (the bushing) that fits snugly around the grief stern while allowing it free vertical motion. This arrangement lets the weight of the drill string drive the drill bit downward while efficiently transferring the turning force from the motor to the drill bit.

The hoisting system. The drilling operation has to be stopped periodically to add lengths of pipe into the drill string. The grief stern has to be detached and moved aside while a new pipe is moved into place and secured onto the top of the drill string. The

Drilling for oil is dangerous. Highly skilled workers must control the drilling, which continues day and night until the absence or presence of oil is confirmed.

A tanker ship pumps petroleum from an oil rig out at sea.

the base of the tower, where it winds a length of cable in and out. The cable passes over a pulley that is mounted on the crown block (the top of the derrick), down to the traveling block (a suspended pulley), and back up to an anchoring point on the crown block. When the cable is wound in, the traveling block rises; winding the cable out lowers the traveling block. The traveling block carries a swiveling hook that is used for lifting and to keep the top of the grief stern steady during drilling.

The circulatory system. The drill bit is lubricated and cooled with specially formulated drilling mud, which is a mixture of clay, water or diesel oil, and chemical additives. The mud is pumped through the central bore of the drill string and returns to the surface through the space between the drill string and the wall of the well. The drilling mud also serves to carry the well cuttings (drilling debris) to the surface and provides a seal to prevent the escape of gas and oil from the well. On occasion, the weight of the mud is not sufficient to hold down the trapped gas and there is a surge of pressure that could cause a blowout—a sudden escape of gas and mud that has the potential to endanger the drilling crew and damage equipment. When this happens, the pressure surge is detected by sensors and the well sealed by automatic blowout preventers until a heavier mud can be prepared and pumped into the well.

grief stern is then attached to the top of the new length of pipe and drilling recommences. All of these lifting operations are done with the hoisting system, which is basically a winch and pulley mounted in a steel tower called a derrick. The winch is secured at

Offshore drilling

The extraction of oil from submarine oil fields has the added complication that the drilling operation takes place in the middle of a sea or ocean. The basic drilling operation remains the same, but the drilling

INFLUENCING FACTORS IN THE FORMATION OF PETROLEUM

Each individual oil field produces a unique variety of petroleum, ranging from viscous, brown-black oils to runny, straw-colored oils. The densities and chemical compositions of different types of oils also vary widely according to their source (see OIL REFINING). Lighter oils are more valuable, since they contain a greater proportion of gasoline and chemically useful substances.

The processes leading to the formation of petroleum are common to all oil fields: sedimentation of organic matter, conversion to kerogen by bacterial action, and generation of petroleum from kerogen by the action of pressure and heat. However, the differences between the exact conditions of oil formation are sufficient to produce a wide variety of types of petroleum.

The principal factors that determine the constitution of the petroleum produced by an oil field are the organic origin of the petroleum, the subterranean conditions under which it was formed, and the age of the deposit.

Organic origin. The types of organisms that live in oceans, seas, and rivers differ from place to place, depending on the local climate and availability of nutrients. This regional variation also occurred millions of years ago when the organisms that formed today's petroleum were being deposited. Each type of organism had a

different chemical composition, so that the starting point for oil formation—rotting organic matter—was different in each case. In addition, the exact strains of bacteria that converted the dead organic matter to kerogen and the conditions of temperatures and air concentration under which these bacteria lived also had an influence on the characteristics of the petroleum that would eventually form.

Subterranean conditions. The temperature of the rocks under Earth's surface increases with depth. Oil shales near Earth's surface do not reach a sufficient temperature to be converted to petroleum, and the organic matter is present as kerogen. At a depth of around one mile (1.6 km), the rock temperature is around 120°F (49°C)—the lowest temperature for petroleum formation to occur. Petroleum formed at this depth tends to be a heavy, dark-colored, tarry liquid. Petroleum that forms at greater depths—and higher temperatures—is lighter, paler in color, and less viscous. Below around 4 miles (6.4 km), the temperature reaches 350°F (177°C)—the point at which natural gas forms rather than petroleum.

Age. The formation of petroleum proceeds very slowly and requires a minimum of around one million years. The majority of usable oil reserves were deposited 10–270 million years ago, and the oldest deposits were laid down more than 600 million years ago.

A CLOSER LOOK

rig must be kept in place over the well, and an outer casing is needed to carry the returning drilling mud to the platform from the top of the bore. Since there is always a risk that a new well will not succeed in finding oil, the expensive drilling equipment must be capable of being moved from site to site relatively easily until oil is found.

Jack-up rigs are frequently used for drilling in waters up to a depth of around 250 ft (75 m). A jack-up is a buoyant platform that typically has three legs that can be vertically raised and lowered. The platform is floated to the prospective drill site with its legs raised. Once in position, the legs are dropped until they hit the ocean floor. Then the platform is raised to a height that is clear of high tides and storm waves. Drilling can then be started.

Semisubmersibles are rigs that can be used in deeper water. Instead of reaching the ocean floor, the legs of a semisubmersible rest on buoyancy tanks that keep the rig afloat. The buoyancy tanks are attached by cable to anchors in the ocean floor, which hold the rig in a fixed position.

The third type of floating oil rig is the drill ship. As the name implies, a drill ship resembles a normal oceangoing vessel but has a drilling rig mounted amidships. Instead of relying on legs or anchors, drill ships use automated propulsion systems to compensate for currents and hold the ship in position.

Advances in drilling technology

The growth of the offshore oil production industry in the latter half of the 20th century benefited greatly from a technique known as deviation drilling, whereby several wells are drilled at angles that splay out from one platform, thereby increasing the productivity of that platform. In the late 1990s, platform productivity was increased even further by a technique known as horizontal drilling. Horizontal wells run through oil- or gas-bearing strata at a shallow angle, which increases the wall area of the well in the productive rock. As a consequence, a horizontal well can be as productive as up to eight vertical wells.

Another advance in drilling technology is the turbine drill bit, which uses the circulating drilling mud to drive the drill bit via a turbine at the bottom of the drill string. The advantage of this technique is that it eliminates the need for the whole drill string to rotate during drilling and thereby saves energy.

Finishing the well

Unless a well has proved to be dry (nonproductive)—in which case it is sealed and abandoned—the newly drilled well has to be prepared for production. Samples are taken at various depths in the bore (the drilled cavity) to locate the most productive zones. The well is then lined with a metal pipe known as a casing. The casing is necessary to prevent leakage into porous strata that might lie above the productive zone and to prevent the entry of water, which could damage the well. Cement is pumped around the casing to hold it in place, and the well is capped with an assembly of valves and connectors known as a

wellhead. An explosive charge is then lowered into the well and detonated at the depth of the productive zone. The explosion ruptures the lining of the well and allows the petroleum to flow into the bore.

PRODUCTION

Petroleum deposits exist under a pressure known as the reservoir drive. The proportion of the total reserve that flows from the well through the action of reservoir drive is known as the primary production.

Primary production

The petroleum in a reserve contains some dissolved natural gas, and there may also be a layer of free natural gas above the liquid petroleum. What happens when the well is opened depends on the type of petroleum deposit and the position at which the well casing is perforated. Opening a well can be likened to making a hole in a plastic soft-drink bottle that has been shaken. A hole made in the neck of the bottle

Taken in Beaumont, Texas, in 1936, this photograph shows a fountain of unrefined oil gushing from an an open wellhead without a derrick.

A jack pump in North Dakota. These pumps, which are sometimes called nodding donkeys, are used where the natural pressure in the oil well is too low to force oil out at a fast enough rate.

(above the surface of the liquid) will cause a froth to escape that consists mainly of gas. This is the point at which a gas-producing well would tap into the reserve—above the liquid-gas boundary. The flow of gas continues until the dissolved gas ceases to bubble out of the liquid. A hole made below the liquid-gas boundary causes liquid to spray out of the bottle, but, as the pressure is released, the dissolved gas bubbles out of the liquid. This is the situation in an oil-producing well, which must tap the reserve below the oil-gas boundary.

A petroleum reserve with no free gas typically yields 25 percent of its total oil content under the drive from the dissolved gas. Where there is a free-gas layer, a primary production of around 35 percent can be achieved. The pressure of the water under the petroleum reserve also contributes to the reservoir drive and can increase the primary production to around 60 percent in favorable cases. As the oil and gas are tapped off, the water level rises and maintains the pressure in the reservoir.

Other recovery systems

After the primary production, more petroleum can be recovered by lowering a pump to the bottom of the well. The pump is driven via connecting rods by an engine at the surface. Pumping relies on gravity to make the oil in the reservoir sink to the bottom. A variety of techniques exist by which the proportion of oil recovered from a reservoir can be increased.

Waterflood. As the volume of oil in a reservoir diminishes, the natural water level rises under the oil layer, and the wells that tap into the reserve at the lowest points stop producing first. The oil flow rate at the remaining productive wells can be improved by pumping water down the nonproductive wells to artificially increase the reservoir drive. This is called a waterflood. The oil-field brine, a water-based solution produced during the separation process, can also be put to use in the waterflood.

Gas injection. The gas injection procedure takes two forms: If there is no demand for the natural gas that separates from the liquid petroleum, it can be injected back into the reservoir to increase the reservoir pressure. Otherwise, an inert gas, such as nitrogen or carbon dioxide, can be injected.

Chemical flood. As the water level rises in the reservoir, some oil gets left behind in the flooded pores. This oil can be loosened chemically by injecting detergent-like materials below the oil-water boundary. The loosened oil then drifts up into the main oil layer.

Steam flood. Reserves of more viscous types of petroleum can be made more productive by injecting steam below the oil layer. The heat of the steam makes the petroleum flow more easily, and the additional pressure helps force the remaining oil toward productive wells.

Fire flood. Fire flooding has the effect of combining a gas injection and a steam flood. Some of the oil at the lower margin of the reserve is ignited and air is pumped in to feed the combustion. The heat of the fire and the steam it produces makes the oil above less viscous and more mobile, and the gases (mainly carbon dioxide) produced by the combustion increase the pressure in the reservoir.

Closing the well

Once a well has reached the end of its working life as a productive or injection well, the equipment at the top of the well has to be removed and the top of the well firmly sealed with a concrete plug. This is necessary in order to eliminate the risk of environmental damage due to oil seepage. Furthermore, the lease agreements that are necessary before a well can be drilled normally stipulate that the site be returned to an environmentally acceptable condition after production ceases.

SEPARATION

The petroleum that reaches the wellhead has to be treated before it can be dispatched for distribution. As the well oil reaches the surface, gases that were dissolved in the liquid petroleum at the high pressure found in the well start to separate. The first separation process simply collects the natural gas as it bubbles out of the liquid. This gas can be used as a fuel in its own right (see GAS INDUSTRY), pumped back into the reservoir, or simply burned off.

The liquid that remains after gas separation is known as wet oil and contains a proportion of brine in suspension. The brine and oil can be separated by heating the wet oil mixture. The effect of heat is to make the mixture less viscous, which allows the droplets of brine to sink out of the oil more rapidly. The brine separation takes place in a long, cylindrical tank. Heated wet oil enters through a pipe at one end of the tank and the brine and crude oil are tapped off separately at the other end. The oil-contaminated brine is disposed of by pumping into the ground.

The crude oil produced by the separation is then pumped to storage tanks to await collection by enormous ships called tankers, or it is pumped to a distribution depot by pipeline.

M. CLOWES

A gas fire at an oil wellhead in the Tumen region of Russia.

See also: OIL TANKER AND BULK CARRIER; PIPELINE.

Further reading:

MacKenzie, J. *Oil as a Finite Resource: When Is Global Production Likely to Peak?* Washington, D.C.: World Resources Institute, 1996.

ALTERNATIVE OIL RESOURCES

By the mid-1990s, over 650 billion barrels (27.3 trillion gallons, 103 trillion liters) had been extracted from Earth's petroleum reserves and another trillion barrels are believed to exist in exploitable petroleum reserves. However, at a typical worldwide extraction rate of 24 billion barrels per year, this represents only around 40 years of supply.

A further reserve of 10 trillion barrels of petroleum is potentially available by advanced extraction techniques for existing fields and from two main alternative sources: oil shale and tar sands.

Oil shale. Shale is the mixture of kerogen and rocky material that is the source rock for petroleum formation when it occurs at a sufficient depth underground. Deposits closer to the surface can be artificially converted to petroleum by heating, which breaks down the kerogen. Extraction of petroleum from shale is much more expensive than the extraction of natural petroleum because mining and heating operations are required. Furthermore, shale contains only around 10 percent oil by weight; the remaining 90 percent, which is an oil-contaminated rock, presents difficulties in disposal.

Tar sands. Tar sands are deposits of viscous, tarry oils that are mixed with sand in underground seams. The petroleum can be extracted by pumping steam into a borehole to make the oil less viscous; the oil then rises through a second borehole. Extraction from tar sands has two main advantages over shale oil extraction: no mining is necessary and no rocky waste is produced.

Biofuels

In addition to the petroleum-like resources, a synthetic version of petroleum can be produced from starchy plants such as sugarcane and wood. The starting materials are first fermented to produce ethanol or methanol (both of which can be used as fuels), then converted to synthesis gas and finally synthetic petroleum by chemical processing (see FUELS AND PROPELLANTS). The petroleum can then be refined and modified in the same way as natural petroleum. Although the additional processing costs make synthetic petroleum more expensive than the natural material, biofuels are a renewable and potentially unlimited resource.

LOOKING TO THE FUTURE

OIL REFINING

Oil refining is the industrial activity that extracts useful products from crude petroleum

A drop of heavy crude oil—the starting material of refining processes—falls from a glass tube.

Scientists believe that most petroleum deposits were formed from the remains of tiny marine organisms deposited on the seabed. Over millions of years the action of bacteria and the pressure of sediment above this organic matter turned it into oil (see OIL AND NATURAL GAS PRODUCTION).

The first uses of oil were very basic: where crude oil rose naturally to Earth's surface, local populations would burn it in torches or use it to waterproof wooden boats and cloth. Crude oil (a mixture of petroleum substances) was first refined in Europe during the Renaissance, which began in the 14th century. Crude oil was heated in a pot, and the vapors that boiled at different temperatures were collected separately and condensed (returned to liquid form) by cooling. This process is known as distillation. The materials that were separated in this way were used as medicines and lubricants. Much of the oil was lost by evaporation or simply discarded as useless.

The roots of the modern oil refining industry can be traced back to the 1850s. 1n 1852, British geologist and physician Abraham Gesner (1797–1864) patented a process for making a clean-burning lamp oil by distilling crude oil. This purified oil—known as kerosene—was cheaper than the whale oil that had been used until then and produced less soot than crude oil. It was an immediate success. However, the availability of crude oil for refining was limited to the small amounts that seeped to the surface through rock faults. Then, in 1859, U.S. engineer and speculator Edwin Drake (1819–1880) struck oil at his well in Titusville, Pennsylvania. Discoveries of oil reserves in California and Texas soon followed, and large quantities of crude oil became available for refining into kerosene for lamp oil.

New technology for changing demands

At first, crude oil was distilled to produce kerosene lamp oil, lubricant oil, and paraffin waxes. The low-boiling mixture—called gasoline—boiled off before the kerosene. Gasoline had no commercial use at the time and was discarded. However, this situation soon changed. In 1889 the first gasoline-powered automobile was introduced and, by the start of the 20th century, the demand for motor-fuel gasoline was well established and growing.

As automobile ownership increased, more and more petroleum had to be distilled to produce the required volume of gasoline. Since only 25 percent of the content of a typical crude oil was found to be suitable for use as motor gasoline, the remaining 75 percent—most of it heavier (of higher boiling point) than gasoline—was waste material.

The yield of gasoline from petroleum was improved by the introduction of the cracking process (see page 942), which converts high boiling point hydrocarbons (carbon-hydrogen compounds) into smaller, lower boiling point molecules. In this way, kerosene and heavier fractions can be used to provide more gasoline. A modern refinery can turn more than 50 percent of crude oil into useful gasoline.

Plastics from refinery by-products

The adoption of cracking had an unforeseen bonus. When a hydrocarbon molecule is cracked, the fragment it loses is often a small gas molecule containing two or three carbon atoms, hydrogen atoms, and a double bond (a double linkage between carbon atoms; see the diagram on page 941). These molecules are ethylene (C_2H_4) and propylene (C_3H_6). For years, these gases were simply burned at the refinery.

In 1934, British conglomerate Imperial Chemical Industries (ICI) found that ethylene molecules could be made to polymerize (form chains) by heating them to 210–390°F (100–200°C) at 2000 times

CONNECTIONS

● The **GASOLINE** and **ORGANIC CHEMICAL INDUSTRIES** are major consumers of oil refinery products.

● The **OIL AND NATURAL GAS PRODUCTION** industry provides the raw materials for oil refining.

CORE FACTS

■ Industrial oil refining originally developed to produce kerosene for oil lamps.

■ A modern oil refinery can turn more than half of the processed volume of oil into gasoline.

■ Refinery processes are classified as separation and conversion processes. Separation processes isolate groups of compounds, while conversion processes induce chemical change.

atmospheric pressure. The product was polyethylene. In 1953, German chemist Karl Ziegler (1898–1973) discovered a catalyst for making polyethylene more economically by using much lower pressures. His discovery was followed in 1954 by Italian chemist Giulio Natta's (1903–1979) application of a similar catalyst system to propylene polymerization that had not been possible by the high-pressure method. These developments provided a useful outlet for ethylene and propylene and spawned a new sector of the petrochemical industry.

Crude oil quality

The content of crude oil varies enormously from one oil field to another. All types of oils are mixtures of hydrocarbons with small quantities of sulfur- and nitrogen-containing compounds. The majority of the hydrocarbon content is present as straight-chain paraffins—molecules with long chains of carbon atoms joined in a line by single bonds. The next most important compounds in crude oil are the naphthenes, hydrocarbons that are based on rings of five or six carbons (cyclopentanes and cyclohexanes). The final class of compounds are the aromatics, which are based on a six-carbon ring that is held together by alternating single and double bonds (represented by a circle inside a hexagon).

Crude oil from wells in Pennsylvania, Iran, and Iraq consists mainly of straight-chain paraffins and is a good source of gasoline. Crude from Venezuela contains a high proportion of naphthenes and is described as naphthenic or asphaltic. Crude from Borneo is unusual in that it contains a high proportion of aromatics, which are useful raw materials for plastics, pharmaceuticals, and dyes (see CHEMICAL INDUSTRY, ORGANIC). Other crudes, such as those from Texas, are intermediate between paraffinic and asphaltic crudes and are known as mixed-base oils.

Separation processes

Separation techniques are used to isolate the components of crude oil and split up the mixtures of products resulting from other processes.

Fractional distillation. Crude petroleum—a mixture of hydrocarbons with 3 to 40 carbon atoms per molecule—is first heated to around 750°F (400°C) by pumping it through a heated pipe. At this temperature, the oil becomes a mixture of liquids and gases. The mixture passes into a column, where the liquid falls to the bottom and the vapors rise. The column is a tall steel tower with bubble plates—trays that fill the diameter of the column—at intervals through its height. The bubble plates are pierced with capped metal pipes—bubble caps—through which the rising vapors pass and bubble through the liquid hydrocarbons that have collected in the plate (see the diagram on page 942).

Each bubble plate is cooler than the one below, and the hydrocarbon vapors rise until they reach a bubble plate that is below their boiling point, where they liquefy. If there is an outlet from the bubble plate, the fraction collected contains those

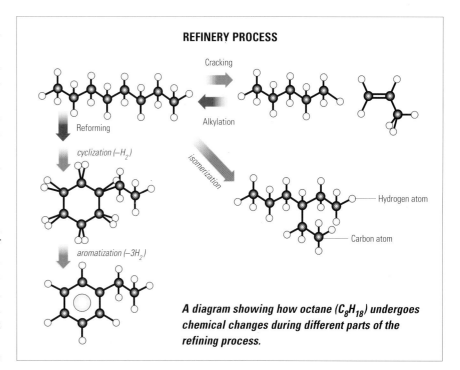

REFINERY PROCESS

Cracking

Reforming

Alkylation

cyclization (–H₂)

isomerization

aromatization (–3H₂)

Hydrogen atom

Carbon atom

A diagram showing how octane (C_8H_{18}) undergoes chemical changes during different parts of the refining process.

hydrocarbons that boil between the temperature of that plate and the temperature of the next outlet below (which is hotter). If there is no outlet, the liquefied hydrocarbons simply overflow onto the plate below. Some hydrocarbons (those with up to four carbon atoms) do not liquefy in the column and leave the column as a mixture of gases. The exact fractions that are collected depend on the crude oil used.

Vacuum distillation. At pressures below atmospheric, the boiling points of liquids drop. This phenomenon is used in vacuum distillation, where it allows liquids to be separated at lower temperatures

---

THE FUTURE OF REFINING

An oil refinery embraces several separation and conversion plants. The composition of the mixtures of products from these plants depends on the starting mixture, the reaction time, the temperature and pressure conditions, and the type and activity of the catalyst in the reactor. Changing any one of these factors changes the blend that comes out.

In most cases, some of the output of one plant is fed into other plants, so that a change in temperature, flow rate, or any other variable in one part of the refinery will have consequences—directly or indirectly—throughout the plant.

Current developments include near-infrared sensors that constantly monitor the composition of product streams without having to take samples and wait for results (see ELECTROMAGNETIC RADIATION; SPECTROSCOPY). Based on the analysis, the control system can feed instructions forward to the fractionation plant to modify the separation of products. Instructions can also be fed back to the reactor to change, say, its operating temperature or pressure.

In a further development—the "thinking" refinery—a processor would use the input from control systems throughout a refinery to determine how to modify the conditions in each plant to obtain the required final product mix. Such a refinery would be likely to produce a better quality of product with less waste.

Ideally, future refineries will require only a few simple instructions to switch between different types of crude oil—including synthetic crudes from natural gas or biofuel—and match the product range to the market demands at any time.

LOOKING TO THE FUTURE

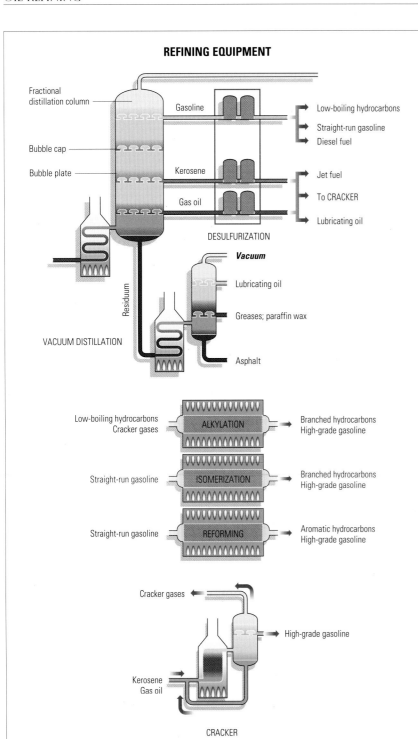

REFINING EQUIPMENT

Fractional distillation column

Bubble cap

Bubble plate

Gasoline

Kerosene

Gas oil

DESULFURIZATION

Low-boiling hydrocarbons

Straight-run gasoline

Diesel fuel

Jet fuel

To CRACKER

Lubricating oil

Residuum

VACUUM DISTILLATION

Vacuum

Lubricating oil

Greases; paraffin wax

Asphalt

Low-boiling hydrocarbons
Cracker gases

ALKYLATION

Branched hydrocarbons
High-grade gasoline

Straight-run gasoline

ISOMERIZATION

Branched hydrocarbons
High-grade gasoline

Straight-run gasoline

REFORMING

Aromatic hydrocarbons
High-grade gasoline

Cracker gases

High-grade gasoline

Kerosene
Gas oil

CRACKER

PETROLEUM DISTILLATION FRACTIONS

Fraction (approximate)	Boiling range	Carbon atoms
Refinery gas	up to 105°F (40°C)	1–4
Gasoline	105–390°F (40–200°C)	5–11
Kerosene	350–575°F (175–300°C)	11–16
Gas oil	530–720°F (275–380°C)	15–18
Residuum	over 720°F (380°C)	16+

From the residuum (vacuum distillation):

Lubricating oil	–	16–20
Greases	–	18–22
Paraffin wax	–	20–30
Asphalt	–	30–40

than would be needed in a normal distillation. In a refinery, vacuum distillation is used to separate oils, greases, and waxes from the high-boiling liquid at the bottom of the fractionating column.

Conversion processes

The two main customers of the refining industry—the fuel and organic chemical industries—require hydrocarbons that are structurally different from those that are present in the original oil. These are produced by the processes that cause chemical changes in the separated hydrocarbons.

Hydrodesulfurization. The distilled hydrocarbons contain small amounts of sulfur compounds that would damage the catalysts used in subsequent processes and cause sulfur dioxide pollution if the hydrocarbons were burned as fuel. The fractions are each treated with hydrogen in the presence of a cobalt catalyst. The sulfur is converted to hydrogen sulfide, a form in which it can be removed.

Cracking. When hydrocarbons are heated to around 1000°F (540°C), they start to shake apart. The carbon chains split into fragments and some molecules with double bonds are formed—the higher the cracking temperature, the smaller the fragments. Few cracking units use heat alone (thermal cracking); most use a honeycomb zeolite catalyst (catalytic cracking) that allows them to run at lower temperatures of around 800°F (425°C).

The cracking process is particularly useful because it converts heavier fractions, such as kerosene, into fuel-grade mixtures suitable for internal combustion engines. This fuel burns more smoothly than the gasoline that comes directly from the fractionating unit (see GASOLINE). At the same time, cracker gases—small molecules with double bonds—are produced. These are starting points for numerous products, including plastics.

Alkylation. Gasoline can be produced by reacting cracker gases with fractions that are too light to be used in gasoline. The process is carried out in long reactors that contain an aluminum chloride catalyst. The products—mainly branched-chain hydrocarbons—are used in high-grade gasoline.

Isomerization. The proportion of branched hydrocarbons in straight-run gasoline can be increased by isomerization, a process in which molecules effectively break up and recombine in a different form. The equipment and catalyst used for isomerization are similar to the alkylation process.

Reforming. When gasoline fractions are heated with a platinum catalyst, they curl up to form ring compounds called aromatics. Aromatics are used to help gasoline burn and as starting materials for nylons, polyesters, and polystyrene.

M. CLOWES

See also: CATALYST, INDUSTRIAL; PLASTICS.

Further reading:
Bacon. R, *et al. Demand, Prices and the Refining Industry.* Oxford: Oxford University Press, 1990.

OIL TANKER AND BULK CARRIER

Oil tankers and bulk carriers are single-deck cargo ships that carry liquid or solid cargoes

Towering pumps are attached to an oil tanker docked in the Sumatra straits, Indonesia.

In 1859, the drilling of petroleum in Titusville, Pennsylvania, founded the world's oil industry (see OIL AND NATURAL GAS PRODUCTION). Two years later the sailing brig *Elizabeth Watts* took the first cargo of American oil to London in barrels in a voyage that lasted 45 days. Even at this early stage in the development of the industry, it was clear that loading oil in individual barrels was an uneconomic means of transporting it. For this reason, eight years later a ship named the *Charles* was designed specifically to carry oil with metal tanks built inside the hull.

However, there were two major problems with this new method. The containers took up a substantial amount of valuable load space and, since oil was strictly a one-way cargo from producer to consumer,

the tanks then had to be scrapped at the end of the voyage so that the ship could sail home with some other cargo. The other main problem lay in the nature of the cargo. The possibility of oil leaks and gas escaping created a serious fire hazard, which was demonstrated when the *Charles* burned out after only three years of service.

Tanker design

The first purpose-built tanker, the *Gluckauf*, was built at Newcastle-upon-Tyne, northeast England, in 1886. It was the first ship to have a row of fixed full-width tanks filling most of its hull, with accommodation for the crew and machinery positioned at the stern. The use of electric lighting on the ship helped to reduce the fire hazard, although it was still possible for gas to leak. Because cargoes were often unloaded by pumping from the tankers into barges, which then transferred the oil to the refineries, there were still plenty of opportunities for a stray spark to cause an explosion resulting in fire.

Modern tankers are built to follow essentially the same plan as the *Gluckauf*, with a hull made up of a series of almost identical tanks. The increased use of welding, rather than riveting, helps to ensure oil-tight joints. Since the cargo is liquid, tankers need no conventional hatches or deck cranes; instead they use a complex system of pipes for loading and unloading. Because a tanker's deck is not pierced by large open hatches, and because the density of the cargo is similar to that of seawater, tankers tend to sit relatively low in the water.

CORE FACTS

- The first cargo of American oil to cross the Atlantic was shipped in barrels aboard a sailing brig in 1861. It took 45 days to reach London.
- Modern tankers have heating coils in their tanks to keep the oil from thickening in cold weather and making unloading difficult.
- When tankers transport dangerous chemicals, they carry them in center tanks that are flanked by side tanks filled with less hazardous cargoes for added protection in a collision.
- Some dual-purpose bulk carriers are fitted with oil-tight holds with open hatchways, so they can carry oil or ore on different voyages.

CONNECTIONS

- Oil spillages from tankers has caused environmental damage and made **POLLUTION AND ITS CONTROL** a concern for the oil industry.

- **RADAR** is used to chart the position of other ships over long distances. In this way, a ship's course can be negotiated safely.

SPECIAL BULK CARRIERS

In the mid-1950s, the Labrador oil fields in northeast Canada created a market for ships that could carry ore during the summer and oil during the winter, when many ore ports were choked with ice. These dual-purpose bulk carriers have oil-tight holds that are used for liquid or solid cargo. Ore is carried in central tanks, flanked by water-filled ballast tanks on either side, and a double bottom below the ore tanks. When oil is carried all the tanks are used, but cargoes are not mixed because damaged bulkheads (the partitions between separate tanks) may allow oil and gas to leak into other cargo areas, where sparks might cause ignition.

Grain ships have special problems. If the cargo shifts in heavy seas, the ship can capsize; several ships were lost in this way during the last century. For this reason, grain bulk carriers have special grain-tight bulkheads, and care is taken to ensure that the holds are filled to capacity to avoid any danger of movement.

Some bulk carriers are designed to carry a very wide range of cargoes, including ore, coal, grain, phosphates, and crude oil or other liquid cargoes. Others have their own loading and unloading equipment, including conveyors, derrick cranes, and clamshells (see CONVEYOR; CRANE).

A CLOSER LOOK

In Alaska, a tanker pumps the remaining oil from the hull of the leaking **Exxon Valdez.**

Loading and unloading

Tankers have two sets of pipes for unloading cargo from their tanks. The main, high-suction pipes run several feet above the bottom of the tanks to avoid sucking out the sludge that collects on the tank bottoms. The low-suction pipes (also known as stripping lines) are, by contrast, set low enough to remove the sludge and debris from the tank bottoms during the cleaning process. Suction pumps transfer the oil out of the tanks and into pipes that are connected via terminals on the deck to the storage installations on the shore.

Larger tankers have cranes or boom posts on deck to lift the heavy pipes that connect the ship's system to the shore installations. Since empty tanks usually contain oil or gasoline vapor, which carries a high fire risk, inert gases are usually pumped into them to prevent any spark from touching off an explosion. Cold weather causes oil to thicken, which can cause pumping problems. To prevent this, the tanks have built-in heating coils.

Tankers are used for carrying many different types of oil products, and for this reason the tanks have to be cleaned regularly using the stripping lines. The practice of flushing out tanks with heated saltwater from the sea causes marine pollution and has been opposed for environmental reasons (see POLLUTION AND ITS CONTROL). In any case, heated saltwater also has the disadvantage of being highly corrosive and soon starts to erode the ship's steelwork. Regular repainting is not enough to guard against this; different types of plastic coating provide more expensive, but more effective, protection against this form of corrosion.

Tankers and supertankers

Most tankers operate regular schedules between fixed loading and unloading points. Voyages tend to be reasonably simple and straightforward, with very little need for any complex maneuvering. This means that a tanker's engines and propulsion system can be designed for a specific operating speed, or RPM, which in turn helps to improve its economic viability. Even the largest tankers have only a single propeller, and automatic control systems eliminate the need for the large crew that would normally be required for vessels of this size.

On the busiest shipping routes, the larger the tanker, the lower the cost of transporting each barrel of oil. For this reason, up until the oil crisis of the early 1970s, tankers had continued to grow larger and larger over the years. By then, the most sizable ships stretched a quarter of a mile (0.4 km) from bow to stern and carried half a million tons of cargo each. However, while supertankers certainly made sound economic sense, there were serious safety and environmental implications that were increasingly demanding consideration.

The enormous size and weight of these ships meant that they took a great deal of time to turn, stop, or even slow down. Traditional routes such as those through the Suez and Panama Canals and whole

A liquid-cargo tanker is capable of carrying up to 39 different products, ranging from edible oils to petroleum products. Extra storage space is provided by the above-deck tanks.

stretches of the U.S. east coast were out of bounds to them for this reason. When tankers reached points on their designated route where shipping lanes converged through narrow straits or channels, their slow reactions often caused severe hazards.

Even with radar in place to give advance warning of other traffic traveling far ahead, piloting tankers could still prove to be unpredictable. In particular, deep-draught tankers could run aground easily as they approached land-based refineries, often with devastating consequences for the environment. In 1989, the *Exxon Valdez* tanker ran aground in Alaska, causing a massive oil slick across 3200 sq miles (8300 km²) of coastline. This event necessitated a costly and complex cleanup operation to reduce the environmental damage.

Safety measures have been put in place by the oil industry to help reduce the pollution caused by tankers. These include fitting some tankers with double hulls to minimize the quantity of oil that will be lost in the event of an accident. In addition, inflatable floating booms (long, flexible tubes) can be used to contain the spill in the short term, since oil forms a layer on the surface of the water. The spilled oil can then be sucked into tanks and removed.

Specialized tankers

The increasing bulk of supertankers limited these ships to destinations where onshore terminals coincided with deep-water berths; however, smaller tankers were still needed to reach other ports. In fact, the oil industry relies on several different sizes of ships, from the largest supertankers down to the smallest coastal tankers, which are able to reach any harbor with the appropriate unloading facilities. Very often these ships load and unload from bigger tankers in sheltered coastal waters.

As demand for natural gas has increased in recent years, specialized tankers have been built to carry liquefied gases. Though these ships are similar to oil and gasoline tankers, the nature of their cargoes imposes special requirements. The gas has to be cooled to −260°F (−162°C) in order to liquefy it before loading. This low temperature has to be maintained for the whole voyage and until the liquid can be pumped ashore at the destination.

At these temperatures steel tanks would become dangerously brittle through metallurgical changes, so the tanks have to be made of a nickel-steel alloy or

---

NAVAL TANKERS

Naval tankers have a more unpredictable life than merchant tankers. They operate at higher speeds and perform more complex maneuvers in confined waters. This means that they need to devote more space to machinery and usually have twin screws for greater control (see PROPELLER). Furthermore, they need to be able to replenish other ships with fuel and various supplies at sea.

During the early part of World War II (1939–1945), Atlantic convoy escorts often had to be refueled from a tanker sailing with the convoy. Usually this was done by trailing a hose from the stern of the tanker, which was picked up by the warship that needed refueling. The hose would be hoisted on board and connected to the ship's own fuel tanks, but the procedure was laborious and could not be attempted in bad weather.

Faced with the need for regular refueling in the vast Pacific Ocean, the U.S. Navy pioneered more efficient techniques. Naval tankers were built that could travel as fast as other warships and sailed as part of a task force. They were fitted with booms that could be hoisted outboard to carry large-diameter hoses over to the decks of warships that were sailing alongside. Each tanker could refuel two ships at a time with the minimum of delay and in all but the worst of weather conditions.

A CLOSER LOOK

OFFSHORE TANKER MOORINGS

A tanker at an offshore gas off-loading facility in Chesapeake Bay, Maryland. The pipe that takes the gas to land can be seen at bottom right.

When supertankers were introduced, they proved to be too large for many ports. Sometimes the problem was solved by unloading part of their cargoes into smaller tankers before they reached their final destination, but this was not always convenient. So the oil companies started to develop moorings that could be used to unload tankers offshore.

The first such mooring was called the single point mooring (SPM) and consisted of a vertical post that was fixed to the seabed. It had a swiveling head that carried connections to a seabed pipeline, and this linked the mooring to an onshore oil-storage installation. The advantages of this system were that the ship could be secured to the mooring and respond to any shifts in wind and tide while unloading its cargo in comfortably deep water.

A later development was the single buoy mooring (SBM). It replaced the fixed structure of the SPM with a floating buoy tethered to the seabed by a set of radial chains. The SBM also has a swiveling head, which allows the tanker to swing while unloading her cargo. Finally, the more elaborate ELSBM, or exposed location single buoy mooring, was developed so that tankers could load cargoes from offshore production platforms where they might be exposed to storm conditions. The largest ELSBMs have a helicopter pad and accommodation for crews to carry out repairs and maintenance, as well as a seabed pipeline linked to the production platform.

A CLOSER LOOK

their design and layout to oil tankers, which have tanks that extend across the full width of their hulls. More dangerous chemicals are carried in central tanks. The side tanks on the ship are then filled with cargoes that would cause less environmental damage if they were to leak in the case of a collision.

Bulk carriers

The economic factors that made it more efficient and viable to carry oil in bulk in a ship's own tanks, rather than in individual barrels in a cargo hold, soon began to apply to many other types of bulk cargoes. These bulk cargoes include coal, iron and other mineral ores, and grain, molasses, wine, and sugar.

From the mid-1950s on, more and more merchant ships were built specifically to carry these cargoes in ever greater quantities. By 1991, there were more than 4500 bulk carriers at work on the world's trade routes, with a total deadweight in excess of 110 million tons (100 million tonnes). Bulk carriers have continued to increase in size in the same way as oil tankers, with the largest ships often weighing hundreds of thousands of tons.

As bulk carriers became more popular, different types emerged for handling specific cargoes or combinations of cargoes. For example, mineral ores are very dense, so ore carriers have large ballast tanks along their sides. When sailing without a cargo, the tanks are filled with water to improve stability in heavy seas. A deep double bottom below the cargo holds provides another safety measure. This raises the center of gravity of the cargo slightly, reducing the strain on the ship's structure when coping with rough conditions. Bulk carriers may have as many as 20–25 tanks.

Like tankers, bulk carriers sail between suitably equipped ports on the busiest routes. Dockside handling equipment includes clamshells and suction machinery to load and unload their cargoes. Ore carriers generally have very large hatchways so that clamshells can reach all parts of the holds to extract the cargo at the destination port.

D. OWEN

See also: MECHANICAL HANDLING; OIL AND NATURAL GAS PRODUCTION; SHIP AND BOAT.

aluminum that can stand up to cold conditions. To prevent the tanks and their contents from absorbing heat from outside, they have to be surrounded by heavy layers of insulation.

Other tankers have been built to carry different types of chemical cargoes. Some of these are specialized ships intended for one particular trade, such as carrying liquid sulfur, which must be kept above 246°F (119°C) to prevent it from becoming solid. Others are used for the transportation of a whole range of different chemicals, depending on the voyage, and the ships are designed according to the relative hazards presented by these chemicals. Less hazardous cargoes are carried aboard ships similar in

Further reading:
International Chamber of Shipping, Oil Companies International Marine Forum, and International Association of Ports and Harbors. *International Safety Guide for Oil Tankers & Terminals (ISGOTT)*. London: Witherby, 1996.
Kemp, P. *Oxford Companion to Ships and the Sea*. New York: Oxford University Press, 1994 (reprint).
Nalder, E. *Tankers Full of Trouble: The Perilous Journey of Alaskan Crude*. New York: Grove Press, 1994.
Wildenburg, T. *Gray Steel and Black Oil: Fast Tankers and Replenishment at Sea in the U.S. Navy*. Annapolis, Maryland: U.S. Naval Institute Press, 1996.
Willis, J., and Warner K. *Innocent Passage: The Wreck of the Tanker* Braer. Trafalgar Square, 1994.

OPERATING ROOM

An operating room is a special hospital room where surgical procedures are performed

The operating room is part of the operating department within a hospital. The department itself may be located on the same floor as the intensive care unit, the labor ward, and the emergency room. There will also be easy access between the operating department and the wards, laboratories, and medical imaging departments. The operating department is divided into four sections, with increasingly restricted access to protect the patient in the operating room from infection.

The operating department layout

The reception area, which is where the patients and staff enter and leave the department, has one entrance. Beyond this is a limited-access zone, with offices, a staff break room, and a recovery room. After the operation, the patient is kept under careful watch in the recovery room, which is like a mini-intensive care unit, fitted with oxygen, an electrocardiograph, and other monitoring equipment (see MEDICAL MONITORING EQUIPMENT).

The operating room itself lies within a restricted access zone and is directly connected to a number of other rooms. The scrub room is where doctors and nurses scrub their hands and forearms with antiseptic, using faucets that are operated by the foot or elbow. They also put on sterile gowns, boots, masks, and caps. The gowns are green or blue, rather than white, because these colors are less tiring to the eyes. The preparation room is where equipment carts and packs of sterile instruments are made ready for each operation. Sterile surgical supplies are either prepared within the department or in a dedicated sterilizing unit in the hospital. All surgical waste has to be disposed of promptly and according to special safety procedures. Finally, the utility room is where samples to be sent to the laboratory for analysis are kept and where soiled linen and other waste material from the operating room are disposed of.

Care is taken to plan the traffic in and out of the operating room itself. The patients are normally transported to surgery through ward doors in their ward bed, which is fitted with wheels. All the doors the patient passes through must be especially wide.

CORE FACTS

- The operating room is part of a set of rooms known as the operating department.
- The general layout of the operating department is designed to protect the patient from infection.
- The operating room is designed with features such as lighting, flooring, and a bed that enables the surgeon to work safely and effectively.
- The surgical team employs several procedures to make sure no surgical equipment is left inside the patient.

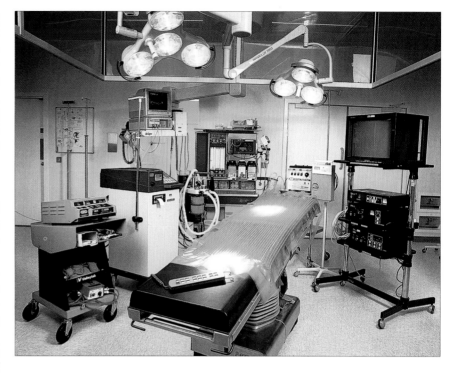

Inside the operating room

All surfaces inside the operating room are made of a washable plastic, and the joins between walls, ceiling, and floor are designed to be easy to keep clean. The floors are made of an antistatic material to eliminate the danger of sparks, which could otherwise ignite anesthetic gases. Sterile air is pumped into the room and is changed completely several times a day. This removes not just microorganisms—which could otherwise cause infection—but also anesthetic gases exhaled by the patient. The temperature is kept at 68–72°F (20–22°C) and the humidity (moisture) between 40 and 60 percent to protect the patient from hypothermia, for body heat is lost easily under anesthetic (see ANESTHETICS).

Pipes and electrical cables run along the ceiling to keep the floor clear and are fed down into two panels—one for the surgeon and one for the anesthetist. These supply electricity for medical instruments, oxygen, and suction to remove blood from the part of the body being operated on. There are two clocks on the wall: one showing the time of day, the other showing the time that has elapsed in the operation. There are also light boxes on the wall for inspection of X-ray films and other images.

The light above the operating table is very bright so that the surgeon has the best possible illumination over the operating area. Halogen lamps are used, which provide an intense light while giving off less heat than filament lamps would, and a system of lenses and mirrors ensures that the light does not cast a shadow. The light is also designed so that it can be moved easily to direct the illumination wherever the surgeon may need it.

A modern operating room. The table in the center is covered with a water-filled mattress that is used to keep the patient warm. The table is surrounded by pieces of equipment that supply anesthetics and monitor the condition of the patient.

CONNECTIONS

- **ANESTHETIC** is administered to the patient in the operating room before and during **SURGERY**.

- The operating room should be as close to the **INTENSIVE CARE UNIT** and the **MEDICAL IMAGING** department as possible.

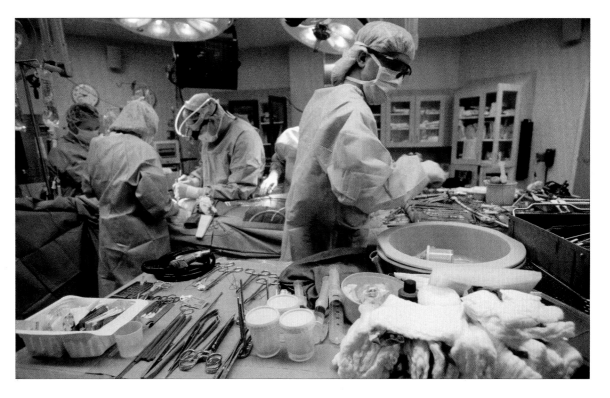

A heart bypass taking place in an operating room. The operating room is equipped with many sterilized instruments that the surgeon may elect to use during the course of the operation.

The patient lies on an operating table. This is made in five sections, which can be adjusted either separately or together by a control panel at the head of the bed or by pedals at its foot. Both the patient and the table are covered by sterile towels. Like the operating gowns of the medical staff, these are usually green or blue so as not to tire the eyes.

A diathermy unit is usually fitted close to the bed. This contains a probe that is heated by an electric current. The surgeon uses it to control bleeding, because it can seal up the ends of tiny blood vessels.

Operating room procedures

For efficient and safe surgery, each member of the team has his or her own allotted duties. The surgeon and the scrub nurse must keep themselves sterile at all times and are not allowed to leave the operating room during the operation. The scout nurse is responsible for taking supplies to and from the operating area, and does not come into direct contact with the patient. A team of anesthetists is responsible for administering anesthetics, a vital procedure that takes place throughout the operation.

The patient's breathing and circulation monitors are fitted with alarms to alert the staff to mishaps, such as accidental disconnection of a ventilator. It is also important to keep count of the instruments, clips, and swabs used during the operation. A swab is a folded piece of absorbent cotton gauze used to apply antiseptic before an incision is made or to absorb blood during the operation. There is a strict routine for keeping count of these items to ensure none are left inside the patient by mistake. Packs of swabs and sponges are not undone until both scrub and scout nurse are ready to count them out. These are recorded both on a form and on a wall board. Each swab and sponge is fitted with a tiny tag that would show up on an X-ray should one accidentally be left inside the patient. Swabs will normally be weighed as they are removed from the patient's body after counting and double-checking the count. This gives an estimate of the amount of blood that has been lost during the operation.

S. ALDRIDGE

See also: AMBULANCE AND EMERGENCY MEDICAL TREATMENT; ANTISEPTICS AND STERILIZATION; BLOOD TRANSFUSION; MEDICAL TECHNOLOGY.

Further reading:
Fuller, J. *Surgical Technology.* 3rd edition, Philadelphia: W.B. Saunders. 1994.
Surgical Principles. Edited by I. Taylor and S. J. Karran. New York: Oxford University Press, 1996.

THE HISTORY OF THE OPERATING ROOM

Surgeons used to perform operations in the hospital ward, but by the late 18th century the idea of doing surgery in a special room took hold. The oldest surviving surgical amphitheater is in the Pennsylvania Hospital, first used for an operation in 1804. The operations were performed without anesthetic, so the surgeon prided himself on being quick. The idea was to provide medical students with instruction in both surgery and anatomy. However, this led to many operations becoming a theatrical spectacle, with the admission of the general public and audience applause.

It was only in the late 19th century—when the germ theory of disease was finally accepted by surgeons—that the importance of keeping infectious agents away from the operating site was realized. Surgeons exchanged their unwashed frock coats for white gowns, and the audience was confined to watching from behind a glass screen. Nowadays, a camera lens—incorporated into the light over the operating table—allows students to watch and learn from an operation on closed-circuit television.

HISTORY OF TECHNOLOGY

ORE EXTRACTION AND PROCESSING

Ore extraction and processing yield pure metals from mineral deposits in Earth's crust

Metals are usually found combined with other elements in substances known as minerals. Earth's crust is rich in deposits of various minerals. When extraction of pure metal from a mineral is economically worthwhile, the mineral is known as an ore. Some mineral deposits are too inaccessible or contain too low a concentration of metal to be considered as ores. Prospecting and mining produce ores from Earth's crust (see MINING AND QUARRYING; PROSPECTING). Various physical and chemical operations must then be applied to the ores to obtain the metal from them. These operations are divided into three main stages: concentration of the ore, conversion into metal, and refining of the metal. In concentration, the ore is separated from impurities. Conversion involves breaking the chemical bonds that the metal makes with other elements in the mineral. Depending which method of conversion is used, the metal may require further purification; this process is known as refining.

CORE FACTS

- The three processes involved in extracting a metal from its ore are concentration, conversion, and refining.
- The process used for conversion depends on the chemical nature of the ore.
- Zinc, lead, iron, and tin are obtained by reacting their ores with carbon.
- Aluminum, sodium, potassium, calcium, and magnesium are obtained by electrolysis of their ores.

The abundance of metal ores

Aluminum is the most abundant metal in Earth's crust, accounting for 8.1 percent of its mass. It is followed by iron (5 percent), calcium (3.6 percent), sodium (2.8 percent), potassium (2.5 percent), and magnesium (2.5 percent). These figures include soluble ores, such as sodium chloride, which are found in large quantities in seawater. By contrast, other metals (including some of the most useful, such as copper, zinc, and uranium) account for less than 0.1 percent of Earth's crust. Fortunately, these metals are not evenly distributed over Earth's surface, or it would not be economically worthwhile to extract them. Instead, they are concentrated in certain areas: there are rich deposits of copper in Chile, Canada, Kazakhstan, and Zambia, for example.

Only gold, silver, and platinum occur principally in their elemental forms (that is, uncombined with other elements). The rest occur in chemical combination—chiefly with sulfur, oxygen, and chlorine, all of which react readily with metallic elements. The most common ores are the sulfides, which are simple compounds of metal and sulfur. Copper, lead, and zinc sulfides are particularly important minerals. The next most common are the oxides, which are metal plus oxygen, of which aluminum and iron oxides are the most important. Salt (sodium chloride, NaCl) is an important chlorine-containing mineral. The carbonates (compounds of metal with the carbonate group, CO_3^{2-}) also form significant deposits. Calcium, iron, and magnesium carbonates are important minerals.

CONNECTIONS

- The extraction of metals from their ores is a very complex process that requires a lot of **ENERGY RESOURCES**.

- A good **INDUSTRIAL DESIGN** is needed to ensure that the process is being performed as efficiently as possible.

An ore crushing mill reduces the size of the ore grains to make the extraction process easier.

Concentration of ores

Even the richest ore deposits are mixed with dirt and rock, which must be removed before the metal can be extracted. Once the ore has been mined, the first stage in concentration is to break it up into tiny pieces. This involves a process called comminution, which is a combination of crushing and grinding of the crude ore particles. Mechanized crushers produce particles that are 0.4–0.6 inches (1.0–1.5 cm) in diameter, and these then go into a grinding mill, where they are pulverized.

Next, the ore particles are separated out from impurities such as sand, clay, or rock, typically by one of three processes: magnetic separation, gravity separation, or froth flotation. In magnetic separation, powerful electromagnets are used to pick up particles of ores from the mixture, leaving impurities behind (see MAGNET). This method can only be applied to the separation of any ore that is magnetic, such as hematite (an important iron ore). In gravity separation, ore and impurities are separated according to their density. The crude ore is placed on a sloping table and powerful jets of water are used to wash the heavier particles to one end, leaving the finer and lighter particles at the other end.

The third method, froth flotation, is the most widely used. It depends on adding a chemical known as a frothing agent to a suspension (undissolved mixture) of the crude ore in water. The frothing agent can change the surface properties of both the ore and the impurities. The surface becomes either hydrophobic (water-hating) or hydrophilic (water-loving). In practice, the frothing agent is chosen deliberately so that the ore particles are the ones that become hydrophobic. Air is then bubbled into the suspension. The hydrophobic ore particles attach themselves to the bubbles, while the hydrophilic impurities stay in suspension. The air bubbles with their attached ore particles form a froth on the surface of the mixture. This is skimmed off, leaving impurities behind in the water.

Whichever separation method is used, the next stage is generally dewatering. This reduces the water content of the ore either by filtering or by letting the ore settle. Finally the ore is dried by exposing it to hot air. It is then ready for transportation to the site where conversion from ore to metal takes place.

From ore to metal

The chemical process by which a metal is removed from its ore is known as reduction. There are two main ways of doing this, depending on how strong the chemical bonds are between the metal and the other elements in the ore compound.

The first method is smelting. This involves melting the ore with substances known as fluxes. The resulting melt separates into two layers. The top layer is a mixture of impurities called slag, while the bottom layer is impure metal. Many fluxes contain carbon, usually in the form of coke (a type of fuel made by heating coal in a confined space to remove its more volatile and reactive components, such as hydrocarbons and sulfur). Thus, in the case of an ore comprising zinc oxide, the carbon atoms combine with the oxygen to form carbon oxides, leaving zinc metal. Other metals that can be produced by smelting their ores include iron, tin, and lead (see IRON AND STEEL PRODUCTION).

However, the more reactive metals such as sodium, potassium, magnesium, and aluminum form very strong bonds with oxygen in their ores, and these cannot be broken by smelting with carbon. The only way to extract these metals is to pass an electric current through the molten ore. This process is known as electrolysis (see ELECTROLYSIS). Refining metals through electrolysis is a similar process.

Refining metals

Refining removes the final impurities from a metal that has been extracted from its ore. It leaves the metal pure enough to be used in commercial applications. In fire refining, oxygen is blown through molten metal. The impurities combine more readily with the oxygen than with the metal, therefore they can be burned off, leaving the pure metal behind. Fire refining is used to purify copper and lead as well as for producing steel from pig iron. Very high purity metals can be made using a form of electrolysis. The impure metal is made into the anode (positive electrode) of an electrolytic cell, with another sheet of metal acting as the cathode (negative electrode). When current is passed through the cell, metal ions from the anode deposit onto the surface of the cathode, forming a layer of very pure metal.

Aluminum. Aluminum is extracted from its ore, bauxite (aluminum oxide), by electrolysis. First, impurities such as silicon and iron oxides are removed from the bauxite by froth flotation. The melting point of bauxite is too high to make its electrolytic extraction economic, so it is dissolved in another aluminum compound called cryolite. The melting point of the mixture is 1560°F (850°C), and passing an electric current through it maintains this temperature throughout the electrolysis. The process uses a great deal of electrical energy, so an aluminum plant is normally built close to a source of cheap electricity, such as a hydroelectric power plant (see HYDROELECTRICITY). World production of bauxite is 80 million tons.

Copper. The most important ore of copper is the sulfide ore, copper pyrites. This contains only a small percentage of copper, so it is concentrated by froth flotation. Copper is obtained from the ore by heating it in air, which causes a complex set of reactions to occur. One by-product of these reactions is the gas sulfur dioxide, which is formed by the combination of the sulfur in the ore with oxygen in air. Bubbles of gas are given off by the impure copper as it solidifies, giving it a blistered appearance. The crude "blister copper" is then refined by electrolysis. Around 20 million tons of copper pyrites are produced each year worldwide.

Zinc. Sphalerite, the main ore of zinc, is a sulfide. It is usually roasted in air to form zinc oxide, and the zinc is then extracted from this either by electrolysis or by smelting. For electrolysis, zinc oxide is dissolved in sulfuric acid to form zinc sulfate. When an electric current is passed through the zinc sulfate solution, zinc metal is liberated.

Smelting of zinc is done using a blast furnace similar to those used in the production of iron (see BLAST FURNACE). The zinc oxide is mixed with coke, which reacts with the oxygen to produce oxides of carbon and zinc metal. The furnace operates at 2550°F (1400°C). Zinc boils at 1665°F (907°C), so it is a vapor under these conditions. It exits the furnace with waste gases, and can be condensed (cooled) to a solid in a separate vessel. The process is essentially a form of distillation (a process for separating chemicals in which a substance boils and is then condensed and thereby separated from impurities with different boiling points). Refining of the zinc is done by further distillation.

Tin. Cassiterite, or tin dioxide, is first roasted in air to remove sulfur impurities, which commonly occur in the tin-containing ore. Then the oxide is reduced in the presence of carbon in a furnace at

CHARLES MARTIN HALL AND PAUL-LOUIS-TOUSSAINT HÉROULT

Charles Martin Hall (1863–1914) invented the electrolytic method of extracting aluminum from bauxite, which enabled the widespread use of the metal. Born in Thompson, Ohio, Hall became interested in aluminum while he was still a student of chemistry at Ohio's Oberlin College. He graduated in 1885 and formulated his aluminum extraction method only eight months later. Although Hall found it hard to secure financial backing at first, he was eventually successful and went on to found the Aluminum Company of America.

The discovery of the electrolytic process for isolating aluminum was made independently at around the same time by French chemist Paul-Louis-Toussaint Héroult (1863–1914). While Hall had been studying the chemistry of aluminum in Ohio, Héroult had been conducting similar studies at the École des Mines in Paris.

Hall and Héroult became involved in a lengthy legal dispute over who had really invented the process but eventually reached an agreement on joint patent rights. By 1914, the Hall-Héroult process (as it is now known) had brought the cost of aluminum down to just 18 cents a pound; aluminum had previously been as expensive to extract as gold.

Charles Martin Hall at the age of 23.

PEOPLE

2190°F (1200°C), forming impure tin. Depending on the grade of metal required, fire refining or electrolytic refining is then used. Tin can also be refined by distillation to obtain a very high grade of metal.

Lead. The main ore of lead is galena, a form of lead sulfide. It is roasted in air to obtain lead oxide. This is then reduced by coke in a process similar to that used in a blast furnace to obtain lead metal. The product is up to 95 percent pure and may contain elements such as silver or bismuth impurities. These elements may be recovered through a range of different refining methods.

Titanium. Titanium has been extracted from rutile (titanium dioxide) on a large scale only since the 1950s. The extraction involves a chemical process that is very different from the methods used to extract other metals. First, titanium oxide is reacted with chlorine to form titanium tetrachloride. This is fed into a large, sealed, steel vessel and reduced with liquid magnesium. The extracted titanium is protected from contamination by performing this part of the extraction in a chemically inert (unreactive) atmosphere of argon gas rather than in air.

Uranium. Uranium is found in over 200 minerals and is present, at least in tiny amounts, in most parts of Earth's crust. The main types of uranium ore, uraninite and pitchblende, are often found in water-filled volcanic fissures and veins. These ores contain oxides of uranium. The first stage of uranium extraction is to roast the ore. This removes impurities such as carbonates and sulfur and dries out the clay in the ore. Then the uranium is removed by a process called leaching. Leaching involves washing the ore with acid or alkaline water solutions. This creates a solution of complex uranium ions. The solvent is then boiled off, leaving the uranium salts as a bright yellow solid commonly known as yellowcake. Yellowcake is then treated with powerful chemicals, such as hydrogen fluoride gas, to yield uranium metal.

S. ALDRIDGE

See also: ALLOY; BLAST FURNACE; ELECTROLYSIS; MATERIALS SCIENCE; METALWORKING; MINING AND QUARRYING; NONFERROUS METAL.

Further reading:
Craig, J., B. Skinner, and D. Vaughan. *Resources of the Earth: Origins, Use, and Environmental Impact.* New York: Prentice Hall, 1996.
Raymond, R. *Out of the Fiery Furnace: The Impact of Metals on the History of Mankind.* Philadelphia: Pennsylvania University Press, 1991.

ORGANIC FARMING AND SUSTAINABLE AGRICULTURE

Organic farming and sustainable agriculture produce food using traditional, nonintensive methods

Organically produced fruit and vegetables are free from all agricultural chemicals and fetch a higher price at the market.

Modern agriculture is an extremely intensive industry that uses high levels of inputs, such as fertilizers, pesticides, and powered machinery, to achieve high crop yields. Intensive farming methods, together with the development of genetic engineering, have raised crop and livestock yields to levels that were considered unachievable half a century ago. However, this improvement has not been without drawbacks. Intensive farming has been criticized for harming the environment, wildlife habitats, and water supplies; for neglecting the welfare of livestock; and for accelerating soil erosion (see POLLUTION AND ITS CONTROL). In addition, scientists are increasingly concerned about potential human health problems caused by the continued high use of pesticides and other agricultural chemicals on food crops. Some of these chemicals are very stable and gradually accumulate in the food chain, which makes it difficult to assess their long-term impact. The large energy demands of modern agriculture are a further concern, particularly if fossil fuels become less readily available, and therefore more expensive, in the future (see ENERGY RESOURCES).

There are various agricultural practices that seek to address or avoid the problems of modern intensive farming. Organic and sustainable farming are two of the most important alternatives. Both are gaining popularity in countries where intensive agriculture is predominant, and they have much in common with the traditional agriculture of many regions.

THE ORIGINS OF ORGANIC AND SUSTAINABLE FARMING

Many of the methods adopted by contemporary organic and sustainable farmers have been around for centuries. As modern agricultural systems, however, they have their origins in the 20th century, generally as a conscious reaction to conventional agriculture. Austrian philosopher Rudolf Steiner (1861–1925) inspired the biodynamic farming movement of the 1920s. His holistic approach advocated using methods to work with ecological patterns and natural cycles. In the 1930s, British agriculturalist Albert Howard demonstrated a natural farming system that promoted recycling nutrients to the soil.

Biodynamics and Howard's system have much in common with organic and sustainable approaches. Other pioneers did much to popularize similar

CORE FACTS

- Organic farming and sustainable agriculture are systems that reject many aspects of the increased intensification of modern agriculture.
- Organic farmers avoid using synthetic agrochemicals and employ traditional husbandry methods.
- Sustainable agriculture promotes a long-term, largely self-sufficient and environmentally benign way of farming, using natural substances and good husbandry.
- Organic farming and sustainable agriculture produce lower yields than conventional methods but can be equally profitable. Both methods are increasing in popularity and economic importance.

CONNECTIONS

- Compared to intensive **ARABLE FARMING**, organic and sustainable farming use almost no artificial **FERTILIZER** and help preserve precious **ENERGY RESOURCES**.

- All organic and many sustainable farmers reject **GENETIC ENGINEERING**.

A manure spreader at work on an organic farm in North Dakota.

Rules and regulations

Specific legal standards exist for organic farming in many countries. These define which substances and methods may be used in order for farm products to qualify as organic. Although the standards vary from country to country, all of the codes preclude the use of synthetic chemicals. Other requirements include treating livestock humanely, limiting damage to the environment, and prohibiting the use of genetically modified organisms (see GENETIC ENGINEERING). The standards are often strict and may apply not only to agricultural methods but also to the processing and packaging of the final product.

There are various bodies that regulate organic farming practices, all of which provide certification when their standards are met. There are over 40 in the United States, operated either by private organizations or by individual states. There are currently proposals by the U.S. Department of Agriculture to implement new national standards. These plans are controversial, however, since the proposed standards are less rigorous than the existing regulations.

Organic techniques

Organic farmers have developed various techniques to ensure satisfactory yields, to control pests and weeds, and to maintain soil structure and quality. Emphasis has been placed on improving the long-term fertility and structure of the soil, rather than concentrating on the short-term needs of the current crop. The intention is to retain a wide variety of beneficial insects and other wildlife that will act as natural predators for crop pests. Mixed livestock and arable enterprises are common, since manure is a very important organic fertilizer.

Although organic systems try to avoid many aspects of modern intensive farming, the use of technology remains as important. For example, tractors and mechanized equipment are common. Indeed, organic farmers may use a wider range of advanced cultivation equipment than conventional farmers, because careful soil preparation is an important way of controlling the growth of weeds and providing good growing conditions. Furthermore, research continues into the development of technologies specifically designed for organic systems. An example is the development of green manure crops. These fast-growing crops are plowed back into the soil, where they decompose and act as a fertilizer. Special blends of such crops have been developed that provide a predictable combination of useful soil nutrients when they decompose.

Crop rotation, in which a piece of land supports a different crop each year, is particularly important in organic agriculture. This practice preserves the soil structure and the nutrients it contains, and it prevents the buildup of specific pest species, which is often a major problem in intensive arable farming (see ARABLE FARMING).

Mulching, a very popular organic technique, involves covering the soil surface with an opaque material to stifle the growth of weeds and to retain

concepts. Certain environmentally motivated agricultural methods came to be defined as organic in the 1950s, and this term has become widely recognized. Sustainable and organic agriculture have grown steadily in acceptance since the 1960s, mainly because the limitations and problems associated with conventional farming have become more evident (see AGRICULTURE, HISTORY OF).

ORGANIC FARMING

Organic agriculture avoids using synthetic chemical fertilizers, livestock feed additives, pesticides, and herbicides (see PESTICIDE AND HERBICIDE). Instead, organic farmers rely on varied husbandry methods and the use of natural substances, such as compost or manure, as fertilizers (see FERTILIZER). Today, organic farming and food production is an important sector of the economy in the United States. It has expanded by 20 percent each year since 1990, and its value was estimated at over $4 billion in 1998.

PERMACULTURE

Permaculture—or permanent agriculture—is a philosophy of agriculture that shares many ideas and practices with organic and sustainable farming. The concept was first developed in Australia in the 1970s.

Permaculture is an environmental design system that aims to create long-term productive environments that serve many human needs while maintaining the stability and diversity inherent in natural ecosystems. Techniques such as intercropping, mulching, and composting are actively encouraged. An example of a permaculture design is the establishment of a "forest garden," in which various vegetables, shrubs, and fruit trees are grown together and where every plant is carefully chosen to provide a product or benefit. Permaculture designs are not generally applicable to commercial farming, but they demonstrate many important agricultural principles.

A CLOSER LOOK

moisture. Among the materials that can be used are plastic sheeting and crop residues. Some of these materials will also add nutrients to the soil as they rot. Mulching can be used in several ways. For example, straw can be piled around the bases of tomato plants to suppress competing weeds. Alternatively, plastic sheeting can be stretched over a piece of land to kill off existing weeds and prepare the ground for planting using the heat of the sun. Crops can then be planted through small slits cut in the sheet. Organic lettuces are often grown this way.

Companion planting is an organic farming method that is especially suited to horticulture or greenhouse growing. It is based on the ecological principle that plants will grow more vigorously when in association with certain other plants. For example, onions and carrots are often grown alongside each other, because the strong aroma emitted by the onions will mask the aroma of the carrots. The carrot fly, which locates carrots by their scent, is therefore less likely to infest and spoil the carrot crop. Companion planting is basically a variation on the practice of intercropping, where different crops are mixed on the same plot.

If pests become a problem, several organic insecticides exist. Most organic insecticides, including derris and pyrethrum, are made from plant extracts. They are considered less harmful than chemical pesticides because they are less toxic and decompose into harmless compounds soon after their use. Nonetheless, all insecticides are used sparingly, usually only when other methods have failed. Organic growers may also use a biological control—they may introduce a natural predator of a pest organism to the area of cultivation (see BIOLOGICAL CONTROL). For example, whitefly can be controlled in greenhouses by the introduction of a parasitic wasp.

Profitability

Organic agriculture nearly always produces lower yields than its conventional equivalent. For example, wheat yields are typically 25 percent lower. Despite this reduction in yield, however, organic farming can be at least as profitable as any other method. Organic methods have lower input costs and a different cost structure; organic farmers spend much less on fertilizers and pesticides, but they generally spend more on labor and cultivation compared to conventional farmers. The profitability of organic enterprises is also helped by the fact that their products can fetch higher prices than produce that is farmed conventionally.

SUSTAINABLE AGRICULTURE

Sustainable agriculture aims to produce foodstuffs without depleting soil nutrients over the long term through the establishment of self-sufficient, diverse, and stable farming systems. Emphasis is also placed on the social impact of agricultural activities, and the importance of the farm's contribution to the local community is recognized. Sustainable farmers aim to produce a variety of crops, grown either in a

rotation or intercropped, and some degree of mixed arable and livestock farming is also desirable. Farmers aim to minimize the use of inputs from outside the farm environment where possible. For example, plant residues can be recycled as compost, which is used as a replacement for chemical fertilizers. Similarly, seeds are saved from the harvest to plant the following year.

Workers feeding conifer branches into a shredding machine. The resulting wood chips will be spread over the ground to enrich the soil and prevent weeds from growing—a process called mulching.

Sustainable agriculture in practice

Many of the techniques used in sustainable agriculture are similar or even identical to organic methods, and many sustainably farmed enterprises are certified organic farms. However, sustainable agriculture does not have any specific standards, and it is broader and more general in scope than organic farming. Many groups have been established to promote the practice of sustainable farming, and there are several research programs in U.S. universities, including the University of California, Davis, and Michigan State University, that are dedicated to the improvement of its methods.

These farmers are harvesting soybeans on an organic farm in Illinois. In sustainable agriculture, human labor supplements or replaces machinery whenever possible.

Sustainable techniques

Sustainable agriculture seeks to reduce its nonrenewable energy inputs, especially fossil fuels. Minimizing the use of agrochemicals is important, because their industrial production consumes significant quantities of energy (see CHEMICAL INDUSTRY, INORGANIC). On-farm energy consumption is also kept as low as possible, and the use of mechanized equipment is kept to a minimum. In many cases, human labor is used instead. For example, seed placement may be done by teams of planters rather than by a tractor-drawn drill machine. Horses and other draft animals may be used to pull plows and other implements on some farms (see HORSE-DRAWN TRANSPORT; PLOW).

On-farm technologies can also help to reduce energy requirements. An example is the decomposition of manure slurry to produce methane-rich gas, which can be burned to heat greenhouses or other farm buildings. This often takes place in a small methane digester, where slurry is stored in an airtight tank, and the gas (a mixture of methane and carbon dioxide) is collected and stored in a second tank. Gas is piped away from this tank for use, and the decomposed slurry is used as fertilizer.

Modern irrigation projects require energy to construct (see IRRIGATION AND LAND DRAINAGE), and natural water supplies may be depleted by high levels of water extraction. Therefore, sustainable farmers prefer to use small-scale local irrigation designs, choosing crops that do not require high levels of irrigation and using techniques such as mulching to retain soil moisture. Rainwater can be collected and stored in tanks to supplement irrigation supplies by installing gutters on farm buildings.

Transporting farm produce is another costly and energy-demanding activity. Reducing transportation requirements by seeking out local markets in which to sell farm produce is one solution to this problem. Many smaller farmers have made a concerted effort to form links with local consumers, such as by the establishment of a farmers market, where farmers sell their produce directly to the end consumer. The absence of intermediaries increases the farmer's profits and keeps prices low. Where long-distance transport cannot be avoided, fuel and labor costs can be pooled by forming a transport cooperative with other local farmers, whose goods can all be shipped together. Similar cooperative arrangements can be formed to share the costs of buying equipment, building and maintaining storage sites for bulk commodities such as grain, or processing produce.

Profitability

Sustainable agriculture aims to be economically and environmentally sustainable. Large capital inputs, which most farmers can obtain only by taking out loans, are avoided; the farm instead attempts to finance its operations using nothing but its own profits. There is thus no requirement to make a large profit to repay large loans, and so a sustainable farm can survive with much lower profit margins than those needed by an intensive farm.

T. ALLMAN

See also: AGRICULTURAL SCIENCE; AGRICULTURE, HISTORY OF; AQUACULTURE; ARABLE FARMING; BIOLOGICAL CONTROL; CHEMICAL INDUSTRY, INORGANIC; ENERGY RESOURCES; FERTILIZER; FOOD PRESERVATION; GENETIC ENGINEERING; HORSE-DRAWN TRANSPORT; IRRIGATION AND LAND DRAINAGE; LIVESTOCK FARMING; PESTICIDE AND HERBICIDE; PLANT BREEDING AND PROPAGATION; PLANT HORMONE; POLLUTION AND ITS CONTROL; SOIL SCIENCE; WASTE DISPOSAL, RECYCLING, AND COMPOSTING.

Further reading:
Newton, J. *Profitable Organic Farming.* Cambridge, Massachusetts: Blackwell Scientific Publications, 1995.

SUBSISTENCE FARMING

Millions of people—mainly in tropical regions in the developing world—survive by subsistence agriculture. Subsistence farming does not aim to produce crops to sell but to supply the needs of those tending the plot—often a single family living on the land. Any surplus produce is traded for essential equipment or for food that cannot be grown on site.

Subsistence farming is characterized by a high diversity of crops grown in a relatively small plot, either in rotation or by intercropping. Livestock are common, especially poultry and pigs, which can feed off waste products or forage for themselves. The crop diversity must produce a year-round supply of food, and also allow the farmer to cope with the failure of any one crop. Labor requirements on the plot are broadly continuous throughout the year.

Traditional farms are self-sufficient and sustainable by necessity, because external inputs are usually very limited. Subsistence farmers use a range of simple technologies appropriate to the local conditions to enable them to obtain the maximum diversity of products from their smallholdings. Subsistence farms often achieve reasonable productivity, supporting those who farm them for years.

A CLOSER LOOK

OUTPUT AND DISPLAY DEVICE

Electron tubes and flat-panel technologies are used to display alphanumeric characters and images

Displays for viewing computer output and other visual information are ubiquitous in modern life. Computers are now incorporated into all kinds of equipment, so the requirements for size, shape, cost, ruggedness, and other attributes of the display device have become more diverse. This has driven the development of many new technologies for visual information displays (see COMPUTER).

Display devices can be compared in terms of their visual and technical characteristics. The format may be either portrait (page) mode, in which the display is taller than it is wide; or landscape mode, the standard television format, in which the reverse is true. A few specialized displays use a square format, and some computer monitors can be physically rotated to switch between the portrait and landscape formats. The overall size of a display may range from the 3-inch (8-cm) screens of pocket televisions to projection displays suitable for theaters and stadiums. The aspect ratio of a display is the ratio of the width of the display to its height.

All types of displays, from the earliest television sets to the latest flat-screen displays, create pictures in much the same way. Letters, numbers, and other characters are built up from groups of dots known as picture elements, or pixels. Each pixel can be turned on or off (addressed). For color displays, the pixels each consist of three sub-pixels: red, green, and blue. These are the primary colors of light, which can be combined to produce the desired hue.

Electron tube displays

Several types of display devices are based on the electron tube. In a glass vacuum tube, an electric current is applied to a filament heater that warms the nearby cathode (negative electrode) to the point where electrons start to escape from its surface. A high voltage is applied between the cathode and anode (positive electrode), which attracts those electrons toward the cathode and accelerates them to a high speed. The movement of the charged particles may be controlled with electrostatic or magnetic lenses, which can change the direction of the beam. When the

A U.S. Special Forces soldier uses a laptop computer designed to be used in the field. The screen uses a liquid crystal display.

electrons pass through or strike some types of materials, the material's molecules become excited and emit light in a phenomenon called luminescence.

If the luminescence occurs in a gas contained in the tube, the device is called a gas-discharge display. These include the familiar neon signs and the numeric display tubes of the early 1960s, in which individual neon elements could be used to form the digits 0–9. Plasma display panels are sturdy gas-discharge devices that are often used in military applications. They contain transparent, individually addressable conductive elements in the shape of the characters to be displayed. These elements are sandwiched between two glass plates along with the gas.

Cathode-ray tube. The cathode-ray tube (CRT) is best known as the central element in television sets. Electrons are given off by a heated cathode at the back of the tube, then accelerated and steered along the tube of a widening cross section until they hit the inside of a screen at the front. This is coated with a crystalline material called a phosphor, which luminesces wherever it is hit by the beam. In color television receivers and monitors, there are separate phosphors for red, green, and blue (see TELEVISION).

Since the 1950s, engineers have been striving to develop flat CRT displays, the goal being a television that could be hung on the wall like a picture. Some of these devices are based on a thin tube in which the phosphor is parallel to the electron beam, and the beam is deflected by 90 degrees at the last moment to strike the screen. This tends to produce considerable picture distortion, which requires additional circuitry to correct. Some of the flat CRT research programs have been dropped because other flat-panel technologies—particularly liquid crystal display (LCD) devices (see box on page 958)—have now been developed.

CORE FACTS

- Display screens may be monochrome, gray scale, or color.
- Pixels are the individually addressable groups of dots, or picture elements, in an image display.
- Many older display devices are based on the electron tube, including the cathode-ray tubes (CRTs) used in televisions and computer monitors.
- Semiconductor and liquid-crystal technologies have become preeminent in electronic displays and small flat-panel screens.

CONNECTIONS

- The latest technology used in **PHOTOGRAPHY** allows images to be displayed instantly on a **COMPUTER** screen.

- Three-dimensional images can be displayed using **HOLOGRAPHY**.

During his visit to Mexico in 1999, Pope John Paul II addressed a crowd of 120,000 on a giant video screen at the Azteca stadium in Mexico City.

Vacuum fluorescent devices. Vacuum fluorescent devices are simple variants of the CRT in which a small tube and low-voltage phosphor are used, generally to produce an alphanumeric display. Bright and inexpensive, these were popular in electronics products, such as pocket calculators and alarm clocks, but they have now been largely supplanted by LCDs.

Field-emission display. In a field-emission display (FED) each pixel has a tiny cathode; the screen serves as the anode. When a high voltage is applied to a cathode, an electric field results that attracts electrons from that cathode to the screen. The cathodes do not need to be heated, which reduces the power consumption of the device.

Electroluminescent displays. Electroluminescent displays do not use electron beams. Instead, they are essentially light-emitting capacitors, two flat electrodes (at least one transparent) with a layer of phosphor between them. When a voltage is applied across the electrodes, the phosphor luminesces. Commercial applications of electroluminescent devices have been limited by their cost and power consumption. However, they have been used in military and industrial applications because they are rugged, and because their efficient yellow phosphor corresponds to the color to which the human eye is most sensitive.

Semiconductor displays

Light-emitting diodes (LEDs) are semiconductor devices that are bright, inexpensive, use relatively little power, and generate little heat. They first became available as small on-off indicators and quickly replaced the incandescent bulb for most such applications. The first LEDs were red, but soon green and yellow were developed (the three stop-light colors are ideal for instrument displays).

Some of the earliest LEDs had seven linear elements in a rectangle—two on each side and one each at the top, middle, and bottom of the rectangle; they could represent the numbers 0–9 and most letters of the alphabet. Red LED displays were widely used in electronic calculators until they were largely replaced by LCDs, which use even less power. LEDs still sometimes supplement them for viewing in darkness. Larger arrays of LEDs are used in signs for advertising, traffic messages, or other information that must be changed periodically.

Special displays

Besides computer displays and alphanumeric readouts, displays have been built to address many special needs. Virtual reality headset displays are worn close to the eyes and are designed to make users feel they are located inside a computer-generated scene. At the other extreme, video displays hundreds of square feet in area are used in arenas. The brightness required for outdoor displays is often achieved by using removable modules of red, green, and blue display tubes as the individually addressable pixels.

S. CALVO

See also: COLOR; COMPUTER GRAPHICS; ELECTRON TUBE; ELECTRONICS; IMAGING TECHNOLOGY; TELEVISION AND COMPUTER MONITOR.

Further reading:
Electro-Optical Displays. Edited by M. Karin. New York: Marcel Dekker, 1992.

LIQUID CRYSTAL DISPLAYS

Liquid crystals are composed of long organic molecules that tend to align themselves parallel to each other. When an electric field is applied, the molecules change alignment, and light passing through the material becomes polarized. A liquid crystal display is constructed by sandwiching the material between transparent electrodes and polarized film. Images are formed by polarizing selected segments (pixels) of the display at ninety degrees to the polarization of the film, thus causing those pixels to appear black. Pixel elements each containing red, green, and blue filters are used to produce color LCD displays.

LCDs have overtaken even cathode-ray tubes (CRTs) in popularity because of their thinness, low cost, light weight, and low power consumption. Laptop and even palm-top computers with LCD screens have completely replaced the early suitcase-sized portable computers with their small CRTs and made mobile computing a practical option. LCD readouts are found in all sorts of instrumentation and consumer electronics.

LCD screens cannot yet compete with CRTs for mass-market home television receivers because large, bright LCD screens are still difficult and expensive to produce, and the viewing angle is somewhat restricted. But they are likely to increase in popularity as advances in manufacturing technology and increased competition bring down their cost still further.

A CLOSER LOOK

PACKAGING INDUSTRY

Packaging is the process of enclosing a commodity for safe and convenient storage, transportation, and sale

Packaging began with the onset of commerce. Initially its use was mainly limited to commodities such as wines and other liquids that could only be transported in containers of some kind. The earliest packaging methods involved containers made of skins and clay, and glass bottles.

With the introduction of mass production during the Industrial Revolution in the 18th century, the packaging of products took on a new significance and economic importance. Factory owners found it necessary to set up packaging departments and to devote staff exclusively to the business of packing up manufactured goods for transport and safe storage. Packaging materials and methods changed and improved systematically with the ongoing development of other technologies, particularly materials technology, and also began to develop technologies of its own. Today, packaging has become a major industry in its own right, involving costs to companies of billions of dollars annually.

Purposes of packaging

At each stage of the packaging process, secure means of identification or coding of the contents must be provided. The goods must be protected from the risks of damage from rough handling during transportation and from environmental hazards during storage and movement, including moisture, unduly high or low temperatures, exposure to air and light, and contact with harmful microorganisms or with corrosive or contaminating chemicals. Packaging must satisfy these requirements at a cost that is only a small proportion of the value of the contained goods.

Stages of the packaging process

Packaging methods vary with the nature of the product to be packaged and are influenced by such factors as its weight, bulk, fragility, and intrinsic value. Different packaging methods are also required depending on whether the goods are solids, liquids, or gases, and whether they will be handled by humans or machines.

In a food warehouse, a forklift truck is used to transport cans filled with fruit cocktail.

The general packaging process usually comprises three separate stages:

Primary packaging. The first stage is primary packaging. This is the process of separating the bulk commodities into individual packeted quantities of an appropriate size for selling to individuals. The primary packaging must be filled, sealed, and labeled appropriately. The primary packaging of drinks involves sealing the liquid inside bottles or cans.

Secondary packaging. The next stage is to collect the primary packaging into larger, secondary, packages of suitable size for short-term storage by the retailer. The secondary packaging of drinks involves packaging groups of bottles or cans together in cardboard boxes or trays.

Tertiary packaging. The secondary packages are collected into still larger units of appropriate size and weight for bulk handling, storing, and shipping. This stage is tertiary packaging.

Paper and cardboard packaging

By far the most widely used material for packaging is cardboard. The United States is the world's largest producer of paper and paper products. Slightly more than half of all U.S. paper production is consumed in converted paper products such as cardboard containers and boxes (see PAPER AND PAPERMAKING). Cardboard containers are produced in a very large range of sizes, shapes, and strengths. Almost half of them are required for the storage and transport of primarily packed food products. In small, simple cartons, the cardboard is usually solid, but larger

CORE FACTS

- Packaging has several functions: to protect goods during handling; to divide bulk commodities into quantities of suitable size for storage, distribution, and retailing; to identify the goods through labeling; and to attract purchase.
- Packaging commonly involves three stages, known as primary, secondary, and tertiary packaging.
- Packaging materials include paper and cardboard, plastic, wood, metal, and expanded polystyrene.
- Standardized steel containers are now used to transport bulk goods in specialized vehicles.

CONNECTIONS

- Plastic sheeting is sometimes used to package bales of hay for **FARM STORAGE**.

- Labeling on primary packaging usually features brightly designed **PRINTING** to attract customers.

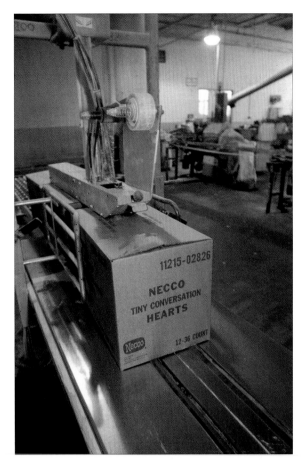

A machine applies adhesive tape to secure cardboard boxes containing candy.

around a mandrel, then, while the lining remains on the mandrel, wrap the outer cardboard around the mandrel and glue its side and bottom end. The double-layer carton is then moved to the filling point.

Other packaging materials

Other common materials for packaging include wood, plastics, glass, and metals such as aluminum and tin-plated steel.

Wood packaging. Wood crates have traditionally been used for packaging goods weighing more than 220 lbs (100 kg) per item. Since the development of forklifts, however, wood pallets have largely replaced crates. This change has been associated with the widespread use of tough plastic sheeting to hold heavy and bulky items together. Building materials, such as bricks, and other similar products are now commonly packaged in this way.

Plastic packaging. Plastics are used in enormous quantities to make a wide range of containers of all sizes for packaging liquids and other types of loose materials (see PLASTICS). The use of plastics for containers has substantially replaced other materials such as tinplate for commodities ranging from perishable foods to highly corrosive liquids. Squeezable plastic tubes are used to hold toothpaste, pharmaceutical creams and ointments, cosmetics, and other substances. Plastics in foam or expanded form are extensively used for protective purposes in packaging (see the box on page 962). Food packaging includes microwavable containers and breathable plastic to keep vegetables fresh.

Glass packaging. Glass containers have also been largely replaced by plastic containers. However, glass is still used to package some liquids and other loose products. Glass bottles and jars can be cheaply produced in large quantities by molding machines and can be reused or recycled. They are resistant to corrosives and are suitable for packaging foodstuffs and cosmetics (see GLASS AND GLASSMAKING).

Metal packaging. Tin-plated steel cans are still widely used, mainly for foods but also for paints, varnishes, polishes, waxes, and aerosol sprays. Thin-walled aluminum cans are used for packaging beers and soft drinks (see BEVERAGE; METALS).

cartons are made tougher and more durable by using corrugated and laminated cardboard. Cardboard for containers has notable advantages as a packaging material. It has a high ratio of strength to weight, can easily be printed upon, and is widely available in flat, precut sheets that are folded into shape. Cardboard also readily lends itself to the production of boxes by ingenious cutting designs.

Manufacturers of cardboard containers supply their products as piles of flat precut blanks. In some cases the blanks are pre-glued. These are assembled at the packing point, either by hand, often using shaping forms (mandrels), or by machine. Blanks are commonly cut in such a way as to allow containers to be assembled from single sheets without the use of adhesives or adhesive tape. This is done using shaped tabs that lock together when folded in the correct sequence. Machines are often used to assemble such containers in high-speed mechanical packing. Glues, adhesive tapes, and heavy-duty staples are commonly used in the forming and sealing of large containers.

Many of the lighter cartons, such as milk cartons, are designed exclusively for machine handling. Pre-glued blanks can be packed into a magazine in a carton-forming machine. The blanks then pass through machines that open them, fold the bottom ends, and heat-seal them by melting the pre-applied glue. The carton is then filled with the intended product, and the top end is heat-sealed. In this way, hundreds of cartons are processed each minute.

More elaborate double-layer cartons such as those used for breakfast cereals require even more complex machines. These form the inner lining

Filling primary packaging

Except in very small-scale production plants, filling primary packaging with the appropriate goods is now almost entirely automated. Vacuum suction or controlled flow under gravity can be used to fill containers with liquids and granular solids. Filling machines are commonly custom designed for the particular material and can achieve rapid rates of container filling. Drink cans can be filled by a single machine at a rate of up to 2000 cans per minute. Small cartons or bags can be filled with dry, powdered material at a rate of over 1000 per minute. Viscous materials, such as syrups or honey, are necessarily filled much more slowly.

Filling machines may operate by weighing the quantity of product before filling. Rapid methods of

electronic weighing with automatic control of flow can be used to speed up the process. Machines may also weigh the container and contents together, then move the container on or shut off the supply when the appropriate weight is reached.

Closing and sealing

Glass packaging uses a variety of closures, including screw-caps, twist-off caps for jars, and crowns—the metal caps that are crimped onto the bottle and require a bottle opener for removal. These are sealed over the mouth of the filled containers by machines that perform a series of operations as the container moves on a carousel (a belt that moves around the machine; see the picture above).

Materials for inner bag linings can be sealed by applying heat and pressure. Many cartons are laminated with a plastic material that is adhesive when hot, then closed by the application of heat and pressure. Other cartons are closed by more conventional gluing, either with wet glue or with adhesives that are active when heated.

Most metal food cans are either three piece (a cylindrical body to which two round ends are attached) or two piece (a cup-shaped body that needs only one end). In either case, the end is attached by first forming a flange on the mouth of the body. The end is then put in place and a sealed by a machine that rolls the edge of the end over the flange and then flattens the resulting seam against the side of the body. In the case of three-piece cans, one end is applied before the contents are filled.

Labeling

Labeling is also usually fully automated. Cans are rolled over pre-glued paper labels, and sticky labels are often mechanically applied or blown by air onto plastic containers. Bottles may be pre-labeled in the glass plant as part of the molding process or have preprinted expanded polystyrene labeling applied during the bottle production process.

Beverage cans are labeled while empty. The can spins on a mandrel and is brought into contact with a blanket (a curved rubber pad) to which the inks for the design have been applied. The can is then varnished using a roller before being placed on a conveyor that passes through an oven at around 360°F (180°C). The oven hardens the varnish.

Wrapping machines

Wrapping may be a primary, secondary, or tertiary packaging process, and machines are used for all three functions. Items such as cheeses and fresh meats are often packaged by wrapping, which is done by machine. Transparent plastic film is the most common material used and it is sealed by heat.

RECYCLABILITY

Packaging consumes enormous quantities of natural materials that, once used, are commonly discarded as garbage and are thus wasted, either being destroyed by incineration or being buried in landfill (see WASTE DISPOSAL, RECYCLING, AND COMPOSTING). To try to reduce these environmental disadvantages, the packaging industry has begun to make packaging that is easier to recycle. The main materials concerned are paper, glass, plastics, and metals.

Given the will on the part of local authorities, glass, paper, and aluminum can be successfully and economically recycled. However, there is currently little demand for recycled plastics, and the problems and expense of separating waste plastics into the various types make plastic recycling even less economically attractive (see POLLUTION AND ITS CONTROL).

WIDER IMPACT

Ships loaded with containerized freight in Oakland Docks, California.

In wrapping machines the product itself is usually the mandrel for the wrapping action. Alternatively, thermoform wrapping systems use a flexible or semirigid plastic that is heated to soften the material and then formed by pressure into a cavity. This is then moved to a filling point, where the product is inserted. A seal is created by means of a further sheet of plastic that is applied to close the wrap. Often the air is evacuated from inside the wrapping before the final heat sealing. Speeds of up to 600 wraps per minute are common.

Secondary and tertiary packaging

Secondary packaging is the grouping of primary-packaged items into sets, which are then secured together in a second package. The process need not involve total enclosure. Drink cans are secondarily packaged in packs of four, six, or eight cans by means of plastic ring carriers. These packs are then packed into tough, shallow cardboard trays that are wrapped in a layer of plastic.

Cardboard cartons of many sizes are routinely used to accommodate groups of 12, 18, 20, or 24 bottles or cans. Machines for packing these groups of items may use preformed, open, rectangular-section cardboard tubes. These are erected and the contents to be packed are pushed in from both ends. The ends are then closed and secured shut by gluing or tape sealing. Other systems set up the contents in the manner in which they will occupy the container and then wrap the carton around them.

Tertiary packaging may use larger carboard containers or crates, but, increasingly, shrink-film bundling is being used. Tough plastic sheeting is applied by machine to secure together groups of secondarily packaged items into units of appropriate size for storage and distribution purposes.

Containerization

A major development in packaging is the process of containerization. Since the 1960s, this has become the principal method of international transportation of all types of packaged goods. Containerization can be considered to be quaternary packaging in which the form of the final package is standardized. This standardization is of significant functional and economic importance because it allows solid commodities to be treated as identical units for purposes of handling and movement.

These standardized containers are made from steel. They are commonly 8 ft (2.4 m) wide, 8 ft (2.4 m) tall and range from 20 to 40 ft (6 to12 m) in length. They can be transported by road, rail, or sea in vehicles specially designed to carry them, either singly or in large numbers. Containerization for road or railroad transportation began early in the 20th century, but the method did not become widespread until the second half of the century when its advantages began to be appreciated for large-scale movement of goods by sea. Designing ships specifically for container transportation has made this a major feature of oceangoing trade. These bulk carriers transport containers not only in their holds but also on their open decks.

The development of container ships led to the production of massive dockside container-handling equipment to allow exceptionally fast loading and unloading. Container-handling docks also provide facilities for the rapid movement of containers, mainly by road vehicles, to and from the loading and unloading points (see OIL TANKER AND BULK CARRIER).

R. YOUNGSON

See also: DESIGN, INDUSTRIAL; ERGONOMICS; FOOD PRESERVATION; MECHANICAL HANDLING; RETAIL INDUSTRY TECHNOLOGY.

Further reading:
Active Food Packaging. Edited by M. L. Rooney. New York: Blackie Academic & Professional, 1995.

EXPANDED POLYSTYRENE

Expanded polystyrene is one of the most successful packing and protective materials ever developed. Polystyrene—a synthetic polymer—is an excellent electrical and thermal insulator and is resistant to attack by acids and alkalis (see ACID AND ALKALI). Polystyrene is a thermoplastic material with a low melting point. Small pellets of it can be impregnated with the volatile substance isopentane. When these are heated in a suitable mold, the isopentane evaporates, the plastic partially melts, expands, and foams, and the pellets fuse together to form expanded, or foamed, polystyrene. In this way very low-density packing items or containers can be formed quickly and cheaply to any required shape.

Expanded polystyrene is tougher than unexpanded polystyrene. It is compressible and so provides cushioning against shocks. It is readily molded into shapes to fit around complex equipment while forming an outer shape that can fit securely into a strong carton. This combination provides excellent protection to delicate products such as personal computer monitors, hi-fi equipment, and other domestic goods. A principal disadvantage of custom-made expanded polystyrene packaging material is that its resistance to degradation by biological action makes it an environmental pollutant. An example of biodegradable packaging is biodegradable cornstarch, which is used for packing peanuts.

A CLOSER LOOK

PAINT AND SURFACE COATING

Paint and other coating substances are used to decorate and protect surfaces

Paint and other surface coatings, such as varnish or enamel, form a barrier between a surface and its surroundings. Originally for mainly decorative purposes, surface coatings are used today as much for their protective properties as for their appearance. Buildings, vehicles, and furniture that are painted, varnished, or otherwise coated look better and last longer than those that are left in their natural state.

PAINT

Paint is a suspension of solid pigment in a liquid known as the vehicle. A suspension is not the same as a solution—the pigment particles are distributed among the vehicle but not dissolved in it. The vehicle is made up of a polymer, known as the binder or film former, and a solvent. The binder produces a continuous film that adheres, or sticks, to the surface being painted and holds the pigment in place. The solvent reduces the viscosity of the paint so that it flows more easily (see PLASTICS).

CORE FACTS

- Surface coatings, such as paint, make a barrier between a surface and its environment.
- Paint consists of pigment suspended in a polymeric vehicle that is either dissolved or dispersed in a solvent or in water.
- The vehicle spreads the paint over the surface, while the pigment covers and obscures it.
- Surface coatings include enamels, lacquers, polishes, and varnishes.

The history of paint

Paint has been used for a very long time. Cave paintings found in Lascaux, France, and Altamira, Spain, date from at least 15,000 B.C.E. They show hunting scenes painted in yellow, brown, red, and black. The paints used were probably charcoal and colored ores mixed with water and animal fats.

The Chinese made pigments by heating mixtures of plant material and inorganic compounds c.6000 B.C.E. By 1500 B.C.E. the Egyptians had discovered indigo and madder—blue and red dyes derived from plants. These were mixed with substances such as albumen (egg white), beeswax, gelatin, and gum arabic to make them spread and stick to surfaces.

In about 200 B.C.E. the Chinese used cellulose derivatives from the sap of the sumac tree, *Rhus verniciflua,* to make the first lacquers. Linseed was known by the Romans as a medium for dispersing pigments to make paints, but the widespread use of linseed oil and white lead oxide for making protective coatings only started in the 17th century.

The composition of paints today

The basic composition of paint has changed little over the years. What has changed is the nature of the components. Paints also include a number of additives—chemicals that improve the application characteristics of the liquid paint or the properties of the finished film of dried paint.

Pigments. The pigment provides the color of the paint, obscures the original surface, and contributes to the protective action of the paint. The most important pigments are white, and for many years

CONNECTIONS

● The Egyptians were the first to discover indigo, a plant extract, which they used in **DYES AND DYEING** to produce a blue **COLOR**.

● The majority of **COLORANTS AND PIGMENTS** are now based on copper or iron oxides.

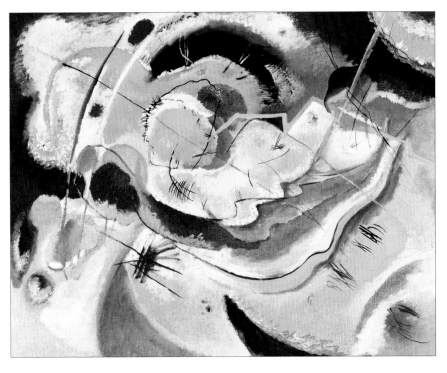

Improvisation ("Little Painting With Yellow"), by Russian artist Wassily Kandinsky (1866–1944) in 1914, shows the enormous range of colors available in oil paint.

white lead oxide was used. However, lead oxide has now been removed from most paint because of its toxicity. Modern white and pastel-colored paints now contain titanium oxide as the main pigment. Reds, yellows, and greens were also provided by toxic lead compounds and chromate salts. Most of these have now been replaced by pigments based on iron or copper oxides. Phthalocyanines are green and blue pigments; carbon in the form of fine soot is used to provide black (see COLORANTS AND PIGMENTS).

Extenders. Expensive pigments are often supplemented with cheap, semitransparent solids known as extenders. Careful use of these increases the solid content of the paint, making it more resistant to wear without diluting the pigment's coloring effect. Talc, mica, and kaolin are typical extenders.

Binders. The choice of binder depends on the paint's intended field of application, since it is the binder that forms the film in the final paint. The final covering's flexibility, hardness, and resistance to wear are mainly due to the properties of the binder.

The most common binders are alkyds—polyester resins made from natural oils such as linseed, soybean, castor, and coconut oils. The exact properties of these resins can vary considerably between oil types and even batches of the same type. High-performance paints have binders made of synthetic polymers—commonly acrylics, polyurethanes, synthetic polyesters, and epoxies (compounds containing an oxygen atom bonded in a triangular structure with two carbon atoms)—that can be tailored to the uses of the paint and manufactured more reliably than natural-oil-based polymers.

Solvents. The main function of the solvents in a paint is to reduce the viscosity (thickness and stickiness) of the binder resin sufficiently for the paint to be applied by brush, spray, or other means. Typical solvents include hydrocarbons, ethers, esters, and alcohols (see SOLVENT, INDUSTRIAL). The solvents evaporate after the paint has been applied.

The solvent blend must be well matched to the binder so that the paint retains its properties for a period of at least six months under typical storage conditions. The solvents must keep the pigment and resin well dispersed during this time, and should not react with other components of the paint. Otherwise viscosity or color changes could occur. Finally, the solvent blend should make the paint dry quickly enough to avoid running while remaining liquid long enough to flow evenly over the surface.

Water-based paints—formulations in which a substantial part of the solvent blend is water—are gaining importance because of their reduced content of often harmful and polluting solvents. Since few resins dissolve in water, most water-based paints are made using an emulsion—a dispersion of resin in water. A small amount of solvent is needed to help the resin form a continuous film.

Additives. Paints contain small percentages of specialty chemicals that perform a variety of functions. Dryers are catalysts that promote reactions between the film-forming components of the paint, making it dry and harden more rapidly (see CATALYST, INDUSTRIAL). Surfactants—chemicals similar in function to detergents—make the paint spread more effectively, improve the smoothness of the surface, and suppress the formation of bubbles. Waxes can improve scratch resistance, while flame retardants help to resist fire. Water-based paints often contain biocides to help prevent attack by fungi or bacteria.

Types and uses of paint

Paints may be classified according to the type of resin they contain, since this has the most direct influence on the suitability of the paint for an application.

HOW PAINT IS MANUFACTURED

Paint manufacture normally starts with a solution of the main film-forming resin in solvent or water. Pigment and other solids, such as wax powders, are added to the resin solution in a high-speed disperser, which is like a large kitchen blender. The pasty mixture of pigment and resin solution at this stage is known as the grind base. It consists mainly of pigment aggregates dispersed in a resin solution.

In order to obtain a good gloss and the full coloring potential of the pigment, the individual pigment particles have to be separated. This can be done in a ball mill, which is a large metal barrel mounted on its horizontal axis. The ball mill is partly filled with ceramic balls that tumble over each other as the mill rotates. The pigment suspension is ground between the tumbling balls, and the mill is left to rotate for a number of hours until the pigment particles are fully dispersed.

An alternative to the ball mill is the sand mill, which is a metal cylinder loaded with sand. A rotating shaft passes through the center of the cylinder, and metal disks on the shaft agitate the sand. The grind base is fed in at one end, and the pigment particles are separated by being ground between the moving sand grains. A filter at the other end holds back the sand but allows the dispersed grind base to pass out of the cylinder. The dispersed grind base is then made into paint by adding any remaining resins and additives, together with enough solvent to "let down" the paint to its final viscosity.

A CLOSER LOOK

There are three main fields of application for paints as protective coatings: Architectural paints are used on the inside and outside of buildings; these include home decorating paints and wood paints, which provide specialist protection against rot. Industrial paints are used on factory production lines to coat many different types of objects. Finally, specialty coatings are used for tasks that require particular additives. These coatings include ship paints with antifouling compounds to prevent algae buildup, paints used in road markings, and slippery paint to keep burglars from climbing up drainpipes.

There are over a dozen classes of paint resins. Paints containing polyester resins, mainly alkyds, are the most widely used for decorative, industrial, anticorrosion, and wood painting. Paints with acrylic resins are very durable and are used for decorative, automobile, industrial, anticorrosion, and wood painting. Epoxy-based paints have good adhesive properties and resistance to corrosion (see ADHESIVE). They are used for marine, automobile, anticorrosion, flooring, and industrial applications.

How paint is applied

Multiple coats of different paints may be applied to cover a surface. The first coat, known as the primer, aids adhesion to the surface and improves corrosion resistance. The second coat, the undercoat, guarantees a smooth covering, while the topcoat, or finish, is responsible for the final appearance. The topcoat may be gloss, matte, or eggshell (semigloss).

Some paints come in 100 percent powder form, as pigment particles dispersed in a binder without solvent. These paints, known as powder coatings, avoid the use of environmentally harmful solvents. They are applied to metal objects using an electrostatic spray gun, which imparts a negative charge to the powder as it is blown onto the object to be coated. The object, which is grounded, attracts the charged particles through an induced positive charge (see ELECTRICITY AND MAGNETISM). Any spray that misses the target is collected in the spray booth and recycled, so there is practically no wastage. The powder-coated objects are then heated in an oven, where the powder melts and forms a film.

Powder coatings are exceptionally hard and scratch resistant, making them ideal for coating domestic appliances and automobile bodies. The use of current powder coatings is, however, limited by the stippled appearance of the final film, which is unpopular with many consumers.

OTHER SURFACE COATINGS

Vitreous enamel, lacquer, polishes, preservative coatings, sealants, and varnishes are other surface coatings. These are used for a variety of purposes.

Vitreous enamel

Vitreous enamel—or simply enamel—is a thin layer of glass and pigment that is melted onto a metal surface to form a coating. An enamel layer is hard, glossy, and resistant to corrosion, scratching, and

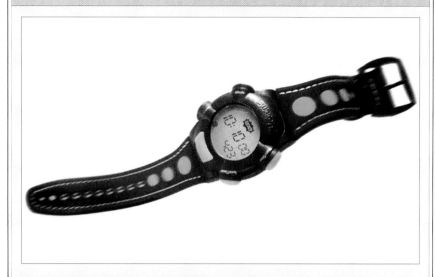

LUMINOUS PAINT

The greenish yellow glow of this luminous watch comes from phosphors.

Paint can be made to glow in the dark by the addition of a substance that emits light. Radium—a radioactive element—was used first in luminous paints to make dials on watches and control instruments on planes. However, radium also causes cancer and was a health hazard to people handling it.

Today, dials and signs that are visible at night are normally made with paints containing phosphors. These are compounds—zinc sulfide and calcium sulfide are examples—that emit visible light for some time after being excited by exposure to ultraviolet radiation.

A CLOSER LOOK

staining. Many household objects, such as bathtubs, washing machines, stoves, and refrigerators, are enameled to increase their durability.

In an enameling process, powdered glass particles of diameter 0.0016–0.0028 in (0.04–0.07 mm) are mixed with clay and water to make a suspension. Chemicals to help the mixture adhere to the metal surface are also added, along with titanium oxide if a white enamel is to be made. This is sprayed over the surface to be coated, which must be completely clean for the enamel to bond effectively to it. The coated object is then baked in a furnace until the surface temperature reaches 1470–1560°F (800–850°C) for a few minutes. During this time, the glass melts and bonds chemically to the metal surface. The object is then cooled. In decorative enameling, pigments of various colors are added to the mixture, which may give a transparent, opaque, or translucent coating.

Lacquer

Lacquer is a solution of a film-forming substance in a volatile solvent that is used to coat wood or metal. When the solvent evaporates, the lacquer hardens and forms a glossy film. It is usually applied in layers and may be colored by adding pigments. The basis for the original Chinese lacquers was a solution of cellulose derivatives obtained from the sap of trees. Synthetic derivatives of cellulose, including nitrocellulose, form the basis of some modern lacquers.

A worker at a cloisonné workshop in Beijing, China, applies enamel paints to a copper vase. In cloisonné, the blocks of different colors are separated by metal wires or strips.

Polishes

Most polishes contain some form of wax and are used to protect surfaces from scratching and staining. Polishes form a hard surface film that can be rubbed to give a smooth, glossy finish that enhances the appearance of the object. They also repel water, which can otherwise cause cracking and swelling in porous materials such as wood.

Waxes are long-chain hydrocarbons that come from organic or mineral origin. Plant waxes used in high-gloss polish include carnauba wax, which comes from a Brazilian palm tree. One of the most commonly used animal waxes is beeswax, found in polishes for wood furniture. Paraffin wax from petroleum is also widely used in polishes.

Preservative coatings

Preservative coatings are used mainly to protect wooden surfaces from fungal attack. Creosote is a complex, tarry mixture of hydrocarbons obtained from coal that may be used to coat wood. Creosote has to be used with care, since some of its components pose a health hazard to humans. Antifouling paint contains chemical agents, such as tributyl tin oxide, that are toxic to marine organisms. Its main use is in coating the hulls of ships to prevent algae or barnacles from accumulating, though it may also be applied to the legs of piers, jetties, and oil platforms. Self-polishing paints guarantee that a permanently smooth finish for the hulls of racing yachts can be created. They gradually dissolve in water so their surface is always fresh and smooth, and this helps to reduce the boat's resistance to motion through water.

Sealants

Sealants are compounds similar to adhesives. They are generally used to fill gaps or joints between surfaces and to join building materials, such as concrete, glass, wood, and steel. A sealant must adhere well to the surfaces that it is applied to, be able to withstand a wide range of temperatures, and block air, dust, and water from entering. The most effective sealants are elastomers (polymer materials that have a rubberlike nature), which are fabricated from silicones, polysulfides, urethanes, and fluoropolymers (materials that contain fluorine atoms and have anticorrosive properties).

Varnishes

A varnish is a transparent liquid that is spread over a surface to form a hard, shiny film when left to dry. It consists of a solution or dispersion of resin in water, oil, or solvent.

Varnishes are used mainly on wood to provide protection and an attractive finish. Their main applications are on floors and furniture and for protecting wooden surfaces on boats—all areas that receive heavy use and suffer abrasion. They are similar to lacquers, except that the polymers in lacquers form a film by evaporation alone, whereas polymers in a varnish also become linked together in a reaction with oxygen from the air. Historically, most varnishes were based on rosin, a polymer taken from dried pinewood. However, modern varnishes tend to be made with synthetic resins, which can be formulated according to requirements and are less likely to crack over time.

S. ALDRIDGE

See also: ACID AND ALKALI; CORROSION.

Further reading:

Morgans, M. W. *Outlines of Paint Technology.* New York: Halsted Press, 1990.
Principles of Paint Formulation. Edited by R. Woodridge. New York: Chapman & Hall, 1991.

PAPER AND PAPERMAKING

Paper is a writing and packaging material made by processing wood, rags, straw, and other fibers

At a paper mill, the quality and consistency of the paper coming off the production line is checked by a production technician. In the papermaking industry, quality-control checks made by experienced people with a trained eye are as vital as automated methods.

The United States is the world's largest producer of paper, pulp, and paper products, followed by Japan. Each person in the United States consumes approximately 675 pounds (304 kg) of paper a year. It is used for the 350 million magazines, 2 billion books, and 24 billion newspapers read in the United States every year.

HISTORY OF PAPERMAKING

Paper is an ancient invention, but except for the introduction of automation the basic processes have changed little over the last 1900 years.

CORE FACTS

- The word *paper* comes from *papyrus*, the reed used by the ancient Egyptians as a writing surface.
- Paper began to be made in great quantities to satisfy the demand for books after the invention of printing with movable metal type.
- The first papermaking mill was opened in the United States in 1690 by German papermaker William Rittenhouse in Philadelphia, Pennsylvania.
- Until the 19th century most paper was made from the cotton and linen fibers of rags. Today, wood pulp from harvested trees or waste lumber is the most common raw material used to make paper.
- Paper is made of many small, separate fibers, usually cellulose, enmeshed to make sheets.

Early history

The invention of paper is attributed to the Chinese, although the precise date is unknown. The person usually credited with inventing papermaking is Ts'ai Lun (c.50–c.118 C.E.) in China in 105 C.E. He made paper from mulberry tree bark, bamboo, and fish nets, and was the first person to write down the process he used. This knowledge was kept secret and remained with the Chinese until about 600 C.E., when it spread to Korea, then Japan, and later Arabia. During the next one hundred years knowledge of the process began to spread westward, mainly along the silk and trade routes, until it reached the city of Samarkand, now in Uzbekistan, in about 750 C.E. Gradually, with the expansion of Arab domination through the countries around the Mediterranean, papermaking spread into Europe. By 1009 the process was known in Spain and Morocco. During the next two or three centuries, Italy, France, and Germany also began papermaking, and it had spread to England by 1488. The first English factory for making paper was set up in 1490. However, papermaking did not begin in North America for another two centuries.

One of the greatest spurs to the spread of papermaking was the invention of printing by movable metal type, which was pioneered by Johannes Gutenberg (1400–1468) in Germany c.1450. Gutenberg's invention led to many more books being printed and many more people learning how to read.

CONNECTIONS

- In the early days of papermaking, a natural source of running water was required to wash the fibers used in the process and to provide the **WATER POWER** for the mill.

- The development of the **PRINTING** industry led to a vast increase in literacy as the production of more books gave the means and motivation to read.

Papyrus showing the Book of the Dead of Heruben: Working in the Fields.

Philadelphia. The site and some of the buildings (although not the mill) have been preserved. The Rittenhouse mill remained the only mill in America until 1710, when a relation of Rittenhouse's established another mill nearby.

Following the Revolutionary War (1775–1783), the number of paper mills continued to grow until, by 1810, there were 185. In order to identify where paper was made, it became a convention to bundle it in set amounts (reams) using a wrapper printed with a picture of the mill; this convention is still followed today. During the following hundred or more years, the papermaking industry continued to grow and became more mechanized.

From handmade to machine-made paper

Until the end of the 18th century, all paper was made by hand. This is a slow and laborious process, although it can produce paper of very fine quality. The first papermaking machine was invented in 1798 by Nicholas-Louis Robert (1761–1828), a Frenchman. In Robert's machine, a hand crank was used to turn a pair of squeezing cylinders, which pressed out the water from the paper and produced a continuous roll rather than single sheets. Unfortunately, Robert was unable to interest investors in his machine, but the brothers Henry and Sealy Fourdrinier, who were part of an English papermaking family, heard about it. They employed an engineer named Bryan Donkin, who had experimented with papermaking and printing, to develop their own machine, and it was patented in 1807. Papermaking machines are still known as fourdriniers (see box on page 965).

The first fourdrinier to be used in the United States was imported from England and erected in Saugerties, New York, in 1827. Following that, American mechanic George Spafford and his partner James Phelps built a fourdrinier machine in Connecticut, which was completed in May 1829. The first cylinder-type paper machine had been invented by English papermaker John Dickinson in 1809. Unlike a fourdrinier, which forms the wet pulp into paper on a flat mesh of wire, a cylinder machine builds up the pulp on a cylinder of mesh. This idea also crossed the Atlantic to the United States: Thomas Gilpin constructed the first cylinder machine in America at Brandywine Creek, Pennsylvania. It produced a sheet 30 ft (9.1 m) wide at a rate of 60 ft (18.2 m) per minute and made the production of paper cheaper and faster. This led to a huge increase in the printing and production of books, newspapers, and journals.

A machine for making brown paper bags was invented by Charles Stillwell in 1883. He developed his machine in Philadelphia, near the very first Rittenhouse paper mill.

MAKING PAPER

Paper is made by hand or by machine either from virgin material such as flax or wood pulp or by recycling old rags or previously made paper.

Previously, literacy had been confined to the aristocracy and the monastic orders. Suddenly the ability to read spread throughout Europe, and demand for materials printed on paper began to grow apace. Paper was still made mainly by hand using rags and flax fibers, but the search was now on for alternatives, of which wood pulp was a favorite.

Papermaking in the United States

Papermaking did not begin in the United States until 1690, although it had been introduced to Mexico by Spain more than 100 years earlier. William Rittenhouse (1644–1708), a German papermaker who worked in the Netherlands for many years, was the first papermaker in the United States. Like all papermakers, he sought a place where there was a good supply of old rags to turn into paper and a source of running water to wash the fibers and power the mill. Rittenhouse's mill was established outside

---

DIFFERENT USES OF PAPER

Although the history of papermaking is associated closely with printing, there are many other uses to which paper may be put. For example, it is commonly used for all types of packaging. This includes making paper bags, tissue paper, decorative wrapping paper, and corrugated cardboard. The brown paper bag for carrying groceries is still a reasonably common sight today.

Paper is used to decorate houses, and there is a vast range of wallpapers. These may range from straightforward plain sheets used to hide cracks and imperfections in plaster walls before painting, to highly patterned, thick wallpaper pasted on to the walls as part of the finish. Some special papers may be used to cover old faulty plaster or to strengthen it. Anaglypta—a thick, embossed wallpaper—is a leading trademark for paper used for this purpose. In Japan, paper has been used for centuries for creating walls and screens to divide the interiors of houses into rooms.

WIDER IMPACT

FOURDRINIERS

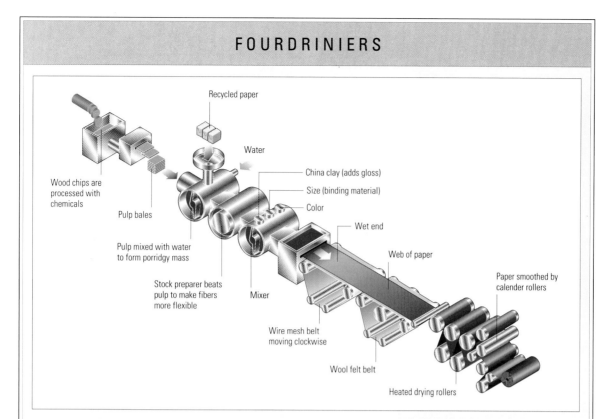

Recycled paper

Water

Wood chips are processed with chemicals

Pulp bales

Pulp mixed with water to form porridgy mass

Stock preparer beats pulp to make fibers more flexible

Mixer

China clay (adds gloss)

Size (binding material)

Color

Wet end

Web of paper

Paper smoothed by calender rollers

Wire mesh belt moving clockwise

Wool felt belt

Heated drying rollers

Fourdrinier's papermaking machine was patented in 1807 and is still the most widely used tool for making paper today. A modern fourdrinier can be 330–660 ft (100–200 m) long and up to 60 ft (20 m) wide; it can produce over 0.6 miles (1 km) of paper every minute it is in operation.

A fourdrinier machine has a wet end and a dry end. At the wet end, wood pulp (roughly 98 percent water) is deposited continuously on a moving horizontal mesh of wire from a vat known as the headbox. As the pulp moves through the machine, water is drained, shaken, and sucked away continuously. When about 20 percent of the water has been removed, the paper fiber is strong enough to pass between squeezing rollers, which extract most of the remaining water. At this stage, a watermark (a pattern embossed in the paper) may be added by a so-called dandy roll. The web, as the forming paper is known, threads its way around perhaps 50 steam-heated rollers called felt dryers (which are actually covered with cotton). Next, it passes through a stack of smoothing rollers known as calenders, after which it is wound onto a continuous reel that can be loaded into a printing press.

A CLOSER LOOK

Handmade paper

Papermaking is still carried out by hand as well as by machine. It can be a very simple process using only basic tools, although great skill is needed in their use to produce a good finished sheet.

Pulp, often made from old rags or directly from flax, is soaked and made ready for use, usually in a large vat of water. The papermaking mold (known as a deckle) is dipped once into the pulp, removed, and shaken by the papermaker in a particular way to ensure that the pulp it holds is spread evenly. The resulting wet sheet of paper is turned out onto a piece of thick felt and another layer of felt is placed on top of it. This sandwich is then pressed to remove excess moisture. The sheet of paper is then removed and hung up to dry.

After this, the dry sheets may be stoned (rubbed by hand) to impart a sheen if required. More commonly, the paper is left in its roughened state, especially if it is to be used for artistic purposes such as hand printing or engraving.

Machine-made paper

The papermaking machines that are used today carry out essentially the same steps but on a much larger scale. Most paper is made from wood pulp, which varies according to its source. Logs from a timber plantation have their bark removed by a machine called a debarker, and then they are cut into small chips and washed.

Next they are heated with a solution of sodium hydroxide and sodium sulfide in an enormous tank, known as a digester. The chips are broken down into wood pulp. This chemical process was developed by German chemist Carl Dahl in 1884. It is known as the kraft process (from the German word *Kraft* meaning "strength"), because it makes pulp stronger by eliminating bark and other unwanted material.

The pulp mush is pumped from the digester into a refining machine that breaks it into individual fibers. The pulp is then washed, screened for impurities, and optionally bleached to make it whiter. (Chlorine dioxide, which has been used to bleach

Paper can be recycled up to eight times. Here, scrap paper is being delivered to a papermill, where it will be used as a raw material.

paper for many years, produces traces of toxic dioxins in the bleaching process, and is gradually being replaced with safer oxygen-based bleaches.)

After this process, it is refined again by beaters, and additives are included, according to the type of paper required. For example, china clay (kaolin) may be added to give the paper glossiness and make it suitable for printing magazines.

The pulp is then ready for papermaking. It is fed into a papermaking machine, where it clings to a horizontal wire screen, despite being mostly water. It is then dried and, as a final step in the process, the sheet is passed between heated rollers to acquire a smooth finish (a process known as calendering) and wound onto a large roll that can later be cut into small sheets. A modern fourdrinier can be more than 330 ft (100 m) long and can produce 3300 ft (1000 m) of paper per minute in a continuous roll.

Recycling paper

It is the paper industry itself that is responsible for most of the recycling that takes place in the United States. But recycling is not as simple as it seems, and paper cannot be recycled indefinitely. After going

through the recycling process for up to eight times at most, the fibers in the paper become too short and weak to be reused.

Much of the paper that claims to be recycled never left the paper mill in the first place: it is simply reused offcuts and rejects. Truly recycled paper (manufactured from salvaged and reused paper, cardboard, and magazines) is known as post-consumer waste. In practice, paper sold as recycled paper or used as packaging is a mixture of reused mill waste and post-consumer waste. Papermakers are often reluctant to increase the proportion of post-consumer waste in their recycled products because collecting, sorting, baling, and transporting it is one of the most expensive parts of recycling. (The rest of the processes needed are highly mechanized and less labor-intensive, which makes them far less costly.) However, after pressure from consumers and bodies such as the Environmental Protection Agency (EPA), recycling has now become a necessary process to reduce the waste sent to landfills (see WASTE DISPOSAL, RECYCLING, AND COMPOSTING).

Once paper has been transported to the mill, the next step in the recycling process is repulping. The bales of sorted waste paper are soaked in large vats, where they disintegrate into fibers. Surfactants (detergents) are added so that, when ink particles start to separate from the paper, they are unable to reattach themselves to the pulp (see CLEANING AGENTS). The pulp is fed through a series of increasingly fine screens, which remove extraneous material (known as "trash"), including floating ink particles. Next, the pulp goes through more cleaning stages in which heat, chemicals, and mechanical action may be used to loosen more ink particles. Finally, the mixture goes into a flotation tank, where calcium soap and other chemicals are added to clean the pulp further. Air bubbles in the mixture float the remaining ink to the surface, where it is skimmed away like fat from the surface of a stew. The clean pulp, free of ink, is treated and loaded into the headbox (feeding hopper) of a papermaking machine. From this point on, the pulp is treated just the same as if it had been freshly made from wood chips rather than recycled.

Old newspapers and magazines are used in different products. Newspapers are used to make tissue and cardboard, while magazines are used to make more newsprint. If the paper was glossy originally, it contains china clay; this is useful in recycling because it helps to separate the ink from the paper.

S. ALDRIDGE

See also: FORESTRY; PACKAGING INDUSTRY; TECHNOLOGY IN ANCIENT CIVILIZATIONS; TEXTILES AND THEIR MANUFACTURE.

Further reading:

Dawson, S. *The Art and Craft of Papermaking.* Asheville, North Carolina: Lark Books, 1996.
Hiebert, H. *Papermaking with Plants: Creative Recipes and Projects Using Herbs, Flowers, Grasses, and Leaves.* Pownal, Vermont: Storey Books, 1998.

ALTERNATIVES TO PAPER

The word *paper* comes from *papyrus*, a reed used by early Egyptians as a writing surface. It was split, pasted in strips, and allowed to dry to form sheets. Other materials used outside Egypt include baked clay tablets, waxed boards, leaves, bronze, and silk. Examples of these writing surfaces have been found in such archaeological sites as Pompeii and Herculaneum in Italy, as well as sites in ancient Troy (in modern Turkey).

By the early Middle Ages (c.700 C.E.), vellum (from calf, kid, or lamb skin) and parchment (mainly form sheepskin) were the most widely used materials. Parchment was used mainly for everyday documents, such as household accounts, messages, and letters. Vellum was reserved for making and writing the beautifully illuminated books and manuscripts produced by the monastic orders.

HISTORY OF TECHNOLOGY

PARACHUTE

A parachute is a fabric canopy that slows the descent of a person or object through the air

When an object is dropped it accelerates through the air due to a force called gravity. The larger the surface area of the object, the slower it falls. This is because a small part of the kinetic energy of the falling object is used to overcome air resistance. Recognizing this principle, Italian artist and scholar Leonardo da Vinci (1452–1519) formulated the first design for a parachute in 1495.

However, it was three hundred years later before the first parachute descent was attempted. In 1783, French chemist and aeronaut Louis-Sébastien Lenormand (1757–1839) jumped from the tower of the Montpellier Observatory, France, holding a 5-ft (1.5-m) umbrella in each hand to slow his descent. Fortunately for Lenormand, his attempt was successful. Fellow French aeronaut André-Jacques Garnerin (1769–1823) perfected a parachute design that he used to land successfully from an exhibition balloon over Paris in 1797. Following his success, Garnerin gave parachute jumping exhibitions throughout northern Europe, including a jump of 8000 ft (2440 m) from a balloon in England in 1802.

Parachuting in the 20th century

In 1912, U.S. inventor Lee Miller was granted a patent on "aerial life-saving devices of the parachute type..." Miller envisioned parachutists saving steeplejacks and others working in high-rise construction, and saw parachutes as essential safety devices for balloonists and pilots. Since then, parachuting has evolved into a challenging sport for civilians and a routine feature of military operations.

Early parachutes were made by stitching together panels of canvas or silk. Cotton has also been used, and most modern parachutes are made using light, strong synthetic fibers, such as nylon. The original hemispherical canopy with a scalloped border is no longer the only form of parachute: modern parachutes come in many shapes, including the rectangular parafoil.

Parachutes open in several ways. In all cases, however, the huge expanse of the canopy traps air and slows the descent of falling objects. Free-fall parachutists pull a rip cord to open the canopy. Static-line parachutes open automatically by a line attached to the aircraft. Automatic parachutes open in response to a timer or a specific air pressure. Parachutes can also be used to slow fast-moving vehicles or aircraft. Parachuting or skydiving is a popular sport. Competition involves precision landings and, in the case of paragliding, seeking the longest flight paths and times (see GLIDER).

Military applications

Parachutes are used by the military to deliver large numbers of personnel and cargo to otherwise inaccessible locations and as an essential life-saving device

A skydiver descends under a hemispherical canopy.

for pilots. Operation Market-Garden in World War II (1939–1945) was the largest airborne invasion in history. It took place September 17, 1944, as more than 50,000 paratroopers from the United States 82nd Airborne Division and troops from Britain and Poland landed in the Netherlands.

Airborne troops use both HALO (high-altitude low-opening) and HAHO (high-altitude high-opening) techniques to reach their targets without alerting the enemy on the ground. These maneuvers can shield troops from both visual and radar observation. HALO involves jumping from aircraft as high as 25,000 ft (7620 m) and free-falling until the last possible moment. HAHO landings use steerable parachutes and global positioning receivers to allow troops to jump from a plane as far as 31 miles (50 km) away from their planned landing position.

J. TEMPLE-DENNETT

See also: AERODYNAMICS; BALLOON AND AIRSHIP; EJECTION SEAT; FLIGHT, HISTORY OF; FLIGHT, PRINCIPLES OF; MILITARY AIRCRAFT; SAFETY SYSTEMS.

Further reading:

Outlaw, B. *FAA Parachute Basics*. Washington, D.C.: Federal Aviation Administration, Regulatory Support Division, 1998.

CONNECTIONS

● Parachute canopies were often made from silk. Since the mid-20th century, however, synthetic **FIBERS** such as nylon were used for their strength and lower cost.

● Some aircraft and **SPACE PROBES** use parachutes as **BRAKE SYSTEMS** when landing.

PARTICLE ACCELERATOR

A particle accelerator increases the kinetic energy of charged atomic or subatomic particles

The European Synchrotron Radiation Facility in Grenoble, France, uses synchrotron radiation emitted as a result of electrons being accelerated around a storage ring. The radiation is emitted in the form of ultraviolet light and X rays.

Particle accelerators are a powerful tool for investigating particles on atomic and subatomic scales. They are used to increase the kinetic energy of particles, which is proportional to the square of their speed. The high-energy particles can then be aimed at a target atom to break it into its constituent parts. The nucleus of an atom is composed of protons and neutrons, while electrons orbit the nucleus. High-energy impacts can break these subatomic particles into quarks and other species.

BASIC PRINCIPLES
Accelerators supply kinetic energy using a powerful electric field. This can be produced between two conductors that have a potential difference in voltage between them. Electron tubes, such as the cathode-ray tube inside television sets, are examples of simple particle accelerators. In these, negatively charged electrons are released from a heated filament called the emitter. The kinetic energy of the electrons is increased by a potential difference between the filament and a target (see ELECTRON TUBE).

Types of particles
Electric fields only affect the speed of particles that have an electric charge. Particle accelerators can accelerate protons and positrons (which are positively charged) and electrons and antiprotons (which are negatively charged). Uncharged particles such as neutrons cannot generally be accelerated.

Energy capability
The energy capability of an accelerator is measured in units called electron volts (eV). One electron volt is equivalent to the amount of energy a charged particle acquires when accelerated across an electrical potential difference of one volt. The standard voltage

in residential circuitry in the United States is 120 volts; this could be harnessed to accelerate a particle to 120 eV. Research accelerators reach thousands, millions, and billions of electron volts (keV, MeV, and GeV, respectively). At least one has produced energies over a trillion electron volts (TeV).

Beam intensity
When comparing accelerators, beam intensity is quoted with energy capability. The beam intensity is the number of particles accelerated per second.

Pulsed and steady beams
Some accelerators produce pulsed beams, others produce steady beams. Accelerators with pulsed beams have another parameter called the duty factor. The duty factor is the percentage of time an accelerator produces a beam.

TYPES OF ACCELERATORS
Accelerators can be classified by whether the particles move in a straight line or follow a circular path.

Linear accelerators
The particles in linear accelerators move in a straight line. There are two basic methods of acceleration:
  Electrostatic acceleration. Electrostatic accelerators use a constant voltage to accelerate particles. The particles are sent from a source supplied with a steady direct current (DC) to a target at ground potential (zero volts). Electron tubes are an example of electrostatic accelerators; they are limited by the size of the potential difference between the source and the target.
  In 1932, British physicist John Cockcroft (1897–1967) and Irish physicist Ernest Walton (1903–1995) built the first electrostatic accelerator powerful enough for nuclear physics research. A high-voltage transformer impelled ions through a vacuum tube at up to 700 keV (see TRANSFORMER).

CONNECTIONS

● Particle accelerators can be used to create **NUCLEAR FUSION** between two nuclei.

● Small accelerators introduce performance-enhancing elements in silicon-chip **INTEGRATED CIRCUITS.**

CORE FACTS

■ Accelerators produce beams of charged particles of controlled intensity with high kinetic energy. The beams may be either pulsed or continuous.

■ Most large accelerators use protons or positrons, which have a positive electrical charge, or antiprotons or electrons, which have a negative electrical charge.

■ Accelerators allow the study of matter by smashing particles into fixed targets or colliding two beams traveling in opposite directions. Detectors track the debris from the collisions, which provide clues about the nature of matter and energy.

■ Accelerators also have many useful applications in medicine and industry.

Varying-field acceleration. An alternative method of acceleration is to use a voltage that varies with time to create a changing electric field. A linear accelerator with a time-varying electric field consists of a series of tubes (called drift tubes) of increasing length through which the particles pass (see the diagram at right). The walls of each drift tube have a potential difference with those of the next tube, creating an electric field between them, which accelerates the particle as it passes from one tube to the next.

Circular accelerators

Circular accelerators are a form of varying-field accelerator. A magnetic field can be used to apply a force to any electrically charged particle in motion. Circular accelerators use electromagnets to bend the path of the electrically charged particles into a circle (see ELECTRICITY AND MAGNETISM; MAGNET).

Cyclotrons. Cyclotrons were the first type of circular accelerator. The first cyclotron, designed by U.S. physicist Ernest Lawrence (1901–1958) of the University of California, Berkeley, used two D-shaped magnets to create the magnetic field. In a cyclotron, the particle passes between two electrodes during each orbit. The potential difference between the two electrodes is switched in time with the frequency of the particle's orbit so that, when the particle passes from one electrode to the other, it is accelerated by the electric field between them.

The diameter of the orbits increases as the particles gain kinetic energy so that they follow a spiral path inside the cyclotron. Eventually the particles reach the edge of the magnetic field, and this poses a physical limitation to acceleration.

Synchrotrons. In a synchrotron, a series of magnets is used to bend the path of the particles into a circle. As the kinetic energy of the particles increases, the magnets increase the magnetic field so that the particles stay in the same-sized orbit.

Storage rings. Storage rings further improve the utility of accelerators. They receive beams from "injector" accelerators and keep the particles circling in a vacuum until enough have accumulated for experimentation. Two storage rings can keep particles traveling in opposite directions until the beams are intersected so that the particles crash together in head-on collisions. These colliders can double the energies of the injector accelerators.

APPLICATIONS

The most powerful accelerators are research tools in high-energy particle physics or nuclear physics laboratories. More modest machines produce beams used to test the composition of materials, sterilize instruments, and to produce radioactive isotopes for a variety of applications by inducing transmutations in the nuclei of target atoms (see NUCLEAR ENERGY). Accelerators can aim particle beams at tumors to kill cancer cells (see MEDICAL TECHNOLOGY).

R. SMITH

See also: PHOTOCELL; RADIATION DETECTION.

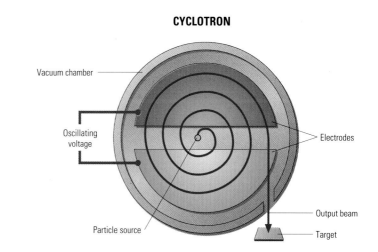

VARYING-FIELD LINEAR ACCELERATOR

Negatively charged drift tube

Positively charged drift tube

Target

Particle source

Particle accelerated between drift tubes

Vacuum chamber

Output beam

As a particle moves through a series of drift tubes, it is accelerated along its course by passing through the vacuum between the tubes.

CYCLOTRON

Vacuum chamber

Oscillating voltage

Electrodes

Output beam

Particle source

Target

A magnetic field causes a particle to orbit. When the particle passes through a vacuum chamber, its energy builds up and it moves outward to collide with the target.

Further reading:

Parsa, Z. *Future High Energy Colliders.* Woodbury, New York: American Institute of Physics, 1997.
Trefil, T. *From Atoms to Quarks: An Introduction to the Strange World of Particle Physics.* New York: Doubleday, 1994.

THE LARGE HADRON COLLIDER

Theoretical physics aims to provide explanations of the fundamental nature of space and time. Theories gain credence if the existence of particles that they predict can be observed—often using a particle accelerator. One such theory—concerned with how particles achieve their mass—predicts that a particle called the Higgs boson would be observed if protons and antiprotons could be made to collide with sufficiently high energy—at energies as yet unattainable using existing accelerators.

The Large Hadron Collider (LHC) under construction at the European Center for Nuclear Research (CERN) near Geneva, Switzerland is scheduled for completion in 2005 at a cost of $5 billion. The LHC will have a 17-mile (27-km) circular tunnel for its storage ring. Injector accelerators will pump protons and antiprotons (the hadrons) into the ring. When the beams cross, the proton-antiproton collisions will produce energies of 14 TeV. This should be enough to help physicists solve some current mysteries and even uncover new ones.

A CLOSER LOOK

PATTERN RECOGNITION

Pattern recognition is the process that computers use to identify recurring patterns in data

Pattern recognition is that part of artificial intelligence that gives computers the ability to extract certain features from a set of data—usually a visual image—and remember those features so that it can look for and recognize them again in other images. Pattern recognition computer programs allow a computer to recognize and manipulate objects without human intervention.

For instance, a computer program that can convert the image of a table into a line drawing would make it possible for a robot waiter to place a plate on the table without breaking either the plate or the table. Likewise, a similar program could be used to compare a picture of an individual's face with a set of stored images of different people and identify the person in question.

Pattern recognition technology is still very much in its infancy, but the possible applications range from producing advanced robots to fast and efficient analysis of visual data such as weather maps, the structural integrity of a manufactured component, and the surveillance of public places.

Humans are great pattern recognizers, and the difficulty of achieving pattern recognition in computers derives from the different ways in which computer and human memories function. In conventional computers, data is stored in numbered locations and retrieved by the location number. In humans, memories are retrieved by association. For example, if someone mentions a new pet bassett hound, we think of a small dog with a long body, short legs, and long ears—a mental model containing the recognizable features of a bassett hound.

Attempts to develop computer pattern recognition that works in the same way as a human brain has fostered the development of neural networks, circuits that share some of the characteristics of nerve cell networks in the brain. Like humans, such networks learn (acquire new memories) by being provided with new information and modifying the connections between different parts of the network.

The stages of pattern recognition

A computer that is learning to read handwritten numbers, for example, begins by building a model of each number by taking each integer (0–9) and breaking it into a set of smaller parts. This is called decomposing. Next, the computer reassembles the parts to form each number's character, using a model it has constructed. This is called reconstructing. To

CORE FACTS

■ Pattern recognition is a technology that allows a computer to extract features from data and search for those features in other data sets.

■ Pattern recognition is a part of artificial intelligence and is used to analyze weather maps, search for faults in manufactured components, and read handwritten words and numbers.

■ Computers can learn to recognize patterns in any data using neural networks—computer circuits that are designed to work in the same way as the human brain.

■ Learning to recognize patterns in complex shapes such as faces requires a lot of processing power.

test the accuracy of the model, the computer then uses a different set of component parts. This is called transforming. The last step is to analyze the new parts to see if they are of the same pattern as the model. This is called recognizing.

The most complex problems are learning (classification) and recognizing. Both require associating two ways of constructing an object with one pattern. Pattern recognition requires a way to decide whether a given object is equivalent to a learned pattern.

Computers approach the classification problem as a mathematical puzzle to be solved. The input to a pattern recognition system is a set of measurements and the output is the classification. The selection of the measurements is important and is done in two basic steps: extracting features and building them into a template or model. These are then classified and that pattern is "learned."

Pattern recognition problems

The magnitude of pattern recognition problems varies widely. For example, a system for determining the meaning of handwritten numbers requires classifying handwritten digits into one of 10 classes. If, instead, the problem is to recognize letters of the alphabet, the problem is to classify each letter into one of 26 classes.

Although computers are still not as good as humans at recognizing handwritten numbers and letters from the Roman alphabet, this pattern recognition problem is a relatively simple one. There are only a small number of features that the computer needs to recognize to differentiate one figure from another, such as the position of a circle next to a vertical line that distinguishes the letters *b*, *p*, and *d*. Recognizing patterns in a complex object such a human face follows the same principles but requires the use of many more component parts.

To recognize patterns in video images, the computer stores an image model of the type of pattern it is to look for. The model represents the shape of the object that the computer is required to identify. The computer is then ready to search input data from a video camera for the presence of a similar pattern (see COMPUTER GRAPHICS; VIDEOGRAPHY).

The computer disregards irrelevant information. For example, a system designed to recognize objects at various distances might disregard the size of shapes. The model is then compared with the information isolated from the input data. If there is a match between an object and the model, the computer recognizes the object in the image as being the same as the one it is looking for. A computer can use this technique relatively easily to identify simple shapes such as squares and circles. However, subtle characteristics—such as those which differentiate a cat from a dog—are harder to isolate and model.

J. TEMPLE-DENNETT

See also: ARTIFICIAL INTELLIGENCE; COMPUTER; IMAGING TECHNOLOGY; ROBOTICS; SOFTWARE AND PROGRAMMING.

IRIS RECOGNITION

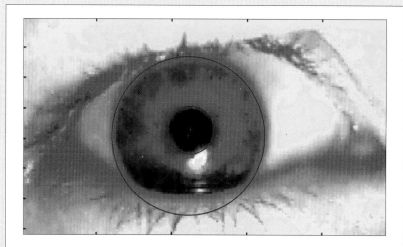

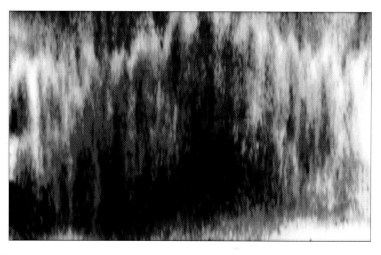

The boundaries of the iris are detected (top), and the pattern analyzed (above).

It may be possible that in the future, people will never have to carry any forms of identification on them such as credit cards, passports, or driver's licenses. Instead, identification will be used that can recognize a person by looking at their eyes. The patterns of the ring of color in the eye are unique to each person and remain the same throughout the person's life, in much the same way as a fingerprint. Technology is already available to recognize people by analyzing this pattern, and several companies are marketing identification devices that use this. The system is highly accurate and is not affected if the person wears glasses or contact lenses.

Since all human irises are essentially the same annular shape, their features can be easily mapped in a polar coordinate system. Applying advanced mathematical techniques to these data then produces a high-resolution characterization that differs obviously from that of another eye. Thus, the image can be used for identification purposes.

A product that accomplishes this, which is being marketed as IriScan, claims to have performed accurate identification in 3 billion cases. IriScan will be used in GTE's Iris Certificate Security system in such applications as teller machines, automatic transit fare collection systems, and money transactions on the Internet.

LOOKING TO THE FUTURE

Further Reading:
Bishop, C. *Neural Networks for Pattern Recognition*, New York: Oxford Press, 1995.

PESTICIDE AND HERBICIDE

Pesticides and herbicides are poisons used to kill unwanted animals, fungi, and plants, particularly in agriculture

A farmer is spraying grape vines with insecticide to kill the pests that would otherwise spoil much of his valuable crop.

CONNECTIONS

● Pesticides are used widely in **CROP SPRAYING AND PROTECTION.**

● Since the environmental implications of pesticide use came to the fore in the 1960s, more and more farmers have been turning to **ORGANIC FARMING AND SUSTAINABLE AGRICULTURE.**

● One alternative to using pesticides is **BIOLOGICAL CONTROL,** in which natural predators and disease-causing organisms are used to control pests.

Animal and microbial pests reduce the yield of food, fiber, and ornamental crops by feeding on them. The most important pests in this group are insects, mites, nematode worms, and fungi. Weeds, on the other hand, are plant pests that reduce the yields of crops by competing with them for nutrients, space, and light. Altogether, damage from pests reduces crop yields by up to 45 percent and has a serious impact on the world food supply and the textile and horticultural industries. In the United States alone, around $20 billion-worth of crops—one-tenth of total production—is lost to pests every year. Without chemical pest-control by poisons called pesticides, these losses would be much greater.

Pesticides are usually classified according to the type of pest they kill. Insecticides, fungicides, and herbicides—which kill insects, fungi, and weeds, respectively—are the most important in terms of amounts used. However, some crops also require the use of miticides or arachnicides, which kill mites and ticks. Other of pesticides include nematicides (for killing nematode worms), rodenticides (rats and mice), and molluscicides (snails and slugs).

History and development

Pyrethrin, a compound that occurs naturally in chrysanthemum flowers, has been used to kill lice since ancient times. Most insecticides, however, have been in use for only the last 100 years or so. Early compounds, the so-called winter washes, were general toxins that had to be applied outside the growing season to prevent them from killing the crop plant

as well as the insect pests. Oils, detergents, lime, sulfur, and organic compounds such as dinitrophenol were all used in winter washes. When DDT was discovered to be an effective insecticide during World War II (1939–1945), it revolutionized insect control, for it was non-toxic to the plant and killed a wide range of different pests. However, this "wonder compound" was soon shown to have a detrimental effect on wildlife and ecosystems, and it was banned in the United States in 1972.

CORE FACTS

■ Pesticides are poisonous substances used to kill organisms that would otherwise destroy, or compete with, crops. They can be naturally occurring but are usually synthetic.

■ Pesticides can be classified in terms of the type of pest they act on: for example, insecticides kill insects, fungicides kill fungi, and herbicides kill weeds.

■ An alternative classification of pesticides is based on the way in which they act on the pest: systemic pesticides are consumed by animal pests or travel up through the roots of weeds; contact pesticides enter the pest by penetrating its outside covering; and fumigants are inhaled by animal pests.

■ Many pesticides have been extremely successful in killing pests and increasing crop yields. However, some are toxic to humans or have serious environmental effects, and for these reasons have been banned or strictly regulated.

The first fungicides were pioneered in France in the 18th century as treatments for wheat seeds. Typical treatments included lime, salt, potassium nitrate, and even urine. Sulfur dusting of vines to prevent fungal infection was introduced in the 19th century, and its place was taken by Bordeaux mixture (copper sulfate and lime), which is still used today to treat vines. In the early 20th century, organomercury seed treatments were introduced for cereals and were widely used until they were banned in the 1970s because of their toxicity to humans.

Early herbicides were inorganic chemicals such as copper sulfate, ferrous sulfate, sulfuric acid, and sodium chlorate. Dinitrophenol, which had been developed as an insecticide, was also used. These compounds were not very selective, however, and they attacked the crop plants. The first selective weed killers, called hormone herbicides, were discovered in the 1940s and included 2,4-D. These compounds imitate natural growth-stimulating hormones called auxins (see PLANT HORMONE): for example, 2,4-D forces broad-leaved weeds to grow so rapidly that they die in the process.

In the last 50 years, there has been a huge increase in the development of safer, more effective, and more specific pesticides. During this time, the growth of the petrochemicals industry has given chemists access to useful raw materials, and there is a better understanding of the physiology and biochemistry of pests so that compounds that kill them—but not their plant hosts—can be developed.

Current use

According to the most recent figures from the Environmental Protection Agency (EPA), 4.5 billion lb (2 billion kg) of pesticides were used in the United States in 1995. This total includes the pesticide types already discussed, as well as wood preservatives, fumigants, disinfectants, and plant growth regulators. In all, approximately 21,000 different products were in use.

The EPA data shows that 77 percent of pesticide use in 1995 was for agriculture, with industrial, government, and homeowner use accounting for the remainder. Total expenditure on pesticides in the United States was $11.3 billion in 1995, corresponding to $43 per citizen. This represents around one-third of the world total expenditure on pesticides. Herbicides are by far the leading class of pesticides, accounting for $14 billion of the world market in 1995, followed by insecticides at $8.2 billion and insecticides at $5.5 billion. Other pesticides accounted for $1.3 billion.

Pesticides are not only used to kill crop pests but also target insects that carry diseases to humans and animals. The rates of malaria, yellow fever, and typhus have all been reduced in various parts of the world as a result of the widespread use of DDT and, more recently, pyrethroids. Mosquito nets coated with insecticide are effective in protecting people who sleep underneath them from transmission of the malaria parasite. Bed nets coated with insecticide

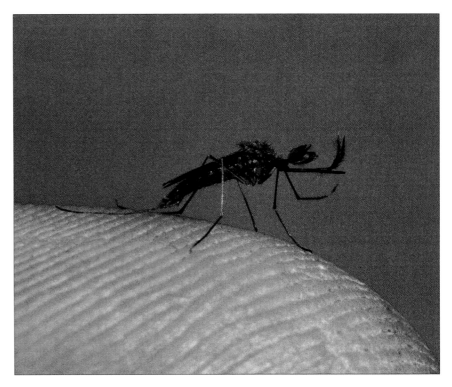

are also being tested for control of the house dust mite, which triggers asthma. Many insecticides are also used widely in gardening (Diazinon, for example) and for clearing houses of termite infestations.

Chemical composition

A wide range of chemical compounds is used in crop protection, both organic (carbon-based) and inorganic (non-carbon-based). In recent years, synthetic organic chemicals have become increasingly important as pesticides (see CHEMICAL INDUSTRY, ORGANIC). Some naturally occurring organic compounds are also important pesticides: for example, nicotine, which is the active ingredient in tobacco, is used as a spray or vapor in greenhouses to control insect pests.

Insecticides are one of the main weapons in the war against malaria, a tropical disease spread by certain species of mosquito.

RACHEL CARSON

In 1962, the publication of *Silent Spring* caused an uproar among chemical companies and deep concern among the general public. The author of this highly controversial and influential book was Rachel Carson, a U.S. scientist and ecologist with passionate convictions about what should be done to prevent the harmful environmental impacts of agricultural pesticides.

Born in Springdale, Pennsylvania, in 1907, Rachel Louise Carson studied at the Pennsylvania College for Women and at Johns Hopkins University before moving to the University of Maryland to teach zoology. Between 1936 and 1952 she was a marine biologist at the U.S. Bureau of Fisheries and the Fish and Wildlife Service, and she published three books before writing *Silent Spring*. These were *Under the Sea Wind* (1941), *The Sea Around Us* (1951), and *Edge of the Sea* (1955).

It took a while for *Silent Spring* to have its impact, but the book eventually helped lead to legislation for regulating the use of pesticides, including the U.S. ban on DDT in 1972. Sadly, Carson did not live to see the fruits of her labors: she was diagnosed with breast cancer during the writing of *Silent Spring* and died just two years after its publication, on April 14, 1964.

PEOPLE

Agricultural workers, wearing protective clothing and gas masks, spray roses in a greenhouse on a plantation in Tabacundo, Ecuador.

By contrast, some inorganic substances, such as arsenic compounds, have been phased out because of their toxicity to humans.

Pesticides enter a pest in three possible ways. Systemic insecticides are ingested by animal pests and are used mainly on animals with biting parts, such as caterpillars. A contact pesticide penetrates the outer covering of the pest and is applied to insects such as aphids, which pierce the surface of a plant and suck out its juices. Fumigants are volatile substances that kill by inhalation and by contact. They are often sprayed onto soil to kill nematode worms, fungi, and weeds. An example of a systemic herbicide is 2,4-D, while a typical contact herbicide is paraquat, which kills only those parts of the weed where it is applied.

Pesticides and herbicides at work

Most insecticides, once they are in the insect's body, work by interfering with its nervous system. These can be classified into four main chemical groups. The organophosphates (OPs), such as parathion and malathion, are the most widely used of the synthetic organic insecticides. They act by blocking an enzyme called acetylcholinesterase, which normally breaks down the neurotransmitter acetylcholine. (A neurotransmitter is a chemical responsible for the transmission of nerve impulses between cells in the nervous system.) If the enzyme is blocked, nervous impulses are transmitted continually, without any control, and the nervous system of the pest is disrupted to the extent that death is rapid. OPs continue to be effective for extended periods. A second group of insecticides called carbamates act in a similar way to OPs, but they decompose and become ineffective more rapidly than OPs.

The earliest insecticides were organochlorine compounds, which include DDT. These act on the nervous system in a different way. The effective transmission of nerve impulses depends on sodium and potassium ions being able to pass in and out of the membranes of nerve cells, through tiny channels.

WIDER IMPACT

REGULATION OF PESTICIDES AND HERBICIDES

Since pesticides and herbicides are toxins and are applied to the food supply, they pose a potential risk to human health. Some pesticides have been shown to be dangerous for infants and small children while increasing cancer risks for adults. The Environmental Protection Agency (EPA) has put strict rules in place to regulate their use in the United States.

First, the EPA may perform up to 100 different safety tests on new pesticides to check for their effect on human health, the environment, and wildlife. Only those that pass the tests are permitted to be used. Then the EPA dictates the wording of the label on the product—to protect both the farmer applying the pesticide and the general public from the dangers of misuse.

The EPA also sets tolerance limits: these are the maximum amounts of a pesticide or herbicide that can be legally applied to crops of a particular food. These are calculated from the maximum amount of the chemical that a person could consume in their lifetime without suffering any adverse health effects (the reference dose). To give an extra safety margin, the EPA sets the tolerance limit at 10–10,000 times less than the reference dose.

The U.S. Food and Drug Administration (FDA) is responsible for monitoring food supplies for pesticide residues. This includes imported food but not meat, poultry, and eggs, which are the responsibility of the Department of Agriculture. Any food in which residues exceed the tolerance level is immediately withdrawn from sale. In 1996, pesticide regulations were further tightened under the Food Quality Protection Act.

The organochlorine insecticides block these channels; so do the pyrethroids, which are synthetic insecticides based on pyrethrin.

Herbicides act on plants in many different ways. One of the most important actions is the imitation of auxins. Also, glycophosphate herbicides work by interfering with the synthesis of amino acids, which are the precursors of proteins. Atrazine and the other triazine herbicides work by interfering with the process of photosynthesis, in which a plant makes carbohydrates from carbon dioxide and sunlight.

Pesticides: for and against

Chemical pest control has undoubtedly reduced crop losses and so had a beneficial effect on the food supply. By keeping disease-carrying insects under control, some pesticides have also had a beneficial effect on human and animal health.

However, the use of chemical pesticides and herbicides does have a number of drawbacks. First, these substances are toxins and potentially harmful to humans, along with animals and plants other than their pest targets. For example, there have been several cases of farmers accidentally coming into contact with organophosphorus insecticides and developing ailments of the central nervous system as a result. Pesticides may also kill the crop plants themselves or the natural predators of the pest; in this second situation, the pest might even benefit from exposure to the pesticide. However, modern research methods in chemistry have yielded compounds that are very specific for the target pest.

Some pesticides (for example, organochlorines such as DDT) are chemically stable and persist in the environment for many years. They contaminate both soil and groundwater, eventually accumulating in the fatty tissues of a wide range of wildlife—particularly predators at the top of the food chain. The animals either die as a consequence or fail to produce offspring. This has caused much concern about organochlorine use in the past (see the box on page 977). In many cases, however, it has been possible to replace organochlorines with alternative pesticides, such as the pyrethroids, which are rapidly broken down.

Finally, all pests are prone to develop resistance, or immunity, to the chemicals that are used to control them. Individuals within a population of pests will vary in their sensitivity to the chemicals, and a few will survive even repeated applications. These go on to breed, leading to a generation with a higher proportion of resistant individuals: an example of evolution by natural selection in action. The problem of resistance is a serious one and means that chemists must continually search for new pesticides and herbicides—a costly and time-consuming process. In the meantime, the more a pesticide is used, the more rapidly resistance to it evolves.

It is unlikely that agriculture will ever be able to do without pesticides completely. These days, many farmers and manufacturers use a system called integrated pest management (IPM), which makes use of

a combination of chemicals, sensible agricultural techniques, and biological control (using natural predators and disease organisms to control pests).

S. ALDRIDGE

See also: AGRICULTURAL SCIENCE; AGRICULTURE, HISTORY OF; ARABLE FARMING; CROP SPRAYING AND PROTECTION; HORTICULTURE; ORGANIC FARMING AND SUSTAINABLE AGRICULTURE.

Further reading:

Copping, L. G., and Hewitt, H. G. *Chemistry and Mode of Action of Crop Protection Agents.* Cambridge, England: Royal Society of Chemistry, 1998.

Pesticides are an effective way of limiting the damage inflicted by the sugarcane-borer, **Eldana saccharina,** *on sorghum crops, an important food in many developing countries.*

EXPLOITING THE NATURAL WORLD

Insects communicate by producing, releasing, and detecting volatile compounds called pheromones. Pesticides based on these natural compounds work by luring pests to a trap to be killed or by disrupting their lifestyle—confusing them during mating, for example—which leads to fewer eggs being fertilized and a subsequent drop in population.

The natural world also produces its own pesticides, which can be exploited. In addition to pyrethrin from chrysanthemums, several potent toxins have been isolated from bacteria. For example, the bacterium *Bacillus thuringiensis* produces a compound called Bt toxin, which punches holes in the gut of many species of insect pests. The gene that produces Bt has been isolated and transferred, by means of the latest genetic engineering techniques, into several important species of crop plants, including cotton and potato (see GENETIC ENGINEERING). These so-called transgenic plants have now been planted throughout the United States and have significantly reduced insect damage.

The genes of plants such as corn and soybeans have been modified to make them resistant to certain herbicides so that the crop plants are unaffected while the herbicide eradicates the weeds among them. However, there is concern that the same genes could eventually transfer to weeds and make them resistant.

A CLOSER LOOK

PHARMACOLOGY AND DRUG TREATMENT

Pharmacology is the study of the properties of drugs and their effects on the body

Drugs come in all colors and receptacles. This is a collection of various medicine bottles, vials, and droppers containing drugs that are used to treat human ailments.

A drug is a substance, either natural or synthetic, that has an effect on the way the body works. Therapeutic drugs are those used in the treatment of disease. Some of these drugs can cure diseases, while others only relieve symptoms. Therapeutic drugs are also called medicines or pharmaceuticals.

Since the beginning of the 20th century, the vast and powerful pharmaceutical industry has saved and prolonged millions of lives worldwide through the use of drugs. The most significant advances have been in the prevention and treatment of infectious diseases (see ANTIBIOTICS; IMMUNOLOGY AND IMMUNIZATION); in drugs based on female hormones, which offer the possibility of controlling the human reproductive cycle; and, to a lesser extent, drugs used in the treatment of early-stage cancer.

There are also effective drug treatments for diseases of the circulatory system and drugs that control, rather than cure, certain mental disorders. Hormone-based drugs—most notably the birth control pill—provide effective birth control by altering the female reproductive cycle. Used in hormone replacement therapies, they can reduce symptoms of menopause and prevent serious conditions associated with it, such as heart disease and osteoporosis.

However, humans are still a long way from having a cure, or even a relief of symptoms, for every disease, and there are still some illnesses for which there are few, if any, effective drugs or preventive therapies. There is, however, a growing emphasis on prevention of some types of diseases, as well as an awareness that drug therapies are not always an appropriate means of aiding recovery.

Diseases for which there is currently no pharmaceutical cure include many diseases of the nervous system, such as Alzheimer's disease and multiple sclerosis; autoimmune diseases, such as rheumatoid arthritis; and common infectious diseases, such as influenza and the common cold (which can be caused by any of some 200 viruses). Chronic conditions such as diabetes mellitus, while controllable by the administration of such drugs as insulin, remain incurable.

In the developing world, many infectious and other diseases remain incurable or uncontrollable until suitable drugs or vaccines can be produced and made widely available. There is also a growing emphasis in developed countries on the prevention rather than the cure of some types of disease, as well as attempts to find alternatives to drug therapies for a number of ailments.

Historical development of drug treatment

Early hunter-gatherers probably discovered quite early that some plants had a beneficial effect on their health. The first historical record of drug use comes from ancient Egyptian papyruses dating from

CONNECTIONS

● Insulin, which is used to treat diabetes, was one of the first products of **BIOTECHNOLOGY** and one of the first made in a bioreactor.

● Chemotherapy includes the drugs used in **CANCER TREATMENTS.**

CORE FACTS

■ Many drugs act at specific sites within the body.
■ Important classes of drugs include antibiotics, analgesics (painkillers), heart drugs, drugs for mental disorders, and cancer treatment drugs.
■ Most drugs are taken orally or are applied locally; some must be given by injection.

1600–1500 B.C.E. These documents mention the application of fruits, vegetables, tree resins (such as frankincense), plant extracts, and minerals to treat certain ailments. For instance, tannins from plant galls (swellings of plant tissue caused by fungi or insect parasites) were used to treat burns, while copper and antimony (a silvery white metalloid element) were used as antiseptics. Such practices were also common in the Assyrian and Babylonian civilizations. The Chinese herbal account, *Pen T'sao*, which dates from c.200 B.C.E., mentions 240 different plant remedies and 125 others of animal or mineral origin.

The Greek physicians Hippocrates (c.460–c.377 B.C.E.) and Galen (129–c.199 C.E.) tried to develop a logical approach to the use of medicines, relying on observation and experience. Another important figure from this era was Dioscorides (c.40–c.90 C.E.), physician to the emperor Nero, who produced a five-volume herbal called *De materia medica*. This describes and documents the use of over 500 plants for relieving the symptoms of diseases and was influential for the next 15 centuries.

However, the effect of drugs could not have a proper scientific basis without a knowledge of human anatomy and physiology. This developed from the 16th century on—along with various other, less scientific beliefs. For instance, the doctrine of signatures suggested that remedies for particular illnesses could be identified by their appearance. Yellow crocus was used to treat jaundice (a liver disease that turns the skin yellow), and red substances, such as wine and rust, were used for anemia, in which a shortage of red blood cells makes the complexion appear paler than normal.

It was not only native plants that were used as medicines. The explorers, missionaries, and traders of the 15th and 16th centuries brought back new plants from distant parts of the world. One of the most important was cinchona, from the bark of a Peruvian tree, which was very effective in curing malaria and other fevers. Another was ipecac, which was the dried root of a Brazilian shrub. Ipecac was used for diarrhea, as an emetic (to make the patient vomit) in cases of poisoning, and for relieving coughs. Quinine, the active ingredient of cinchona, and ipecac are still used today.

Aspirin—currently one of the world's most widely used drugs—also has early origins. In the 18th century, Rev. Edmund Stone, an English parson, reported to the Royal Society that the bark of the white willow tree was effective in relieving fever and pain. The bark contains salicin—a compound related to aspirin—as do other common plants, such as meadowsweet. However, it is thought that the ancient Chinese had used willow bark for fevers as far back as 2000 B.C.E.

Scientific developments

The development of chemistry as a science in the 18th and 19th centuries led to the isolation of the active ingredients of many plant extracts. German chemist Johann Buchner (1860–1917) isolated

This illustration from a 12th-century Dioscorides (c.40–c.90 C.E.) manuscript depicts a medieval herbalist instructing his helpers in the gathering of medicinal plants.

salicin in 1828. Meanwhile, the principles of pharmacology were being developed. French scientist Claude Bernard (1813–1878) showed that curare—a poison that causes paralysis—blocks the nerve impulses that cause the muscles to contract. This link between a action of a drug and its observed effect was a major step forward, since it had been assumed until then that drugs acted on the body as a whole.

INSULIN

A Canadian orthopedic surgeon, Frederick Grant Banting (1891–1941), and a U.S.-born Canadian medical student, Charles H. Best (1899–1978), brought new hope to the millions of people suffering from diabetes through their discovery of insulin. Diabetes was first described in Egypt in 1500 B.C.E. and was nearly always fatal. In the 19th century, it was shown that removal of the pancreas (which produces insulin) caused diabetes. However, it was not until 1921 that Banting found that insulin was the vital hormone produced by cells in the pancreas called the islets of Langerhans. Banting and Best ascertained that insulin was the substance primarily responsible for regulating glucose levels in the blood and, therefore, one of the main factors in human metabolism. They first tried insulin out on a diabetic dog named Marjorie and succeeded in restoring her to health. In 1922, 14-year-old Leonard Thompson, who was dying from diabetes, became the first human to receive insulin. It saved his life.

Scientists obtained their first source of insulin from animal pancreases in local slaughterhouses, and it was first produced at the University of Toronto, where the diabetes research was done. Later, an extraction process was developed by U.S. pharmaceuticals company Eli Lilly & Co. in the early 1920s. By 1926, the commercial production of insulin was under way, and it became possible to work out exact doses for patients. Insulin is now also manufactured by genetically engineered bacteria (see GENETIC ENGINEERING).

HISTORY OF TECHNOLOGY

The leaves of the foxglove plant are used to make the heart drug digitalis. This natural drug stimulates the heart's muscles and is given either orally or, in severe cases, by injection to persons suffering a heart attack.

Doctors were also becoming more scientific in their use of drugs, and another English physician, William Withering (1741–1799), is often credited with carrying out the first clinical trials of a drug. In the late 18th century he performed a series of experiments on the heart drug digitalis, which is extracted from foxglove. Around the same time, anesthetics were also being developed, which are described separately (see ANESTHETICS).

Pharmacopoeias

Written accounts of drugs became increasingly popular during medieval times. Physicians then began to organize their knowledge more effectively, and herbals began to be replaced by pharmacopoeias. These were more formal descriptions of how to make up different medicines, with detailed descriptions of their ingredients. In 1618 the Royal College of Physicians in London produced the first version of the *British Pharmacopoeia*. The first edition of the *Pharmacopoeia of the United States of America* was produced in 1820. These books are still used today and are updated every year. They are the standard prescribing manuals for doctors and list every available drug, along with its effects on disease and reported adverse effects.

Birth of the pharmaceutical industry

English chemist William Perkin (1838–1907) was a pioneer in the chemical industry, having discovered how to make dyes. His methods were taken up by German chemists, who used them to produce drugs as well as dyes. One of the first drugs they made in bulk was salicylic acid, which is closely related to salicin, the active ingredient of willow bark and very effective in the treatment of moderate pain and fever. Aspirin, a synthetic derivative of salicylic acid, was the idea of Felix Hoffmann, a chemist working for the chemicals company Bayer. Hoffmann's father took salicylic acid to relieve the pain and inflammation of arthritis, but it caused severe stomach irritation. Hoffmann synthesized aspirin (acetylsalicylic acid), which was easier on the stomach, in 1897. Aspirin was launched commercially in 1898.

The other great breakthrough in the history of pharmaceuticals was the discovery of antibiotics, which is covered elsewhere (see ANTIBIOTICS). In the 1940s and 1950s, drugs to treat epilepsy, allergy, and mental illness were developed, followed by the first anticancer drugs, known broadly as chemotherapy (see CANCER TREATMENTS). From the 1970s, research and development gathered pace, and there are now more than 6000 different drugs in general use, with more being introduced each year.

Drug dispensing and delivery

In medieval times, apothecaries—the forerunners of today's pharmacists—prepared and prescribed drugs. They would prepare pills and solutions of drugs in water or alcohol to be taken as drops.

In 1843 English chemist William Brockedon invented a tablet-making machine that used mallet blows to compact mixtures of drug and filler powder in a pill-shaped mold. By the late 19th century, tablets, as well as gelatin capsules, had become popular. A British pharmaceuticals company, Burroughs Wellcome, developed an automated tablet-making machine in the early 20th century. Today, most drugs are taken in tablet form. A precise dose of the drug is mixed with an inert powder, such as starch, to dilute it, and with a lubricant, usually talc, to keep it from sticking to the machine. The mixture is then made into granules, which are poured into a set of tablet-shaped cavities. A punch is applied to compress the mixture into a tablet. The tablet is then coated with sugar or a cellulose film to protect it and make it look more attractive. The tablets are then packaged.

Some drugs, however, have to be injected directly into the body because they would otherwise decompose in the stomach. The syringe was invented in the 17th century. The first syringes were made of pewter or other metals. Now most syringes are made of disposable plastic, and used with disposable steel needles, to minimize the spread of infection. However, since injections always cause some discomfort, other methods of delivery are being developed, including nasal sprays, inhalers, eyedrops, and patches that are stuck to the skin.

It is also possible to deliver slow-release formulations of drugs; these deliver a small amount of the drug into the system over a set period of time. This can be more effective than taking several separate doses. One way of administering a slow-release drug is to make a capsule that contains hundreds of

PAUL EHRLICH

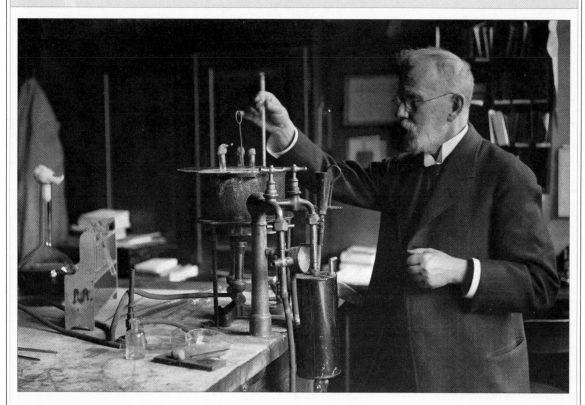

German bacteriologist and 1908 Nobel prize-winner Paul Ehrlich (1854–1915) at work in his laboratory.

Paul Ehrlich was born in Strehlen, eastern Germany (now Poland), and studied medicine in Berlin, where he spent the rest of his career. He tested new dyes developed by the German chemical industry, hoping to find one that would act as a drug against parasites.

Ehrlich is most famous for the development of salvarsan in 1909, an arsenic compound that proved effective against syphilis. He also developed the idea of the "magic bullet"—a drug that would effect its target but leave healthy tissue alone. His work in this field set the scene for the development of sulfonamide drugs in the 1930s and antibiotics in the 1940s.

In Ehrlich's time, the targets were invading microorganisms—but now the target is any diseased tissue. Ehrlich's magic bullet principle is still a strong feature in much of pharmaceutical research in its quest for effective and specific drugs, free of the side effects that can result from interactions of drugs with healthy tissue.

Ehrlich's pioneering work in immunology and hematology (diagnosing disease by blood testing), and his creation of a diphtheria vaccine were other major achievements. Ehrlich was a joint recipient of the 1908 Nobel prize for medicine or physiology.

PEOPLE

tiny spheres enclosing some of the drug. The spheres have varying thicknesses of coating. Those with a thin coat release the drug quickly, while those with a thicker coat release it more slowly. This way, the drug is released steadily into the body from the capsule as more and more of the spheres dissolve.

How drugs work

Many drugs work by interacting with specific molecules in the body. This interaction has a specific effect on how the body functions, such as lowering blood pressure or decreasing the sensation of pain. The molecules that drugs interact with are known as targets and are of two types: enzymes and receptors.

Enzymes are biological catalysts—they speed up chemical reactions in the body to occur fast enough to sustain life. For instance, without the help of enzymes, the reactions necessary to extract the energy from a typical meal would take 50 years in a laboratory. There are thousands of different enzymes in the body, each of which catalyzes a different reaction. All enzymes are protein molecules. A protein is a large molecule made up of a sequence of amino acids—small organic molecules.

Enzyme inhibitors—drugs that block the action of an enzyme—fit into a crevice on the surface of the enzyme molecule, known as the active site. This is where the enzyme substrate—the substance the enzyme reacts with—normally fits. With the inhibitor present, enzyme action cannot take place.

Enzyme inhibitors can be very useful in controlling the body's chemistry to give a therapeutic (curative) result. ACE (angiotensin-converting enzyme) inhibitors are a class of drugs used in the

THE PHARMACEUTICAL INDUSTRY

Drugs are big business. The worldwide pharmaceutical industry is said to be worth around $256 billion in sales per annum, and its annual growth rate is about 10 percent a year. The United States accounts for the biggest market share, at just over 30 percent, and is followed by Japan, then Britain. The world's top selling drug, ranitidine (Zantac), which is prescribed for gastric ulcers, earned its British manufacturers Glaxo Wellcome nearly $1.1 million in 1998. Drugs to treat infectious diseases, heart diseases, high blood pressure, and depression are also highly successful products, as are the thousands of over-the-counter medicines for treating the symptoms of common ailments such as coughs and colds.

However, the costs and risks of developing new drugs are very high. On average it takes about 12 years to get a drug onto the market from its initial stages in the laboratory, and the cost of developing it can be about $350 million. Many thousands of potential drugs fall by the wayside during development because they are toxic, too expensive or difficult to make in bulk, or are just not very effective.

There are three main stages of development. In the research phase, new compounds are investigated, or screened, for activity against a target (such as a pathogen). A company can make thousands of different compounds in one operation. From this, a few promising compounds known as candidate drugs will pass on to the second, preclinical stage. In this, various studies take place. These include tests on animals to assess toxicity, tests to see how long the compound stays in the body, and chemical synthesis to see if the drug can be made in large quantities. If all goes well, the candidate drug will then be tested on humans in clinical trials.

Clinical trials

Clinical trials cannot begin until thorough testing of a potential drug has been carried out in animals. Phase I clinical trials involve healthy volunteers, usually men between the ages of 18 and 65. Often medical students or employees of the drug company will take part in these trials, which usually involve up to 100 people. The aim of this stage is to check for any unexpected adverse effects associated with the drug, rather than to see if it is an effective treatment.

If the drug passes through Phase I without problems, up to 500 patients with the disease the drug is intended to treat will be recruited into a Phase II trial. Phase II trials aim to find out how effective the drug is and to assess how large a dose is needed.

Most clinical trials are done in a standard way: the new treatment is compared either to an existing treatment or to an inactive substance known as a placebo. Each patient is randomly

A factory worker checks drug capsules before they are packaged.

assigned to be given either the new drug or an existing drug, or the new drug or a placebo. Extreme care is taken to ensure that neither the patients nor the individuals attending to the patients know what any patient is receiving, since this could bias the results. This is known as a double-blind test.

If Phase II gives positive results, Phase III begins, which involves thousands of patients, perhaps internationally. If the drug passes Phase III, it is allowed onto the market. However, the manufacturers continue to monitor its progress and often ask doctors to enroll patients into further trials, as well as to report any adverse effects.

A CLOSER LOOK

treatment of heart disease, for example. The ACE alters a molecule in the body, which then raises blood pressure (pressure against the arteries of circulating blood), which is fine in a healthy person, but not so good for someone whose blood pressure is already too high. An ACE inhibitor can keep blood pressure at a safe level and may help prevent strokes (brain hemorrhage) and heart disease, such as coronary thrombosis (blockage of an artery close to the heart).

Receptors are protein molecules that are found on the surface of cells (whereas enzymes are usually found inside the cell). A receptor can alter the chemical activity within the cell if it allows a specific molecule, known as a ligand, to bind to it. Drugs that

act on receptors mimic the action of ligands. There are two different types: agonists and receptor agonists. Both block the receptor's action by binding to the site where the ligand would normally bind.

Agonists (chemical substances that combine with a receptor to start an activity or reaction) make the cell do what the ligand would usually do. Morphine, one of the most potent painkillers used in medicine, acts as an agonist. It binds to pain receptors in the brain, where the body's natural painkillers, known as endorphins, would normally act.

Drugs that act as receptor antagonists produce no action in the cell. Instead, they turn off the action that the ligand would have produced. Important

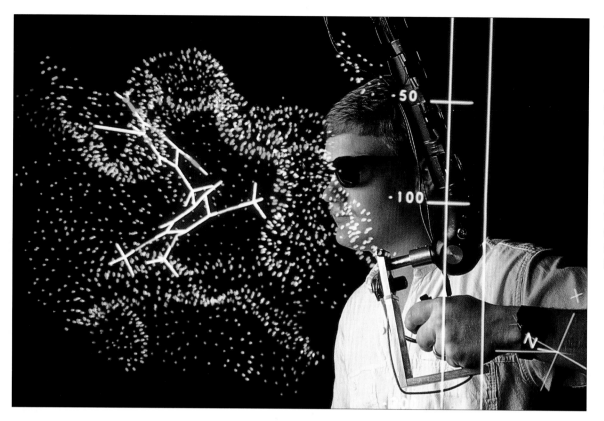

A biochemist uses a virtual reality (VR) system to design a new drug. The drug and its target molecules are represented by dots and lines on a 3-D diagram. A robot arm allows the drug designer to rotate the drug molecule in order to find the best fit with the target molecule. When the drug molecule fails to engage (fit) strongly, the operator feels the force of resistance in the robot arm.

drugs in this category include beta blockers, used to treat high blood pressure and heart disease. They act on receptors whose ligand is epinephrine (adrenalin), which normally gears the body up in a stress situation. It prepares the body for an emergency by increasing blood pressure, heart rate, and breathing rate. If adrenalin cannot bind to its receptor because a beta blocker drug is already in place, then the workload on the heart is eased.

Drug action, therefore, depends on knowing the structures and shapes of enzyme and receptor molecules. These can now be worked out using either X-ray crystallography or nuclear magnetic resonance. Both techniques depend on the interaction of radiation with the atoms in a molecule. The data can be displayed on a computer screen, which gives a picture of the drug's target. Using a computer library of images, potential drugs can then be tested for their fit with the target. This work on the computer saves many months' work in the chemistry laboratory.

The first drugs discovered by computer-aided drug design were those that act against the human immunodeficiency virus (HIV), the virus that leads to acquired immune deficiency syndrome (AIDS). The enzyme's structure, which HIV needs to reproduce itself, and which is known as HIV protease, was figured out in 1989. U.S. scientists used this to pinpoint potential drug treatments, such as bromoperidol, a compound that was already used to treat mental disorders. This search would have taken several months in the chemical laboratory; by computer it took only ten hours.

Although bromoperidol proved too toxic in later experiments, it sparked off the search for new AIDS drugs, which produced some new drugs known as HIV protease inhibitors. These drugs enable HIV-positive patients to live longer, delaying the onset of AIDS-related illnesses from a few months to several years. However, protease inhibitors are expensive and have side effects. They must also be taken on a complicated schedule, which can be difficult for patients to keep up. Moveover, HIV, like other disease-causing microorganisms, may become resistant to the drugs with time, so they must be prescribed with care. However, the lives of many people with AIDS have undoubtedly been prolonged by the advent of computer-aided drug design.

TYPES OF DRUGS

Among the most widely used classes of drugs are antibiotics, analgesics (painkillers), cardiovascular (heart and blood circulation) drugs, psychotropic drugs (for mental disorders), drugs to treat cancer, and hormone-based drugs. Antibiotics and drugs to treat cancer are discussed elsewhere (see ANTIBIOTICS; CANCER TREATMENTS).

Analgesics

Pain is a universal problem, whether it is caused by a migraine headache or terminal cancer. Analgesics, which is the clinical term for painkilling drugs, act in one of two ways. Locally acting painkillers, such as aspirin, obstruct the production of substances called prostaglandins. Prostaglandins are involved in inflammation (dilation of blood vessels, often after tissue damage) and are at increased levels during menstruation, causing menstrual pain. Aspirin and other antiinflammatory drugs, such as acetaminophen (Tylenol) and ibuprofen, reduce inflammation and the pain that accompanies it. Unlike many other drugs, aspirin, ibuprofen, and acetaminophen can be bought over the counter in the United States and

ARE DRUGS OVERPRESCRIBED TODAY?

Some experts are of the opinion that many drugs are over-prescribed, or prescribed to patients for whose conditions they are inappropriate. There are various circumstances under which inappropriate prescription may occur: inaccurate diagnosis and the fact that some patients expect to receive a prescription when they visit the doctor are two examples.

For instance, despite the fact that antibiotic drugs are useless against viral infections, antibiotics may be prescribed on demand by the patient for common viral infections such as colds and influenza—against which they are almost certain to be ineffective. Not only is this costly for the health budget, it also contributes to antibiotic resistance, which is a growing public health problem (see ANTIBIOTICS). Tranquilizers and sleeping pills have also been overprescribed in the past and have led to dependence in some patients. If sleeping drugs are taken long-term, they can actually worsen insomnia.

However, it is thought that some drugs are actually under-prescribed. For instance, many cases of depression could respond to drug treatment, if patients could only be persuaded to consult their doctors. It has also been suggested that antidepressants should be prescribed for longer and in larger doses than is usually the case to keep the condition from recurring. Doctors also tend to be very cautious in prescribing strong painkillers for fear of causing addiction. This often increases pain and suffering for patients with terminal illnesses, where addiction is not likely to be an important risk.

WIDER IMPACT

other countries. In some countries, such as Britain, the number of acetaminophen tablets that can be sold in a pack at any one time is restricted. This places a responsibility on the consumer to follow the instructions on the label and consult their physician if their pain symptoms do not improve.

A hospital pharmacist prepares a prescription for a patient.

Centrally acting painkillers, such as morphine, also called opiates, act on receptors in the brain that stop pain signals being sent to the rest of the body. Opiates have molecules that are similar to endorphins, which are naturally occurring painkillers produced in the body. The opiate molecules lock on to the brain receptor sites that would have been occupied by the endorphins, which means the natural substances are temporarily disabled on withdrawal of regular opiate use. In cases of opiate addiction, more and more of the opiate is needed to allay the discomfort of withdrawal. Medication with opiate drugs is therefore restricted to the treatment of severe pain, such as that experienced in serious injuries, following major surgery, or in terminal illness. Medical use of heroin is illegal in the United States.

Cardiovascular drugs

The heart and the circulation of the blood are essential to life. Heart diseases used to be uncommon, except for rheumatic fever, which is caused by infection. However, coronary heart disease—often caused by the buildup of fatty deposits in the blood vessels serving the heart—is a leading cause of death in the United States and other developed countries. It is known that high blood cholesterol levels are related to the fatty deposits that increase the risk of coronary heart disease, mainly because cholesterol-containing plaques clog the linings of arteries, leading to hypertension (high blood pressure). Where prevention measures such as reducing the proportion of fat in the diet are not enough to reduce high blood pressure or the level of cholesterol, certain drugs may be useful. Statins, for example, decrease the amount of cholesterol in the blood, and beta blockers and ACE inhibitors are the most widely prescribed drugs for decreasing blood pressure.

Since diseases of the circulation are often without symptoms, it is often too late for drug treatment to be given before someone suffers a heart attack or a stroke. These life-threatening conditions are usually caused by a blood clot blocking the blood supply to the heart or brain. Thrombolytic drugs—discovered over the last ten years or so—dissolve these clots and are now part of standard emergency treatment.

Psychotropic drugs

Drugs for mental illness, which act on the brain, are known as psychotropic drugs. Antipsychotic drugs, such as chlorpromazine and clozapine, are mainly used to treat schizophrenia—a serious mental disorder involving tactile and visual hallucinations, auditory hallucinations (hearing voices), and other forms of delusions. Antipsychotic drugs relieve these symptoms and allow the patient to lead a relatively normal life. Until the use of drug treatment, most people with schizophrenia could expect to spend years in a mental hospital. The antipsychotic drugs work by blocking receptors for a chemical in the brain known as dopamine. Dopamine is one of several neurotransmitters—the compounds responsible for transmitting information between brain cells. It is thought that schizophrenia may result from an overactivity of dopamine, which can be reduced by antipsychotic drugs.

The first antidepressants, the other major category of psychotropic drugs, were discovered in the 1950s. Doctors noticed that patients on iproniazid, a drug used to treat tuberculosis, became euphoric. Iproniazid and related compounds were then developed as drugs for depression, which affects around one person in 20 at any one time. It is thought that lowered levels of one, or both, of the neurotransmitters norepinephrine and serotonin may cause depression; most antidepressant drugs work by raising the levels of these neurotransmitters. Fluoxetine—sold under the trade name Prozac—is prescribed for a wide range of mental disorders such as phobias and eating disorders, as well as depression. One of a new category of antidepressants, Prozac acts only on serotonin and has fewer side effects than older antidepressants. Another antidepressant, reboxetine, acts only on norepinephrine. Therefore doctors now have a range of specific drugs available to treat different types of depression.

Other important drugs that act on the brain are hypnotics, to induce sleep, and tranquilizers, to relieve anxiety. In the 1960s, tranquilizers such as diazepam (Valium) were widely prescribed. However, it is now known that even relatively short-term use of these drugs can be addictive, so their use tends to be restricted to extreme cases (for example, to help someone sleep after a bereavement or severe shock) or carefully under the supervision of a doctor.

Drugs based on hormones

Hormones are the chemical messengers of the body's control systems. They are produced and released in tiny amounts by the endocrine glands and travel through the bloodstream until they reach their target, where they lock onto receptors and so alter the activity of the target cell or tissue. The action of hormones keeps the inner environment of the body —temperature, blood chemistry, and so on— constant in order to sustain life.

Hormones also control fertility. The male hormone testosterone is responsible for developing the male sex organs and other sexual characteristics at adolescence, and for the production of sperm. The female hormones estrogen and progesterone are responsible for female sexual characteristics and regulate the menstrual cycle.

Millions of people take hormonal drugs. Some are natural hormones, taken from the human body, while others are synthetic derivatives. Sometimes hormones are prescribed to make up for a deficiency. People with diabetes, for instance, lack the hormone insulin, which is needed to keep levels of glucose in the blood steady. They therefore have to take insulin every day to supply what the body lacks. However, the most common use of hormonal drugs is for birth control. Oral contraception (the pill) first became available in the 1960s and is now taken by 63 million women worldwide. Taken correctly, oral contra-

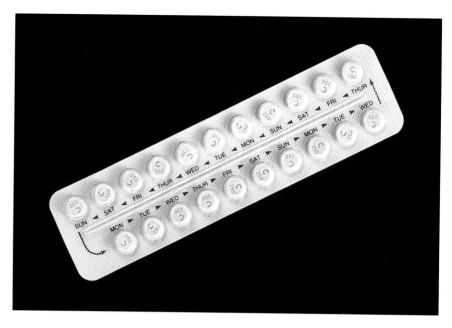

ception is at least 99 percent effective. In other words, if 100 women take it for a year, only one, at most, will become pregnant.

Most oral contraceptives contain synthetic estrogen and progesterone; others contain progesterone only. They work by putting the body into a state resembling early pregnancy, when estrogen and progesterone levels are both high. Under these conditions ovulation—the release of ova (eggs) by the ovaries—does not occur, and if there are no eggs to fertilize, a woman cannot get pregnant. Results of a recent large-scale study on long-term effects of oral contraception show that there is minimal increased risk of thrombosis or breast cancer, contrary to previous thinking. Hormones are also used to help infertile women become pregnant. Fertility drugs contain hormones that stimulate ovulation, sometimes causing the release of many eggs at once (see ARTIFICIAL INSEMINATION AND FERTILITY TREATMENT).

The groups of hormonal drugs broadly known as hormone replacement therapy (HRT) are taken by an increasing number of women during and after menopause. At menopause, which occurs around the age of 50, ovulation ceases and a woman is no longer fertile. Estrogen and progesterone levels fall dramatically, leading to uncomfortable symptoms such as hot flashes, but also to serious conditions such as loss of bone mass (osteoporosis) and consequent hip or spine fractures. HRT consists of estrogen and progesterone to restore the woman's body to its premenopausal hormonal state, alleviating menopausal symptoms, protecting against heart disease and osteoporosis and, according to recent research, reducing the risk of Alzheimer's disease.

S. ALDRIDGE

See also: ANTISEPTICS AND STERILIZATION; INTENSIVE CARE UNIT; MEDICAL TECHNOLOGY; SURGERY.

Further reading:
Ahrens, F. A. *Pharmacology.* Baltimore, Maryland: Williams & Wilkins, 1996.

Oral contraceptive pills are 99 percent effective in reducing the risk of pregnancy. Contraceptive pills usually contain both progesterone, which acts on the pituitary gland affecting the menstrual cycle, and estrogen, which blocks the release of a mature egg each month (ovulation). These pills are marked with the days of the week they are to be taken to insure that a pill is taken every day, since forgetting even one pill in the cycle considerably reduces its effectiveness as a contraceptive.

PHOTOCELL

A photocell is an electronic device that converts light into electricity

A photovoltaic cell designed for use in a spacecraft's solar array. The cell is made of a wafer of silicon protected by a glass plate, which reflects any high-energy ultraviolet light.

CONNECTIONS

● Arrays of photocells are used in **IMAGING TECHNOLOGY** such as digital cameras, which do not use conventional photographic film.

● A **SATELLITE** or **SPACE PROBE** may use a type of photocell to generate electricity from sunlight.

Most people are familiar with the "electric eye" that can cause a door to open when they approach. The electric eye is a photocell (a contraction of *photoelectric cell*) that acts as a switch based on the amount of light that falls upon it. But photocells are not only used to open doors. There are many applications for them in both industrial equipment and consumer products.

Light is a form of radiant energy, and when it strikes certain types of materials, it may affect their electrical properties. It may induce a voltage across the material, alter its resistance, or cause electrons to be ejected from its surface. Each of these effects can be measured, so these materials can be used to detect the presence or absence of light.

The principle behind photocells dates from the 19th century, when scientists began noticing that light sometimes had small but measurable effects on their experiments with electricity. In 1905, German physicist Albert Einstein (1879–1955) developed the theoretical basis for the "photoelectric effect" (the way in which light produces electricity). The paper he wrote on the subject earned him the Nobel Prize for physics in 1921.

Types of photocells

There are three types of photocells: photovoltaic, photoconductive, and photoemissive. Photovoltaic cells are semiconductors (devices that can conduct or insulate electricity, depending upon how they are used; see SEMICONDUCTOR AND SEMICONDUCTOR DEVICE) in which light causes a voltage to be produced across a junction between electron-rich and electron-poor materials. No external voltage source

is needed for a photovoltaic cell to operate, and for this reason these cells have become very important as a means of generating electricity from sunlight (see the box on page 989 and SOLAR POWER).

In photoconductive cells, the incoming light knocks electrons off some of the atoms in the material, which produces an excess of charge carriers and thereby makes it easier for electricity to travel. In other words, the light decreases the material's resistance. A supplementary voltage source must be used in this type of cell; when light causes the resistance to decrease, the current flowing through the material increases. Photoconductive cells are inexpensive to manufacture and respond to very low light levels; they are also more useful with lower frequency radiation (see ELECTROMAGNETIC RADIATION), such as infrared, than the other types of cells.

Photoemissive materials work in a similar way except that their surface properties allow the free electrons to escape from the material altogether. They also require a supplementary voltage source. The photoemissive cathode is generally enclosed in a vacuum tube along with a positively charged anode to collect the electrons so that they can be measured (see ELECTRON TUBE). The purpose of the vacuum is to allow the electrons to travel freely without being scattered by other particles. In order to impart enough energy to the material to knock the electrons from the surface, visible or higher-frequency light is generally necessary.

Applications

Photocells are used in applications where the detection of light is important. The basic electric eye, which signals whether a beam of light has been obscured, is used in door openers, security systems to detect passersby, and automatic toilets and hand dryers in public bathrooms. Photocells are also used in some smoke alarms. In photography, light meters employ photocells to determine whether a flash is necessary. Photoconductive cells are used as infrared detectors in scientific instruments and as low-cost

CORE FACTS

■ Photocells use the principle that light can affect the movement of electrons in some materials.

■ Photocells may be made from photovoltaic, photoconductive, or photoemissive materials. These respond in different ways to incident (incoming) beams of light or other radiating energy.

■ Many types of instruments and equipment use photocells to detect and measure light, including television cameras, fax machines, and pocket calculators.

■ Photovoltaic cells can be used to generate electricity.

sensors for turning streetlamps on at dusk. Low levels of light may be measured using photomultiplier tubes made with photoemissive materials.

Photodiodes are semiconductor devices that can be operated with or without an external voltage. They are often used as digital detectors in optical devices. The photodiode multiplies a current and may be thought of as the solid-state equivalent of the photomultiplier tube. Many photodiodes may be put together in an array to form a charge-coupled device (CCD). CCDs have become increasingly important in imaging and are used as the "eyes" in television cameras, computer scanners, bar code readers, and many other devices (see VIDEOGRAPHY).

Sometimes photocells are used for applications that seem far removed from the simple detection of light. For example, in film projectors, photocells have a role in the reproduction of the audio information. This is encoded by the variations in the density of a gray strip at the edge of the film called the sound track. When the film passes between a constant light source and the photocell, differences in the amount of light that get through are detected and used to reproduce the precise waveforms of the originally recorded sound.

When a piece of paper is fed into a fax machine, photocells measure the reflection of a light source off each point. The resulting information is transmitted to the receiving machine, which is told whether that point should be printed dark or left blank (see FACSIMILE TRANSMISSION).

S. CALVO

See also: ELECTRICITY AND MAGNETISM; LIGHT AND OPTICS; SEMICONDUCTOR AND SEMICONDUCTOR DEVICE; TRANSDUCER AND SENSOR.

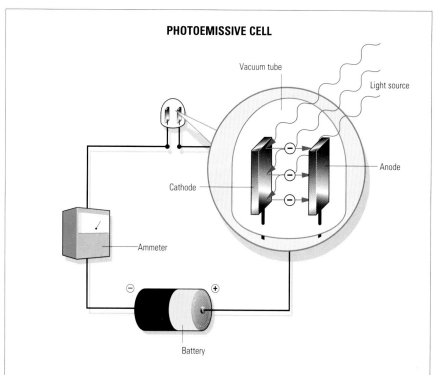

PHOTOEMISSIVE CELL

Vacuum tube

Light source

Anode

Cathode

Ammeter

Battery

A diagram of how a photoemissive cell works. When light strikes the cathode, an increased number of electrons move to the anode, thus increasing the current.

Further reading:

Bhattacharya, P. *Semiconductor Optoelectronic Devices.* Upper Saddle River, New Jersey: Prentice Hall, 1997.

Komp, R. *Practical Photovoltaics.* Ann Arbor, Michigan: Aatec Publications, 1995.

High Resolution Laser Photoionization and Photoelectron Studies. Edited by I. Powis. Chichester, England: Wiley, 1995.

PHOTOVOLTAIC CELLS

Most photovoltaic cells are made of silicon, which is a semiconducting element that can be extracted from ordinary white sand. The most efficient photovoltaic cells, the type used in spacecraft, are made from thin wafers of silicon shaved from a single crystal. To grow a large single crystal, expensive high-grade silicon must be used; half of it will be lost as dust in the slicing process.

Photovoltaic cells are not always made from single crystals of silicon. Amorphous silicon, which has no large-scale crystal structure, can be made into photovoltaic cells much less expensively via vacuum sputtering. In this process, the silicon is fused together from a powder. The electronic properties of amorphous silicon would in theory cause cells made from it to be more efficient than the single-crystal cells. But current manufacturing techniques produce amorphous silicon photovoltaic cells that are only about half as efficient as their single-crystal counterparts. The amorphous cells also tend to degrade somewhat when they are first exposed to light, and their manufacturing processes have been plagued by quality problems that reduce yield. Still, cost considerations are driving research and development efforts to solve these problems, and it is

expected that the amorphous cells will continue to gain in popularity. Amorphous silicon photovoltaic cells are already common in calculators, watches, and other low-power devices.

Photovoltaic cells can generate electricity without the use of an external voltage. As the basis of solar-electric power, they can be used to replace, supplement, or charge batteries in everything from pocket calculators to Earth-orbiting satellites. Arrays of photovoltaic cells can be constructed to cover large areas, such as the roof of a building, providing an important alternative energy source.

Photovoltaic cells are expected to be one of the most important sources of renewable energy in the 21st century. The cost of producing electricity using photovoltaics has fallen dramatically in recent years, from around $1.50 per kilowatt hour in 1980 to around $.10–$.30 per kilowatt hour in1999. Research by the Department of Energy (USDOE) has confirmed that photovoltaic cells could be used to produce electricity anywhere in the United States, even under cloudy skies. According to the USDOE: "Photovoltaics appear to be a long-term and desirable solution to U.S. and global concerns for energy and environment" (see ENERGY RESOURCES; SOLAR POWER).

A CLOSER LOOK

PHOTOCOPIER

A photocopier is a machine that uses light to produce virtually identical reproductions of documents

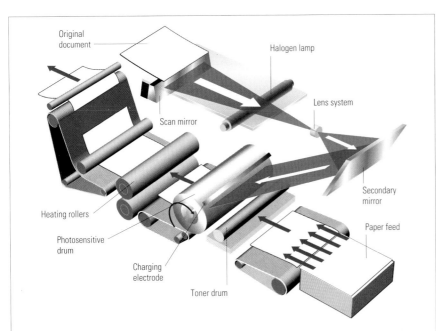

In this type of photocopier a mirror scans across the illuminated document to read the image in narrow sequential strips.

The photocopier is today one of the most common pieces of equipment in offices and other workplaces. The dry-copying system, known as xerography, was invented in 1938 by U.S. physicist Chester Carlson (1906–1968). However, it was not until 1959 that the Xerox company began to produce photocopying machines commercially.

The term *xerography* derives from the Greek word *xeros*, which means dry. This was the first effective copying system that did not involve wetting the material on which the copy was made. Prior to the invention of xerography, document copying involved various projection or contact photographic processes such as microfilming, microfiche production, or photostat production. All those use silver-salt emulsions on plastic or paper and require cumbersome developing, fixing, and drying equipment that use chemicals in solution (see PHOTOGRAPHY).

How a photocopier works

Modern photocopiers are xerographic machines that use an electrostatic copying process. The document to be copied is illuminated in sequential strips from one end to the other by a bright halogen strip light (see LIGHTING). This can be done by moving the light smoothly from one end of the document to the other or by moving the document past a stationary light. Alternatively, the whole document can be illuminated at once and an oscillating mirror will scan the document (see the diagram above). The speed of scanning is synchronized with the rotation of a drum that is thinly coated with a light-sensitive plastic material. A simple lens system forms an accurate

image of the document on the surface of the drum. This image, wrapped around the drum, is the same size as the final copy. The lens system can usually be adjusted to enlarge or reduce the size of the image.

The light-sensitive material on the surface of the drum can retain a strong electrical charge, and the charge at any point on the surface can be dispelled by shining light on it. Before copying, the drum is given a uniform negative charge of static electricity (see ELECTRICITY AND MAGNETISM). When an image is projected onto the drum, the surface parts that bear a very bright part of the image lose all their charge. Dark areas are unaffected and retain their negative charge. Areas of intermediate brightness have a negative charge of intermediate strength.

A very finely powdered black material, the toner, is given a positive charge. Because unlike charges attract one another, the positively charged toner is attracted to those areas of the drum surface that have a negative charge, forming an image. The fine gradations in density of this image correspond to the difference in strength of the electrostatic charge.

A sheet of paper is then moved by rollers close to the rotating drum at the same speed as the drum rotates. This ensures there is no movement between the paper and the surface covered with toner. The paper is also negatively charged, so the image is transferred to the paper by the transfer of toner from the drum. The image on the paper is fragile and can be wiped off, so the paper is passed between high-temperature rollers to fuse the toner into its surface.

Because the light-sensitive drum has a limited life, the most popular system involves the use of a removable and disposable cassette that contains a drum, the associated gearing, and a supply of toner. Such a cassette can produce up to about 12,000 copies before the toner is exhausted and the cassette discarded. A new cassette replaces nearly all the wearable parts of the machine.

Color photocopiers

In 1973, the first color photocopier was produced by the Japanese company, Canon. The laser color copier was launched, also by Canon, in 1986. Color copiers function similarly to black-and-white copiers except that three scannings are required instead of one. Filters resolve each scan into yellow, magenta, or cyan components (see COLOR). Three toners, one of each of these colors, are also needed.

R. YOUNGSON

See also: FACSIMILE TRANSMISSION; PRINTING.

Further reading:

Mort, J. *The Anatomy of Xerography: Its Invention and Evolution.* Jefferson, North Carolina: McFarland, 1989.

CONNECTIONS

● The drum and rollers inside photocopiers are powered by **ELECTRIC MOTORS**.

PHOTOGRAPHY

Photography is the process of making permanent images using light-sensitive materials

Many photographers, professional and amateur, record the wonders of the natural world. High-power lenses have allowed them to capture rarely seen animal behavior and isolated habitats.

Photographic images are everywhere. People's lives are documented in family photographs, and the faces of politicians, entertainers, and sports figures are almost as familiar to us as our own relatives and friends—as are historic photographs of wars and other world events. But 200 years ago, photography did not exist. While the wealthy few may have had the means to commission artists to paint their portraits or even sculpt their figures, the faces of most people's ancestors are lost to history. Painters often warped the truth of an event that they were recording for posterity, and many of their pictures only had symbolic value rather than being faithful to reality.

Today, news photographers record every significant public event, and cameras ride on submarines and spacecraft to explore the world and beyond. The images they record are available almost instantly. Photography also spawned the movie and television industries, providing information and entertainment of unprecedented richness. The world of instant pictures we take for granted today began with the first creation of a permanent image using materials that are sensitive to light (see the box on page 995).

Photography begins with the formation of an image inside a box. Light reflected off an object enters the camera through a small hole, or aperture, generating an inverted image on the opposite wall of the box (see LIGHT AND OPTICS). In order for the image to be recorded, it must fall upon light-sensitive material such as photographic film. The film is then developed with chemicals that bring out the image and prevent additional light from affecting it further. Depending on the type of film, this creates either a negative, which can be used to make prints, or positive slide transparencies. Once the film has been developed, it can be used to print the same photograph over and over again.

Film is not the only means of recording an image. Arrays of solid-state photocells can record a digital image that can be stored on a computer chip. This is particularly convenient when generating images to be stored, displayed, or manipulated by computer. Digital photography is quickly gaining in popularity (see the box on page 999).

The camera

There are many different types of cameras, but they all share the same basic parts. The body of the camera, made of metal or plastic, is the box in which the image is formed. Inside most cameras, there is also a winding mechanism for advancing the film so that

---

CORE FACTS

- Camera optics are designed to focus an image onto a light-sensitive film.
- Developing the film is a chemical process that brings out the image and makes it permanent.
- Film for prints is developed into negatives, and the image is then projected onto photographic paper. Film for slides creates a positive image, and the developed film transparency is simply mounted for viewing or projecting onto a screen.

CONNECTIONS

- Miniature cameras have been developed for the purpose of **INTELLIGENCE-GATHERING**.

- **MILITARY AIRCRAFT** often carry cameras to record tactical information and to assess the damage that has been caused by their attacks.

THE OPTICS OF A CAMERA

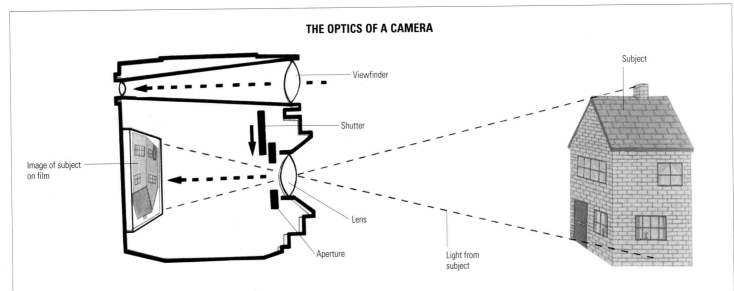

A camera works by focusing the light reflected off an object onto a piece of light-sensitive film. The light passes through a lens that refracts it enough to form a sharp image on the film. The shutter opens for a fixed amount of time, letting light through the aperture to expose the film.

its frames may be exposed in succession. Light enters the camera via a lens, which focuses the light onto the film. The shutter keeps the light out until it is triggered, when it lets light pass through the aperture into the body of the camera and exposes the film for a set period of time.

The size and shape of the camera body depend on the size and format of the film for which it is designed. Common formats include rolls of 35-mm film and easy-to-load cartridges in 110- and 126-film sizes. The disc camera is designed to take film in which each frame is mounted separately around the edge of a plastic disc. A popular camera used at parties and on vacation is the single-use camera, which has a cardboard body in which the 35-mm film is already loaded. Once the film is exposed, the entire unit is sent in for developing, and the various parts of the camera are recycled. Single-use cameras can be easily waterproofed by putting them inside a sealed plastic case, making underwater photography available to the general public.

At the other end of the spectrum, many professional photographers use cameras sized to take larger film, which provides higher resolution images. (Each dot on a high resolution image represents a smaller area than a dot on a lower resolution image, so the high resolution images can be enlarged without becoming blurred). Roll film with 2-inch- (5-cm-) square frames is a good compromise between resolution and portability. When the very sharpest pictures are needed, and speed and convenience can be sacrificed, the view camera is a good option. It uses individual sheets of film as large as 11 by 14 inches (28 by 35.5 cm), and its accordion-like body can be adjusted to change the distance between the film plane and the lens.

Another important way of categorizing cameras is by type of viewfinder. The viewfinder is where the photographer looks in order to frame and focus the picture. The range-finder camera has a viewing system separate from the lens through which the actual photograph is taken. Two mirrors are used to create a double image, and one of the mirrors moves along with the lens as it is focused. The system is designed so that the two images will be superimposed when the subject is in focus. However, mistakes in framing can be made, particularly in close-up shots, because of the difference in viewing angle, or parallax, between the viewfinder and the lens.

Range-finder cameras are not as popular as they once were. They do not generally accommodate the interchangeable lenses often required by serious photographers, and for the point-and-shoot category of user they have been largely replaced by the compact 35-mm camera with auto-focus, a function enabled

AUTOMATED FILM PROCESSING

In the 1970s, drive-through and storefront film processing facilities began competing to offer service in hours instead of days. This was made possible by the development of automated film processing machines, or mini-labs, that use the method by which most photographs are processed today.

Designed for operation by employees with a minimum of training, some mini-labs eliminate the darkroom with daylight-loading hoppers that accept the entire film cassette. Others must back up to a darkroom from which they are loaded, but the rest of the machine, being fully enclosed, can stand in a lit area. Most can process all the common film sizes.

Newer film-developing systems use smaller quantities of chemicals, which makes for easier handling and helps allay environmental concerns. They also employ chemicals packaged in containers that snap directly into the machine, thereby eliminating mixing and pouring.

Mini-labs are ideally suited for developing snapshots quickly and at a reasonable price. However, mini-lab facilities do not generally offer the range of services or on-site expertise provided by the commercial photo-finisher or custom laboratory. For these reasons, it seems likely that there will continue to be a market for a range of photographic services.

WIDER IMPACT

by microprocessors. The camera has set focus positions for each distance range, or zone, in which the subject might be found. Some auto-focus cameras detect the subject's position by bouncing infrared light off it; in others, reflected sound waves or sonar may be used. Some have only a few zones, making focusing somewhat unreliable, while others have dozens. An even more accurate auto-focus system called phase contrast detection does not depend on zones at all and can adjust the lens to any position.

In auto-focus cameras, the viewfinder is simply used to frame the scene. Markings generally indicate where in the field of view the camera will be making its focus determination. This is particularly important if various elements of the composition are at different distances. Simple viewfinders for framing are also used in fixed-focus cameras such as the cartridge and single-use cameras, in which the focus adjustment is factory set for subjects about 8–10 feet (2.5–3 m) from the camera. Other inexpensive cameras have a small number of focusing zones that may be set by the user; for example, close-up, intermediate, and "infinity" (for anything farther than about 15 feet [4.5 m] away).

With the single-lens reflex (SLR) camera, a system of mirrors and prisms allows the photographer to look directly through the lens. Parallax is therefore eliminated, and the viewfinder shows exactly what will appear in the picture. Many types of interchangeable lenses are available for most SLRs, and they have become the most popular choice for those looking for a better-quality 35-mm camera.

The twin-lens reflex (TLR) camera is used mostly by professional photographers, and generally takes 2-inch-by-2-inch (5-cm-by-5-cm) film. It has a separate viewing system, like the range-finder camera, but uses a mirror to reflect the image onto a flat viewing screen many times larger than the usual viewfinder. Some photographers prefer using such a viewing screen when composing and focusing a picture, even though it is seen in mirror image. However, the larger size of the camera makes it hard to transport safely, interchangeable lenses are not generally available, and there is again the problem of the parallax to contend with.

In many cameras, the size of the aperture is adjustable to control the amount of light that reaches the film. This size is referred to as the f-stop, representing the ratio between the diameter of the lens and its focal length. However, only the denominator is given as the f-stop. This is the origin of the somewhat confusing situation in which a larger f-stop represents a smaller aperture and vice versa. The square of the f-stop is inversely proportional to the amount of light that each setting lets into the camera.

The size of the aperture affects the depth of field, which is the range of distance over which sharp focus can be achieved. Depth of field is greater for smaller apertures and for more distant subjects. Often a photographer takes advantage of a smaller depth of field to emphasize a subject and blur out the background. Like the shutter speed, the aperture width is selected

AERIAL PHOTOGRAPHY

This photograph of Central Park was taken from the air through a fish-eye lens.

The first photographs to be taken from aircraft were for military use, but they have since found many other applications in mapping, environmental protection, traffic studies, and archaeology. While simply pointing an ordinary camera down from an airplane or helicopter may produce an acceptable photograph, specialized equipment gives the best results.

Since detail and resolution are important, large film sizes are generally used. Lenses are set for infinity, with a fast shutter speed to reduce the blurring effects of the aircraft's vibration. The cameras may be mounted in a window frame and operated by hand or built into the aircraft's belly and operated by remote control.

Low-altitude aerial shots are useful for photographing large outdoor events; in such cases it may be sufficient to send a radio-controlled 35-mm camera a few hundred feet up, tethered to a kite or a helium-filled balloon. At the other extreme, astronauts have taken pictures from Earth orbit that have shown us an entirely different view of our planet.

A CLOSER LOOK

according to the intensity of light that is available. The aperture may also be adjusted to cause over- or underexposure, depending on the visual effect the photographer is trying to achieve.

The light exposure also depends on the amount of time that the shutter is set to remain open. The shutter speed is given in fractions of a second, such as $\frac{1}{1000}$ or $\frac{1}{125}$. It affects not only the exposure of the film, but also the speed of the action that will be "frozen" in the photograph. If the subject moves a significant amount in relation to the framed scene during the time the shutter remains open, it will appear blurred in the picture. So, for example, a moving car may have to be photographed at a shutter speed of $\frac{1}{500}$ or $\frac{1}{1000}$ in order to freeze the action, while a person walking may be captured with a $\frac{1}{125}$ setting. Of course, sometimes blurry effects are desired in order to depict great speed or for some other reason.

Many cameras have manual shutter settings for time exposures, for example to take star-trail photographs, which show stars and planets as streaks of

WIDE-ANGLE LENS

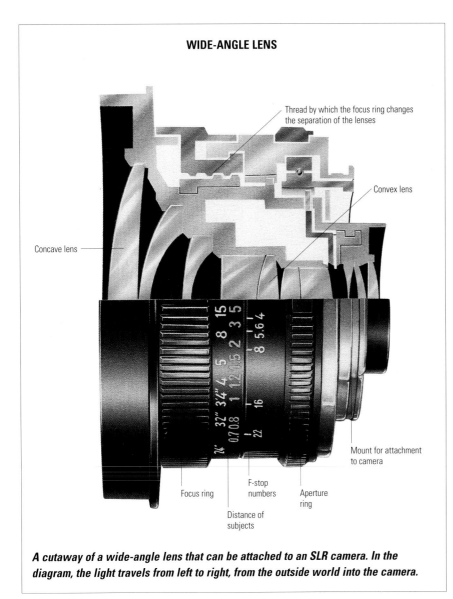

Thread by which the focus ring changes the separation of the lenses

Convex lens

Concave lens

Mount for attachment to camera

Focus ring

F-stop numbers

Aperture ring

Distance of subjects

A cutaway of a wide-angle lens that can be attached to an SLR camera. In the diagram, the light travels from left to right, from the outside world into the camera.

light across the sky. For exposures longer than about ¹⁄₆₀ second, a tripod is generally used to eliminate blurring due to camera movement.

Photographic lenses

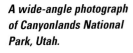

A wide-angle photograph of Canyonlands National Park, Utah.

Light enters the camera via a lens, which may be adjusted with a focusing ring. A lens with a short focal length, the distance between the lens and the point where a sharp image is formed, provides a wide-angle view, taking in an entire scene. Depth of field is greatest with a wide-angle lens. The fish-eye lens is an extreme wide-angle lens with a 180-degree field of view. Wide-angle lenses produce distortion of varying degrees; the exaggerated fish-eye lens actually results in a circular image. The panoramic camera is designed to have an angle of acceptance about twice as wide as that of a standard camera; it can accommodate wide-angle lenses without distortion and is used for photographs of scenic views and portraits of large groups.

The normal lens provides the same view as the human eye from the same distance. For the 35-mm camera, a normal lens is one with a 50-mm focal length, and a lens of this size is generally provided with 35-mm cameras when they are purchased. A macro lens is a normal type of lens that is designed to allow focusing very near the subject, so that close-up shots may be taken.

The long telephoto lens zeros in on a subject and provides a magnified view. Its perspective compresses the scene, shortening the apparent distance between foreground and background objects. A telephoto lens must be carefully focused to get a clear picture of the subject. Since telephoto lenses also tend to be "slow," requiring a relatively long exposure to get enough light to the film, and are heavy as well, they are often used with tripods.

Zoom lenses are those in which the focal length can be varied. They have become extremely popular, because they allow the photographer the flexibility to experiment with framing a variety of shots without changing lenses. They have also made a variety of photographic effects more accessible to the amateur by reducing the need to purchase and carry multiple fixed focal length lenses. Several ranges are available, from wide-angle through telephoto.

Glass or plastic filters may be screwed or snapped onto the lens to screen out particular colors of light (see COLOR). Filters may also be in the form of flexible gelatin sheets affixed to a holder or simply held up in front of the camera. A neutral density filter reduces the light uniformly, without affecting the color. Color-correcting filters are used to

In poor light conditions, photographers can focus natural light onto the subject using reflectors.

compensate for characteristics of the film or lighting; some films, for example, tend to give a bluish cast when used outdoors, and fluorescent lighting often produces a greenish hue. Filters that affect color may also be used to produce a desired artistic effect.

Although filters subtract light of particular color, they are useful in black-and-white photography as well. Film chemicals are not equally sensitive to all wavelengths of light. In black-and-white photographs, this manifests itself as objects showing up lighter or darker than their intended illumination in the scene. Colored filters can correct such effects and increase the contrast between objects. Polarizing filters, which screen for the direction of the incoming light, eliminate haze, glare, and reflections.

Lighting the scene

Without sufficient light, it is impossible to form an image on film. The quantity, quality, and direction of the illumination are also vital in achieving the desired visual effect of light and shadow in the photograph. The amount of light available to the camera is measured with an exposure meter, also called a light meter. The amount of light that is necessary for an exposure depends on the type of film. Older, handheld exposure meters needed to be manually set for the film speed; that is, the sensitivity of the particular film to light. Most cameras now have built-in exposure meters that obtain the value of the film speed from a coded pattern on the film cassette.

Outdoors in daylight, in other brightly lit conditions, or when using very fast film, the exposure meter may indicate that existing light is sufficient for taking the photograph. If not, artificial lighting must be employed. The lighting used for photography may be either instantaneous or continuous. Continuous lighting is generally provided by means of high-wattage photoflood lamps aimed at the subject with reflectors. Instantaneous lighting includes various forms of flash light. Sometimes a double flash is used: the first flash causes the pupils of subjects' eyes to contract, which stops red-eye caused by the eye reflecting the main flash during the exposure.

FILM MATERIALS

Photographic films are layered structures. The topcoat is a hard protective layer of clear gelatin, intended to prevent the film from getting scratched. Underneath the topcoat is the light-sensitive layer of the film, the emulsion. Black-and-white film has a layer that contains crystals of silver bromide and silver iodide. When light hits these crystals, its energy causes a chemical reaction, changing the material's structure. Different areas of the emulsion are affected by the extent to which they have been exposed to the light. This creates a latent image; it cannot be seen until the chemicals used in developing cause the silver metal to be freed from its compounds in the areas that will be black.

Color film has three layers of emulsion. The layers use silver compounds just like in black-and-white film. However, each layer of emulsion is designed to be sensitive to only one primary color of light (red, green, or blue) and forms its own latent image. The red, green, and blue emulsion layers each contain a coupler, a substance that will react with the developing chemicals to form cyan (greenish blue), magenta (bluish red), and yellow dyes respectively. These colors are all that are required to create a full-color image of any scene.

Beneath the emulsion layer is the subbing, an adhesive that holds it onto the base of the film. The base is what we normally think of as the "film"—it is a transparent, flexible strip or sheet of plastic. The plastic used in early films was nitrocellulose, which was highly flammable, and fires occurred frequently, especially in moviemaking where huge stocks of film were warehoused. Today, cellulose acetate, which is much less flammable than nitrocellulose, is generally used. The bottom layer of the film is the antihalation backing, designed to prevent light from reflecting off the film base or the camera itself. Both the topcoat and the antihalation backing are washed away during the developing process.

A CLOSER LOOK

THE FIRST PHOTOGRAPHERS

The first known photograph was taken by Joseph Nicéphore Niepce in 1826.

Some of the principles of forming an image inside a dark chamber, or camera obscura, were known to Greek philosopher Aristotle (384–322 B.C.E.). When light reflecting off an object comes into the chamber through a hole on one side, it forms an inverted image of the object on the opposite wall. If the wall was opaque the image could be viewed from outside.

Techniques were refined during the Renaissance, and inventors began experimenting with improving the image by replacing the pinhole with a lens and using a mirror to turn it right side up. The use of lenses created a brighter, sharper image and allowed the chamber to be made small enough to carry around. But there was still no way to record the image except to trace it onto a sheet of paper by hand.

In the 18th century, chemists discovered that certain silver salts darkened when exposed to light. They made photograms by spreading the salts on paper, placing objects such as leaves or flowers over the salts, and then exposing the arrangement to sunlight. The paper around the objects darkened, but that under the objects, hidden from the light, remained as a white silhouette. However, these early experimenters did not know how to stop the reaction: the whole sheet would soon darken if exposed to light.

The first known photograph was taken in 1826 by French chemist Joseph Nicéphore Niepce (1765–1833), whose process, using a tarry material on a pewter plate, took eight hours to produce a fuzzy image of his rooftop. He also had trouble getting the chemical reaction to stop, so he consulted with his colleague Louis Daguerre (1789–1851). Daguerre built a camera with a polished silver iodide-coated copper plate sitting at the focal point of a lens. After the plate was exposed, he brought out the image with mercury vapor and fixed it with a salt bath that stopped it from developing further. The sharp, clear images produced by this method came to be called daguerreotypes.

At about the same time, British scientist William Henry Fox Talbot (1800–1877) was developing a way to make what he called calotypes—paper negatives in which the dark and light regions were reversed. An unlimited number of positive copies could be printed by shining light through a calotype onto light-sensitive paper that would then be developed. This was a major advantage over Daguerre's process, but the calotypes produced a rather fuzzy picture. Eventually methods were developed using glass plates coated with photosensitive chemicals. These yielded sharp images but could also be reproduced by projecting light through the glass. This was the technology that allowed Mathew Brady (c.1823–1896) to take his famous photographs of the American Civil War (1861–1865), and its widespread use created a photographic record of history for the first time.

Still, photography was for specialists, not for the general public. The glass plates were too heavy to carry around, and the photographer had to have the skills and equipment to develop the photographs. George Eastman (1854–1932), an American bank teller, changed all that. In 1884, he developed a thin film coated with photographic chemicals that could be rolled up into a small container. In 1888, Eastman incorporated this film into a camera called the Kodak. Smaller than a shoe box, it contained enough film for 100 photographs. Once the film was exposed, the camera would be sent back to Eastman's company for the film to be developed and replaced with a fresh roll. Eastman's next major development was the Brownie camera, which he launched in 1900. Cheap and easy to use, Eastman's Brownie made photography more accessible to the general public.

HISTORY OF TECHNOLOGY

Early photographers, working before electric lighting was available, used flash powder, a mixture of chemicals that created a small explosion when ignited, resulting in a flash of light and a puff of smoke. The disadvantages of such a method included burned fingers, singed eyebrows, and the occasional conflagration. Little wonder that when flashbulbs became available, they soon became popular with photographers. Flash powder quickly fell out of use.

Flashbulbs differ from ordinary lightbulbs in that they were intended not to burn over a long period of time, but all at once. For this reason, instead of using a durable filament in an evacuated bulb, they contained shredded foil in an oxidizing atmosphere. A current caused the foil to ignite, creating a flash, and then the bulb would be thrown out and replaced. For the sake of convenience, four-bulb flash cubes and eight-bulb or ten-bulb flash cartridges were developed. While flashbulbs were much safer than flash powder, because the explosion was contained within the bulb, they could only be used once and were a relatively expensive solution to the problem.

Most modern cameras are equipped with an electronic flash. The flash unit may also be packaged separately, as a flashgun that may be handheld, fitted to the camera, or attached elsewhere. Electronic flash units work from battery power stored in a capacitor, which sets off a flash tube good for thousands of flashes. They may include exposure meters, and some allow a range of flash intensities.

Getting it on film

Photographic film is made with light-sensitive materials that can be processed to form a permanent image. Its exact structure and the specific materials that are used are determined by whether it is black-and-white or color and by what its characteristics are to be (see the box on page 995). Black-and-white films and those used for color prints are developed into negatives; the images on the developed film are dark where the final image will be light, and vice versa. In color negatives, not only are the light intensities reversed, but colors appear as their complements. The negatives are then printed to create the positive image. Transparency film for producing color slides does not provide negatives. Instead, the film is developed as a positive image, which is the final product; it is mounted in a small cardboard or plastic frame for use with a projector or handheld viewer.

The response of the film to different wavelengths of light is called its color sensitivity; it is important in black-and-white films as well as in color photography. Most black-and-white films are panchromatic, meaning that they respond to the entire visible spectrum. This produces the most natural representation of the various colored objects in shades of gray.

The corresponding property in color films is called color balance. Daylight and artificial light have different proportions of reddish and bluish light, which will affect the way colors are seen. Most color films for prints are balanced for daylight, but they

have a wide enough response to produce good color in artificial light as well. Color slide films are less forgiving, so separate versions of these films are manufactured for daylight or artificial light.

Films vary in the amount of light they require to form an image. This is called the speed of the film because a faster (more light-sensitive) film will record an image in less time—with a faster shutter speed—than a slower film for a given aperture width and light intensity. Film speed can be expressed as an ASA (American Standards Association) number, which increases geometrically with film speed, or as a DIN (*Deutsche Industrie-Normen*—German industrial standards) number, which increases logarithmically. These two systems have been combined by the International Standards Organization

Modern photographic slide and print film has been laid out for use in a fashion shoot.

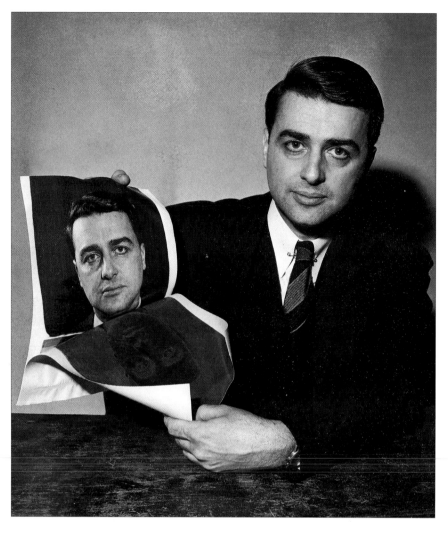

Edwin Land demonstrates the self-developing film he invented in 1947.

look. Faster film tends to be grainy, and enlarging the photograph makes the effect more obvious. It is generally not a concern in standard-size prints. Resolving power is the ability of the film to pick up small details in the image. It is measured by photographing a test chart and determining the number of lines per millimeter that can be individually distinguished. Sharpness is the ability to discern edges between photographed objects.

Bringing out the picture

Developing a photograph is the process of making the chemical changes in the film emulsion visible as an image. For slide film, the result is a positive transparency and the procedure is complete at this point. For black-and-white or color negative film, the negative image is projected onto photographic paper and developed as a positive image.

Today, most snapshots are sent to be developed at facilities offering quick service with fully automated methods (see the box on page 992). However, many photographers still prefer to develop films manually so that so that they can adjust the exposure to achieve the look they want. The photographer's darkroom is so called because parts of the developing process must take place in the absence of light. If the film is removed from the camera while the light is on, it will be ruined. So, in complete darkness, it is taken from the camera and loaded into a reel to be placed in the developing tank.

Several chemicals are used in the developing process. The developer reacts with the silver salts in the film emulsion, resulting in black metallic silver being formed in the pattern of the image. In the case of color film, dyes are developed from the reaction between coupler chemicals in the emulsion and the developer, and the black silver is later bleached out. After a specific amount of time in the developer fluid, a stop bath is used to prevent the reaction from going too far. The fixer, also called hypo, removes

(ISO): an ISO number is the ASA number followed by the DIN number. According to this system, a film with ISO number 400/27 (which is ASA 400, DIN 27) is twice as fast as a film denoted ISO 200/24.

The grain of a film is the tendency of the silver particles it produces to clump during developing. The less grain in a film, the better the picture will

---

PHOTOGRAPHY USING INVISIBLE LIGHT

It is not only visible light that can be used to form images. Other forms of electromagnetic radiation (see ELECTROMAGNETIC RADIATION) also darken light-sensitive substances. A common example of an image formed using radiation other than visible light is a medical X-ray radiograph. Because X rays can pass through material that is opaque to visible light, they are used to take pictures of the inside of objects, usually the body (see MEDICAL IMAGING). The X rays used to take these pictures are produced by machine, but many forms of invisible light occur naturally on Earth and in the night sky.

Heat, or infrared radiation, is one form of invisible light that is abundant in nature. Infrared images are made using silver chloride or silver iodide emulsions.

Infrared photography can be used to make images of warm objects at night, through undergrowth, and even through thin solid walls. False colors are frequently added to distinguish between objects that are at different temperatures.

Similarly, ultraviolet (UV) light can be used to make pictures. UV light has more energy than visible light (infrared has less), and it requires special film and lenses. Glass reflects UV light, and therefore lenses have to be constructed of silica or quartz. UV cameras have filters over their lenses to keep any visible light from getting into the camera so that the image is formed from only UV light. UV photography is important in astronomy and in detecting counterfeit money, for which a UV light source is needed.

A CLOSER LOOK

the unexposed silver compounds from the emulsion. This renders the film insensitive to further light exposure. Generally, a hypo eliminator is used next so that residual hypo does not continue to work; this would bleach the negative over time. Finally, the film is washed with water, often with a wetting agent to prevent streaks.

Photographic prints are created using an enlarger, which projects light via a lens through the negative and onto light-sensitive photographic paper. The process reverses the negative, because less light travels through its darker regions, so these areas of the print will receive less exposure and be lighter. The size of the image, its focus, and its brightness can be adjusted with controls on the enlarger. The exposure time and lens aperture of the enlarger may be set just like those of a camera can.

Photographic papers use light-sensitive emulsions similar to those on film. Papers for black-and-white prints are generally not sensitive to red light, so the darkroom may be illuminated with a red safelight during black-and-white printing. Color papers have layers of emulsion sensitive to red, green, and blue respectively. Filters in the enlarger are used for color adjustment. The photographic papers are processed in a flat tray, using chemicals similar to those used for developing the negative, and then are dried.

Self-developing film was invented by Edwin Land (1909–1991) in 1947 and used in his company's Polaroid Land cameras. Polaroid film includes a chemical pod between two peel-apart sheets, one of which is photographic paper. After the exposure is made, the film is pulled through rollers in the camera to break the pod, freeing the chemicals to do their work on the film emulsion. After the correct amount of time has passed, the protective sheet is stripped off to reveal the finished photograph. Some films of this type must be wiped with fixer once they are dry. Newer integral instant cameras produce a snapshot that pops out of the camera and finishes developing in plain sight. Instant cameras are fun to use and are important tools for scientists or craftsmen checking or recording results during the progress of an experiment or construction project. However, instant pictures are significantly more expensive than ordinary photographic films and are generally inconvenient to duplicate. In addition, their chemistry does not work well in cold-weather conditions.

S. CALVO

See also: ANIMATION; CINEMATOGRAPHY; DIGITAL SIGNALS AND SYSTEMS; IMAGING TECHNOLOGY; LIGHT AND OPTICS; MEDICAL IMAGING; MICROSCOPY; TELEVISION AND COMPUTER MONITOR; VIDEOGRAPHY.

Further reading:

Aaland, M. *Digital Photography.* New York: Random House, 1992.
The *Focal Encyclopedia of Photography.* Edited by L. Stroebel and R. Zakia. Boston: Focal Press, 1993.
Holland, G. *Inventors and Inventions: Photography.* Tarrytown, New York: Marshall Cavendish, 1996.

DIGITAL PHOTOGRAPHY

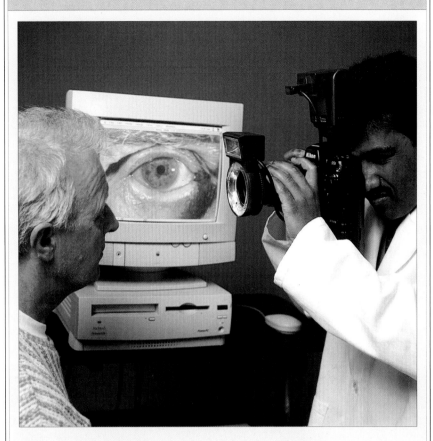

A doctor uses a digital camera to take an image of a patient's eye.

Digital cameras record visual information electronically rather than on film. For applications requiring the best possible resolution, such as book publishing, digital cameras that can scan the image line by line are sometimes used. The process takes about 10 minutes and uses about 100 megabytes (MB) of computer memory per image.

For ordinary picture-taking, mass-market digital cameras employ a charge-coupled device, or CCD, which records an entire scene at once on 4–7 MB and stores it on a computer chip or removable memory module. Some digital cameras look something like handheld video games. They have LCD screens that allow the photographer to see a preview of the image. They also display exposure data and on-screen menus that guide the photographer through exposure options (see OUTPUT AND DISPLAY DEVICE).

To reduce the amount of memory space the image takes up, digital cameras use image compression techniques, which degrade the picture somewhat, limiting the amount it can be enlarged and still yield a quality result. However, this situation is currently improving, and will continue to do so as advances in software and hardware allow more information to be stored in a smaller space and at a lower price.

Digital photography may someday replace film photography for most applications. Most images can now be manipulated and exchanged by computer. Even family snapshots in photograph albums and shoe boxes are gradually being replaced by multimedia slide shows, web sites, and image files attached to e-mail messages. It is much more convenient to be able to input images directly from the camera into the computer than to go through a chemical developing process and then use an optical scanner to turn the prints into a digitized image. The digital technology also has the benefit of reducing the quantity of photographic chemicals flushed into the environment. Doctors are making use of digital image technology for telemedicine (see TELEMEDICINE). By viewing compressed high-resolution images, doctors can study a patient who is many miles away.

A CLOSER LOOK

PIPELINE

Pipelines transport gases, liquids, and powders over long distances using pipe sections, valves, and pumps

Pipelines around the world

Various pipeline designs are now used all over the world. The Trans-Arabian pipeline, built in 1950, carries oil from wells in the Saudi Arabian desert to the Mediterranean port of Sidon more than 1000 miles (1600 km) away. This pipeline rests above ground on supports anchored to the desert floor. The Trans-Alaska pipeline stretches 800 miles (1300 km) south from the oil fields of the North Slope at Prudhoe Bay to the seaport in Valdez. About half of this pipeline sits above ground to avoid melting the supporting permafrost soil; the rest of the pipeline is buried. The Trans-Canadian Pipeline carries natural gas nearly 2300 miles (3700 km), from the border of Alberta and Saskatchewan to Montreal, Quebec. The Export Pipeline in Europe distributes natural gas from Siberia to countries over the 4000 miles (6400 km) along its length.

Pipelines that move large quantities of petroleum products are expensive to build but economical to operate. Because of their efficiency, pipelines distribute more petroleum products worldwide than any other means of transportation.

Overall design

Pipelines are designed for the materials they must handle and the environment they must withstand. The pressure, temperature, and chemical properties of the material to be transported determine the requirements for the interior surface of the pipe and the overall strength of the structure. Strict design codes for pipelines incorporate complex equations that take into account the pipe friction, the viscosity (reluctance to flow) of the fluid, the pressure, the temperature, the speed of travel, and the turbulence of the flow. Curves, joints, valves, and changes in pipe diameter must all be considered in the design of a pipeline, because they affect the flow of the fluid and the resulting stresses on the piping system. Resulting pipe diameters range from 2 to 48 in (5 cm to 1.2 m). Pipes can be made of hardened clay, concrete, aluminum, iron, steel, plastic, or various combinations of these materials.

The Trans-Alaska Pipeline transports oil from Prudhoe Bay to Valdez, Alaska.

CONNECTIONS

● To keep fluids or gas traveling at appropriate speed, **PUMP AND COMPRESSOR** stations may be situated at intervals along pipelines. Pumping stations quicken the flow rate of oil and liquids; compressor stations act on gas.

Transporting liquids through pipes has been practiced since at least 5000 B.C.E. In ancient China, pipes made of bamboo and clay were used to transport water using gravity to force the flow (see WATER SUPPLY AND TREATMENT). Oil and natural gas pipelines were first used in the United States, following the commercial production of crude oil and the development in the 1920s of seamless, electrically welded pipe capable of withstanding the pressures needed to move oil.

Today, oil and gas pipelines use pumps and compressors to move large volumes of material from remote wells to refineries or seaports for further processing and distribution. Pipelines can also move liquid industrial waste, sewage, and slurries (mixtures of small particles and water) of coal, ore, limestone, and so on. Some industries also use pipelines to transport small-grained solids such as sawdust or wheat by blowing air through the pipes.

CORE FACTS

■ Pipelines are widely used to transport a variety of materials, including oil, natural gas, sewage, slurries, and powders.

■ Pipeline operations are automated to ensure safe and efficient operation.

■ Oil and gas travel through pipelines at speeds ranging from 3 to 15 miles (5 to 24 km) per hour.

■ The Trans-Arabian pipeline carries oil from wells in the Saudi Arabian desert to the Mediterranean port of Sidon more than 1000 miles (1600 km) away.

The origin of the Trans-Alaska Pipeline is in an oil field in Prudhoe Bay, Alaska.

The outside environment of the pipeline will determine the exterior surface of the pipe and the support structure that is required. For example, the support structure of the Trans-Alaska pipeline must not disturb the supporting permafrost and needs to withstand freeze-thaw cycles at the soil surface. Pipelines in areas where earthquakes are common must be flexible enough to withstand the force of earth tremors. Similarly, pipelines in areas of heavy snowfall must be designed to withstand the extra weight of drifted snow. In populated areas, pipelines are usually buried underground so that normal land use can continue on the surface. Pipelines running on the seafloor, such as in the North Sea, are coated in concrete to protect them from corrosion and to keep them from floating free of the bottom. All pipeline materials must tolerate the expansion and contraction of caused by temperature changes in the moving fluid and the environment.

Operating pipelines

Pipelines use pumping stations or compressor stations every 30 to 150 miles (48 to 240 km) to overcome the effects of gravity and friction. Compressor stations keep natural gas moving at about 15 miles (24 km) per hour by maintaining the pressure as high as 2000 lb per sq in (13.8 million pascals), which is roughly 136 times atmospheric pressure. Pumping stations for oil and liquids often use centrifugal pumps that admit fluid, increase the speed at which it is traveling with an impeller (a propeller-like device) and send it on along the pipeline.

Because pipelines are designed and built for specific pressure, temperature, and flow-rate conditions, control equipment is crucial to their safe and efficient operation. Control is automated for pumps, valves, and compressors and the drivers that power them—electric motors, steam turbines, gas engines, diesel engines, or gas turbines. Computers analyze sensor data communicated from points along the pipeline and make adjustments to ensure continuous movement of the fluid. In addition, control equipment allows the transport of different petroleum products in batches along the same pipeline. Mixing between batches can be prevented by placing a pig (rubber sphere) between different products. At the delivery point, measuring devices called densitometers are used to identify the materials by their density when they arrive at their destination. Sensors also activate alarms, shut down pumping stations, and close valves in case of leaks or fires.

P. WEIS-TAYLOR

See also: OIL AND NATURAL GAS PRODUCTION; OIL TANKER AND BULK CARRIER; WATER SUPPLY AND TREATMENT.

Further reading:

Ahmad, H. *Gas Pipeline Renewal: Insertion Technology.* Houston, Texas: Gulf Publishing, 1990.
Kennedy, J. *Oil and Gas Pipeline Fundamentals.* Tulsa, Oklahoma: PennWell Books, 1993.

UNDERWATER PIPELINES

Building pipelines across deserts, mountains, tundra, and farmland demands heavy machinery for digging, specialized welding and inspection, and the construction of pumping stations and support structures. However, laying pipelines underwater is probably the most difficult operation of all.

Underwater construction requires all these steps to be conducted from ships and barges, which are exposed to storms and waves. The pipe must be able to tolerate the corrosive properties of the water and be maneuvered against buoyancy and currents. Final inspections and tests can be carried out only by divers working on the seafloor.

Despite these problems, underwater pipelines are now an invaluable part of oil production and distribution. Today's pipelines operate at depths of as much as 525 ft (160 m) for distances of hundreds of miles, delivering millions of barrels of oil per day to onshore refineries.

A CLOSER LOOK

PLANT BREEDING AND PROPAGATION

The breeding and propagation of plants are fundamental to the success of many types of agriculture

Crop plants such as corn have been bred from wild plants by humans over several thousand years. Modern breeding techniques have given rise to many more specialized crop types that can be grown successfully in huge monocultures.

CONNECTIONS

● Some forms of **BIOTECHNOLOGY**, such as **GENETIC ENGINEERING** techniques, are being used widely in plant breeding to produce novel strains with special traits.

● Although many of the procedures used are different, **ANIMAL BREEDING** is very similar to plant breeding in that artificial selection is used to produce organisms with particular favored characteristics.

● **HYDROPONICS** is a method of growing plants that uses nutrient-filled water rather than soil.

Plants are thought to have been first brought under cultivation about 10,000 years ago, when the earliest farmers collected seed from edible wild plants and planted them (see AGRICULTURE, HISTORY OF). Seeds from the most useful individual plants would be used and those from the poorer plants rejected, established a trend of crop improvement over time. Human skill in propagating plants successfully became vital to the survival of early agricultural societies. Over many years, crop plants began to differ significantly from their wild ancestors, becoming domesticated and often unable to survive in the wild. Wheat (*Triticum* species) and peas (*Pisum sativum*) were domesticated in the Middle East at least 8000 years ago, and corn (*Zea mays*) was cultivated in Central America 7000 years ago.

Once crops had been domesticated, their development over time in various regions led to the formation of distinct "land races," each adapted to the conditions in which it was established. Work with these races led to the development of modern breeding techniques at the beginning of the 20th century.

PLANT BREEDING

Plant breeding is the genetic improvement of plants (see the box on page 1004), typically to increase qualities such as high yield, oil content, and seed size in crop plants or ornamental appeal in decorative plants. In practice, the end goal of the plant breeder is generally to produce a new strain of plants displaying a wide range of favored traits, such as size, frost or heat tolerance, and, increasingly importantly, disease resistance. Novel strains may be patented (see INVENTION AND INNOVATION).

Selection—the basic breeding tool

Breeding starts with the selection of existing plants that display useful traits; these plants are the raw material for the development of a new strain. The most basic selection system, which has been practiced for centuries, is called mass selection. This simply involves taking seed only from the most favored plants to use for the next crop. How the second crop turns out may then be used as a basis for evaluating the parental crop; this is called progeny testing. Selection must be made on the basis of inherited traits, rather than on characteristics due to environmental factors, such as variations in soil type. Therefore, progeny testing is generally preferable to selection based solely on parental appearance. Plants must also be grown in similar conditions for accurate comparison to be made. Mass selection and progeny testing are applicable to all plants, but more complex breeding practices are usually only appropriate for certain types, depending on the plant's breeding system.

CORE FACTS

■ Plant breeding is the genetic enhancement of plant quality, and propagation is the controlled reproduction of plants.

■ Breeding aims to produce new improved plant types, whereas propagation generally aims to replicate existing types.

■ Modern technologies such as genetic engineering and tissue culture, as well as more traditional techniques, are now used in plant breeding and propagation.

Breeding self-pollinating plants

Some of the most important food crops, such as wheat, rice, and beans, normally reproduce by self-pollination—that is, each plant is fertilized by its own pollen. These inbreeding plants tend to be relatively genetically uniform, because there is only one parent and so one set of genes. Also, a plant variety is likely to "breed true" for many generations—that is, produce offspring with the same characteristics. Therefore, the breeder must create more genetic variation, from which selection can then proceed.

Inducing two separate plant varieties to cross-pollinate artificially produces genetic variation. This is usually done by physically removing the male parts of all the flowers on one plant before they have shed their pollen, forming an all-female plant; pollen from the desired male plant is then manually placed on the female plant's flowers. These pollinated flowers are then covered to exclude any other pollen. Artificially pollinating plants is a laborious and delicate procedure that must overcome the specific mechanism that each self-pollinating species possesses to deter cross-pollination.

This process will produce a generation of hybrid (cross-bred) plants, called the F_1 generation by breeders. These plants will be genetically similar to one another, because the parents were genetically uniform. F_1 plants are then crossed by the same method, producing an F_2 generation. This will display genetic variation between plants, because the genes of the F_1 generation will have been randomly recombined so that plants no longer breed true. This diverse population is the starting point for selection.

There are two main breeding methods that can be applied to the F_2 generation: the pedigree method and backcross breeding. Pedigree breeding aims to combine the best features of the two original strains. Those members of the F_2 generation displaying the best combinations of desirable traits are selected and allowed to self-pollinate naturally. This process is continued for several generations (F_3, F_4, F_5, and so on), during which time repeated selection produces distinct true-breeding lines of plants. These differing lines can be subjected to various field trials to evaluate their performance. For example, they may be inoculated with molds to test their resistance to infection by fungal plant pathogens (see AGRICULTURAL SCIENCE). Finally, the best lines are identified and subjected to confirmatory trials before being launched as a new strain. The whole process typically takes at least 12 plant generations to complete.

Backcrossing is used to introduce a specific characteristic into an otherwise satisfactory existing strain. An artificial cross is made between the existing strain and a plant with the desirable trait (often a wild relative). The resulting F_1 is then backcrossed with the parent from the existing strain, and members of the F_2 generation exhibiting the desired trait are selected. This process is continued for several generations. After about six such backcrosses, the offspring should be very similar to the original parent from the original strain, but with the addition of the

A false-color electron micrograph of two protoplasts (naked cells) of the tobacco plant (Nicotiana tabacum) undergoing fusion. Hormones are used to stimulate the cell wall to regrow. Microinjections of DNA are also sometimes added to protoplasms.

useful characteristic from the wild type. Allowing these plants to self-pollinate would produce a true-breeding line, which could be considered a new strain. For example, this procedure was used to put resistance to a disease called chestnut blight from Chinese chestnut trees (*Castanea mollissima*) into American chestnut trees (*Castanea dentata*), while still retaining the appearance of the U.S. species.

Breeding cross-pollinating plants

Cross-pollinating plants are those that outbreed—that is, plants that are normally fertilized by pollen from a different plant of the same species. Important cross-pollinating crops include sugar beet and white clover. These plants display great genetic diversity and never naturally breed true, producing a very wide range of types available for selection. The first task when breeding such diverse plants is to reduce overall variability by removing undesirable traits.

Cross-pollinating plants can be induced to inbreed by artificial self-pollination, which is usually done by manipulation of the plant's floral parts. This is continued for many generations, with selection at every generation, until true-breeding lines result. Two desirable inbred lines can then be combined by cross-pollination; this is a hybridization process.

Hybridization

The production of hybrid strains is a very important plant breeding technique. It is done by cross-pollinating two inbred lines; this must be done artificially in the case of natural self-pollinators. The F_1 hybrids thus produced are generally more vigorous than the inbred parents because of the increase in genetic variation compared to the parental types. This phenomenon is called hybrid vigor, or heterosis.

PLANT GENETICS

Chromosomes within the cell nucleus of nearly all plant cells contain DNA, the genetic material. Genes are sequences of DNA that determine specific aspects of inherited characteristics; since plant cells are usually diploid—containing pairs of each chromosome—each gene is usually present in a pair. If both copies of a gene are of the same form, a diploid plant can be said to be true breeding for that gene. Male pollen and female ovules are haploid, with one copy of each chromosome and hence of each gene. Pollination is the fusion of pollen and ovule to restore the diploid condition in a seed, which can then grow into a new plant. Genes are usually rearranged during this fertilization process, producing a new combination in the seed.

Many plants have more than two copies of each chromosome and each gene in their cells because of various features of the plant reproduction process. Such plants are said to be polyploid, and this feature (which is very rare in animals) makes their genetics much more complex. Many polyploids are sterile because they cannot form viable sex cells. They must therefore reproduce vegetatively, giving rise to genetically identical clones.

A CLOSER LOOK

The production of F_1 hybrids has contributed greatly to increased agricultural production, most notably in corn, where high-yielding hybrids are now used by most farmers. A disadvantage is the need to purchase new seed each year, because the offspring of F_1 hybrids are more variable than their parents.

Applications of biotechnology
The major limitation of all standard plant breeding methods is the fact that plants must be compatible to be successfully bred. In other words, they must be sufficiently closely related to permit cross-pollination. Various specialized techniques have been developed to allow incompatible plants to be bred.

A botanist carefully manipulates the reproductive organs of a flower. By controlling the pollination of a plant in this way, researchers can increase or decrease the genetic variability of the plant's offspring.

Protoplast hybridization is one such technique. A plant cell can be treated with enzymes to remove its cell wall, forming a naked cell (protoplast). Applying an electrical current or a chemical agent to protoplasts will disrupt their membranes and may induce the protoplasts to fuse. The hybrid protoplast can then be cultured into a viable plant. This can be done with protoplasts from distantly related species. Common practice, however, is to produce hybrids between members of the same family, where compatibility is more likely (such as potato and tomato, both members of the nightshade family, Solanaceae).

Manipulating an organism's DNA to create new genetic combinations is more widely used than protoplast hybridization (see GENETIC ENGINEERING). For example, a DNA sequence from a soil bacterium has been inserted into rape (*Brassica napus*), making the plant resistant to a leading herbicide (see PESTICIDE AND HERBICIDE). Therefore, applying the herbicide will kill weeds without damaging the resistant plant.

A wide range of genetically engineered crop plants have been produced, and a few have found widespread commercial use. There are many field trials in progress, and the potential range of applications of this technology is huge. For example, food crops can be engineered to contain nutrients beneficial to humans or even to contain vaccines.

However, the prospect of wider usage of genetic engineering has attracted controversy. The long-term unpredictability of releasing genetically modified plants into the ecosystem (and the food chain) is a particular concern, especially since such plants may pollinate non-modified plants, with unknown results. There is also the possibility that traits such as genetic resistance to herbicides could transfer to weeds, creating superweeds. Some farmers have expressed concern about the potential for a price-controlled supply cartel (an agreement between companies to limit competition) to develop, particularly since some large companies started to market seeds for genetically modified plants that require treatment with their own brand of agrochemical products in order to grow successfully.

PLANT PROPAGATION
Propagation is the controlled perpetuation or reproduction of plants, the aim of which is to increase plant numbers. It is an essential, basic part of many agricultural activities, including crop farming, horticulture, and forestry.

Sexual propagation
Propagating plants sexually means growing them from seed. This method is cheap and simple and allows plants to be stored in seed form, often for many years. Seeds are also very convenient to transport. They can usually be relied upon to be disease-free, since most infectious agents are unable to pass from a plant into its seeds. The main drawback with seed propagation is the introduction of genetic variation, which means that plants grown from seed can be quite different from their parents.

Seed production is a specialized aspect of horticulture, with methods designed to produce the maximum number of viable, healthy seeds that will grow into plants of a predictable type (see HORTICULTURE). However, the seeds of some plants are harvested from existing populations, rather than being commercially produced; this is the usual pattern for tree seed because of the long period most trees need to grow to seed-bearing age.

Growing young plants from seed may require exposing them to certain treatments to break them out of their dormant state; this is called vernalization. Vernalization breaks down of the tough outer coat of the seed, allowing the seed to sprout (germinate). For example, seeds from apple trees (*Malus* species) require a lengthy period of exposure to cold before they will start to grow. Other methods of vernalization include soaking the seeds in water or abrading the seed surface (called scarification).

Asexual propagation

Propagating plants asexually by vegetative means is a useful practice that exploits the ability of plants to regenerate after damage. It perpetuates plants without altering their genetic constitution, so a desirable plant can be propagated indefinitely with no variation. It is usually also faster than sexual propagation. Methods of asexual propagation include dividing root systems, taking cuttings, layering, grafting, and using natural vegetative structures.

Cut portions of stem, leaf, or root can often be induced to regenerate a whole plant. The portion of the plant used will depend on the species, and the ease of propagation also varies. Some plants require precise temperature and humidity conditions. Treatment of the cut surface with plant hormones often improves success. Plants that grow well from cuttings include sugarcane (*Saccharum officinarum*) and cassava (*Manihot* species).

Layering is a similar technique, but it is done without removing the plant part. For example, a plant stem can be wounded and pegged down into the soil. Roots will develop from the wound, and then the stem can be severed to form a new plant. Alternatively, a ball of moist growing medium, enveloped in plastic to prevent drying out (desiccation), can be placed around the wounded stem. When roots form in this ball, the stem can be cut off and planted independently. Plants such as raspberries are well suited to layering: they form roots without being wounded.

Grafting is an important method for propagating fruit trees and ornamental shrubs. It involves physically joining two different plants to form a combination plant; the root part is called the stock, and the shoot part is called the scion. Both must be closely related, since the technique relies on the two parts being able to form a continuous connection of tissue. There are various grafting methods, but all involve cutting the stock and inserting the scion into the cut. This union must be bound tightly and coated with a waterproof material such as paraffin to retain

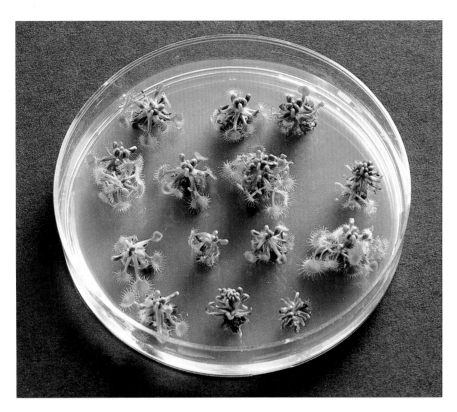

moisture. The two cut surfaces form wound tissue, which will combine to form a living connection. This can create a plant with combined beneficial characteristics—for example, a high-yielding apple scion can be grafted onto a hardy stock. This procedure has been critically important in the U.S. citrus industry and the French wine industry.

Many plants have reproductive structures that can be exploited for propagation. For example, storage organs such as potato (*Solanum tuberosum*) tubers or onion (*Allium cepa*) bulbs can be used to form new plants. Asexual reproductive structures such as the stem runners of strawberries (*Fragaria* species) or the rhizome roots of the iris (*Iris* species) make propagation even simpler.

Tissue culture

Small amounts of plant tissue can be removed and grown in the laboratory on a sterile culture medium; this procedure is called tissue culture. The tissue used can be undifferentiated callus or a shoot tip. With appropriate conditions, the tissue will then regenerate into a plant. The essential conditions for successful growth are the balance of nutrients, and, most crucially, of plant hormones. Tissue culturing is costly and complex, and it is mainly used in research rather than in horticulture. However, some orchids are propagated commercially using tissue culture.

T. ALLMAN

*Round-leaved sundews (*Drosera rotundifolia*), an insectivorous plant, are being grown from tissue cultures. Each tiny plant is a clone of a single cell taken from a parent plant. This makes tissue culturing a useful tool for genetic research.*

See also: AGRICULTURAL SCIENCE; AGRICULTURE, HISTORY OF; ARABLE FARMING; HORTICULTURE; PLANT HORMONE.

Further reading:
Kuckuck, H. *Fundamentals of Plant Breeding.* New York: Springer-Verlag, 1991.

PLANT HORMONE

Plant hormones are substances produced by plants to coordinate their growth and development

There are five types of hormones that control growth and development in plants. A hormone is a chemical messenger found inside an organism that causes specific tissues to behave in specific ways.

Auxins. Auxins are any of a group of plant hormones that affect the growth of the stem tip, leaves, and roots and the development of side branches and fruit. Auxins stimulate certain cells to elongate and inhibit the growth of other cells, depending on the amount and distribution of auxin in the plant tissue. The most common auxin is indole-3-acetic acid, which controls plant functions called tropisms. Tropisms are involuntary movements, such as bending, curving, or turning, in direct response to an external stimulus. When an indoor plant is placed in a sunlit window, for example, the plant grows toward the sun—a process known as phototropism. Although the direct mechanism is not known, many scientists believe that indole-3-acetic acid is destroyed by direct sunlight. The side of the stem that receives less light has a higher concentration of auxin; the cells on this side of the stem are able to elongate more than the cells on the sunlit side, causing the plant to bend toward the light.

Abscisic acid. Abscisic acid is a growth inhibitor that promotes abscission; that is, the dropping of leaves and fruit. Abscisic acid also controls dormancy in seeds until the right season for germination.

Cytokinins. Cytokinins work in opposition to auxins by encouraging the growth of side shoots on stems (lateral buds) rather than the tip. Cytokinins also promote bud formation.

Gibberellins. Similar to auxins, gibberellins play a part in cell elongation. They cause plants to bolt (grow very quickly) and force seeds to germinate. Some are responsible for maleness in flowers. Scientists have identified over ninety different gibberellins, the most common of which is known as gibberellic acid.

Gibberellins were discovered in 1926 by Japanese scientists studying a seedling disease in rice plants. This plant infection is caused by the fungal pathogen *Gibberella fujikoroi* that releases gibberellic acid, causing the rice shoots to grow very long without corresponding root growth. As a result, the seedlings usually die before maturity.

Ethylene. Ethylene was the earliest known plant hormone. The ancient Egyptians used it to ripen figs, while the Chinese used it to force pears to ripen in closed rooms. Ethylene is a gaseous hormone. It acts mainly as a ripening agent for fruit. Ethylene works with gibberellins to encourage seed germination and in opposition to auxin and abscisic acid.

Commercial use of plant hormones

The function of different hormones and their relation to one other is still the subject of much study, but the effects are of great interest to agriculture.

Plant hormones can be put to horticultural and agricultural uses: A small percentage of ethylene, which is produced synthetically in oil refineries, can be used to stimulate the ripening of fruit in greenhouses. Hormone root powder, containing auxin, is often used when propagating plants from twig or leaf cuttings (see PLANT BREEDING AND PROPAGATION).

The manipulation of the genes that are responsible for producing plant hormones has led to the development of new types of individual plants, especially for food. One of the results of this type of genetic modification is the Flavr Savr—a tomato that stays firm for longer.

S. ALDRIDGE

See also: AGRICULTURE, HISTORY OF; AGRICULTURAL SCIENCE; ARABLE FARMING; CROP SPRAYING AND PROTECTION; GENETIC ENGINEERING; PESTICIDE AND HERBICIDE.

Further reading:

Biology and Biotechnology of the Plant Hormone Ethylene. Edited by A. Kanellis *et al.* Boston: Kluwer Academic Publishers, 1997.
Plant Hormones: Physiology, Biochemistry, and Molecular Biology. Edited by P. Davies. 2nd edition. Boston: Kluwer Academic Publishers, 1995.

CONNECTIONS

● Plant hormones are often used in **PLANT BREEDING AND PROPAGATION** to allow people to manipulate the natural growth of plants.

● The successful practice of **FORESTRY** and **HORTICULTURE** has unwittingly relied on the use of plant hormones for centuries.

INDEX

Page numbers in **boldface** type refer to main articles and their illustrations. Page numbers in *italic* type refer to additional illustrations or their captions.

layering 1005
lead 951, 952
lead oxide 963, 964
lenses, camera *993*, 994–5, 996
Leonardo da Vinci 971
light, detection and the photoelectric effect 988
lighting 989, 995–7
linear motors, and maglev trains 887
liquid crystal displays (LCDs) 957, 958
lithium 910
logic gates 901
longitude 902
long-range navigational (LORAN) systems 906

magnesium 908, 909–10, 949, 950
magnetically levitated (maglev) trains 887
magnets, for ore concentration 950
malaria 977, 981
Manhattan Project 923
mapmaking 906
Marsh, Sylvester 890
mass defect 915
mass selection 1002
medical imaging 914
Meitner, Lise 913, 914
Mercator projections 906
mercury, liquid 908
metals 950, 951–2
    alkali 908, 910
    coins 885
    mining for 878–9
    packaging material 960, 961
    precious 910
microactuators 901
microengineering 901
micromotors *899*, 900, *901*
microscopy, atomic force 900, 901
military vehicles **869–73**
mining and quarrying **874–9**
    See also ores.
missiles **880–4**
money and banking technology **885–6**
monitors, television and computer 957
monomobiles 887
monorails **887**
Moog, Robert 898
mopeds 888
Morse, Samuel 886
motorcycles **888–9**
    dirt bikes 931–2
motor scooters 888
motor toboggans 932
mountain railroads and funiculars **890–1**
mulching 954–5
multimedia **892–3**
muon-catalyzed fusion 916
musical instruments **894–8**

Nagasaki 923–4
nanocomputers 901
nanotechnology and micromachines **899–901**
Natta, Giulio 941
natural gas 934, **1000–1**
navigation **902–7**
    guided-missile 881, 882–3
neural networks 974
neutrinos *912*, 913
neutrons, discovery of 912
nicotine 977
Niepce, Joseph Nicéphore 996
nitrocellulose 965, 995
nonferrous metals **908–10**
nuclear energy **911–4**, 921
nuclear fission 913, 914, 917–18, 923–4

nuclear fusion 912, 913, 914, **915–6**, 925, 926
nuclear power **917–22**
nuclear weapons 914, 915, 916, **923–6**
nucleus, of the atom 912, 972

obstetrics and gynecology **927–9**
off-road and amphibious vehicles 871, *872*, **930–2**
oil, crude *See* petroleum.
oil and natural gas production **933–9**, 940
oil refining **940–2**
oil tankers and bulk carriers *936*, **943–6**, 962
omnirange 906
operating rooms **947–8**
opiates 986
Oppenheimer, J. Robert 923
ores 949
    bulk carriers for 944, 946
    extraction and processing **949–52**
    See also mining and quarrying.
organic farming and sustainable agriculture **953–6**, 977
Ørsted, Hans Christian 908
outbreeding, plant 1003
output and display devices **957–8**, 999

packaging industry **959–62**
paints and surface coatings **963–6**
paper 885, 886, **967–70**, 999
    packaging 959–60, 962
papyrus *968*
parachutes **971**
paragliding 971
particle accelerators **972–3**
patents, plant 1002
pattern recognition **974–5**
peas 1002
pedigree breeding, plant 1003
Perkin, William 982
permaculture 954
personal rapid transit (PRT) 887
pesticides and herbicides 953, 955, **976–9**, 1004
petroleum (crude oil) 933–4, 936, 940, 941
    refining *See* oil refining.
    spillages *944*, 945
pharmaceutical industry 982, 984
pharmacology and drug treatment **980–7**
pheromones, for pest control 979
phosphors 957, 965
photocells **988–9**
photocopiers/photocopying 886, **990**
photodiodes 989
photoelectric effect 988
photoemission 988
photography 870, 988, **991–9**
photomultipliers 989
photovoltaic cells 988, 989
phthalocyanines 964
pigments, paint 963–4
pipelines 946, **1000–1**
pixels 957, 958
placebos 984
plant breeding and propagation **1002–5**
plasma (gas), and nuclear fusion 916
plastics 940–1
    uses for 960, 961–2
platinum 875–6, 908, 910
plutonium 920, 921–2, 923, 924
point-of-sale systems 886
Polaris (star) 903
polishes 966
pollination, plant 1003, 1004
pollution 924, *944*, 945, 950
polyethylene, production 941
polyploid cells 1004

polystyrene 962
potassium 910, 950
powder coatings 965
power stations 878, 914, 918, *921*, 922
pregnancy testing 927–8
printing 886, 967–8
progeny testing 1002
propagation *See* plant breeding and propagation.
prostaglandins 985
prostheses 909
proteins, artificial 899–900
protoplast hybridization *1003*, 1004
pyrethrin 976, 979
Pythagoras 894

quarrying 875, 878

radar 870, 882–3, 906
radiation, ionizing 911, 923–4
radioactivity 911, 912–3
radiocarbon dating 914
radio range technology 906
railroads
    and military transport 869–70
    mountain railroads and funiculars **890–1**
ranitidine 984
rape, genetically-engineered 1004
rapid transit systems, personal rapid transit (PRT) 887
reactors, nuclear 918–21
recycling 950, 961, 970
resins 965, 966
rhizomes 1005
rigs, drilling *933*, 935–7
robotics 899, 900, 974, *985*
rockets 880
rooting powder 1006
Rutherford, Ernest 911, 912, 913, 915

SAFEGE system 887
salicin 981
salicylic acid 982
satellites 907
scanners, computer 989
schizophrenia 986, 987
sealants 966
seeds, propagation from 1004–5
selection, plant 1002
semiconductors, in photocells 988, 989
sextants 903–4
shale, oil 939
ships
    container ships 962
    navigation 902–5, 906, 907
    paints/painting *963*, 965, 966
Silent Spring (Rachel Carson) 977
silicon 989
sleeping pills 986
smart cards 886
smelting 950, 951
snow and ice travel 932
snowmobiles 932
sodium *909*, 910, 920–1, 949, 950
solar power 988, 989
sound tracks, film 989
Sperry, Elmer 880
spina bifida 928
split sets 874
stacking, aircraft 906
standard generalized markup language (SGML) 893
stars, navigation by 903
steam-powered monorails 887
steam-powered road vehicles 870
steel, galvanized 909
sterilization (surgical) 927

Stone, Edmund 981
storage rings 973
Strassmann, Fritz 923
streetlights 989
sugar beet 1003
sulfur, liquid 946
sulfur dioxide 950
surgery 927, 929
synchrotrons *972*, 973

Talbot, Henry Fox 996
tanks 870, 872, 873, 931
tar sands 939
thermal imaging 870
Three Mile Island 920
tin 875–6, 909, 951–2
tires 870–1, 889, 930
tissue culture, plant 1005
titanium 908, 909, 952
titanium oxide 952, 964, 965
tobacco plants *1003*
toboggans, motor 932
tomatoes, genetically engineered 1006
tracked vehicles 930, 931
    half-track vehicles 871, 872, 930
    tanks 873
tractors 872, 931
trains 878, 887
tranquilizers 986, 987
transgenic organisms 979
tritium 913, 925, 926
tropisms 1006
Ts'ai Lun 967

ultrasonics, for medical scanning 928, *929*
ultraviolet light 886, 901, 998
unpiloted vehicles 931
uranium 911, 913, 914, 918, 921, 924, 949, 952

V-1 missiles 883
V-2 rockets 883–4
vacuum fluorescent devices 958
varnishes 966
vehicles, military *See* military vehicles.
ventilation, in mines *877*
video displays 958
virtual reality 893, 958, *985*
virtual reality modeling language (VRML) 893
von Neumann, John 899

Walton, Ernest 972
watermarks, on paper 886, 969
wax 966
weeds 1004
wet oil 939
wheat 955, 1002
Windscale, nuclear accident 920
Withering, William 982
World War I (1914–1918)
    military vehicles 870, 872, 873, 888
    trench warfare 869
    weapons 800, 869, 873
World War II (1939–1945)
    horses 871
    military vehicles 870, 871, 872, 888, *930*, 931
    naval tankers 945
    parachute operations 971
    weapons 883, 923–4
wrapping machines 961–2
writing, nano-scale 900, 901

X rays 901, 914, *929*, 998

Ziegler, Karl 941
zinc 908, 909, 949, 951